YOGI BARE

THE LIFE AND TIMES OF A CELTIC LEGEND

JOHN HUGHES

DEDICATION

To my brother Patrick who sadly passed away on
Christmas Day 2012.

YOGI BARE
THE LIFE AND TIMES OF A CELTIC LEGEND JOHN HUGHES

Edited by Alex Gordon

Foreword by Billy Connolly

Published by John Hughes

ISBN 978 1 9046 8488 6

Printed and bound by CPI Group (UK) Ltd, Croydon, CR0 4YY

ACKNOWLEDGEMENTS

I would like to thank the many people who have been indispensable in assisting me to write this book.

Peter Lawwell, the Celtic Chief Executive, who has been an enormous help right from the very start.

Billy Connolly who was kind enough to take time off from his busy tour of the USA to pen the foreword. Well played, Big Yin!

Co-author Alex Gordon and his wife Gerda for assisting in getting the words down in print. I am particularly indebted to Alex for his professionalism, support and guidance throughout. He played a blinder.

The lads at Celtic Quick News - David Faulds, Jim McGinley, Paul Brennan and Tony Warrington - for their much-appreciated assistance and advice.

And, of course, those magnificent Celtic supporters who made my years at the club so very, very memorable. Thank you one and all.

CO-AUTHOR'S NOTE

It was an absolute pleasure and a privilege to be involved in the life story of John Hughes, a true Celtic legend.

With a fair degree of irony, Big Yogi was my dad John's all-time Celtic hero. No-one dared criticise the player around our vicinity in the old dilapidated Jungle. My dad would belt out 'Feed The Bear' with the best of them as Yogi collected the ball, steadied himself and then prepared for one of his wonderful, lung-bursting, legs-pumping slalom runs down the touchline. Truly, it was a wondrous sight when he picked up speed with that long stride of his, the ball closely under control.

Anything could happen when the ball dropped at his feet. There would be a hush around Celtic Park in enthusiastic anticipation before the rafters took a pounding. 'Feed The Bear', was the boisterous chant and off went Yogi on another menacing sortie into enemy territory. Great memories. Great days.

Before the book came to life, John and I were enjoying a quiet pint in a hotel in the south side of Glasgow. The idea was mooted, but nothing materialised. I thought there was so much in Yogi's life that deserved to be seen in print. Some of the stories he told me were insightful, to say the least. Always very interesting, too. Others were just hilarious. However, it looked as though these gems would remain unseen.

It was the middle of December 2013 when my phone buzzed at home. 'Let's do the book,' said John Hughes. There was no preamble. Who could say no?

To be honest, I didn't know what to expect. I was told John would be a very difficult subject to interview. That didn't worry me because I don't interview anyone when I'm involved in a book. I don't turn up with a pre-selected list of questions with a dictaphone at the ready. I much prefer to talk almost randomly with the individual, jot down some words and see where the chat leads us. It's always been my belief you will get so much extra material by taking this possibly unconventional route. And so it proved with Yogi.

We agreed that the Burnside Hotel was the ideal meeting point for the conversations. At first, the arrangement was for a 2pm kick-off until around 4pm every Monday. Soon it became 1pm with most of my scribblings wrapped up by 5pm. Then we moved it to noon with the end of play time now 6pm. I realised this was no chore. I was enjoying our meetings and, thankfully, it transpired, so, too, was John. The extended times just happened naturally. We talked about everything and anything as John opened up about his remarkable life and times, the highs and the lows. I could see an extraordinary book coming to life.

Normally, when you hit the last full stop on a publication, it is greeted with a loud 'Hurrah!' Not on this occasion, though. There was a definite twinge of melancholy. It's not supposed to be fun piecing together over 100,000 words in the race to meet the publisher's strict deadline. However, I had the most enjoyable time working on 'Yogi Bare'.

He has ordered me to write that he was amazed by my knowledge of Celtic. I thank him for that. But I'm going to embarrass the bloke now by saying I found him engaging, generous, honest in the extreme, warm-hearted, fascinating, witty and compelling. Just bloody good company, in fact. During our meetings, we indulged in our obligatory fish-and-chip interlude with John paying one week and me the next.

My old dad would have been delighted. I got to Feed The Bear.

I hope you have as much pleasure reading John Hughes's life story as I had putting it down in print. I can't wait for the sequel.

ALEX GORDON

CONTENTS

FOREWORD
by BILLY CONNOLLY

John Hughes, or Big Yogi as he became lovingly regarded, swept into the sixties at Celtic Park in much the same way as the sixties swept into all of our lives, bringing a message that nothing we knew was going to remain the same!

The Celtic of the early sixties were going through a bad patch, but that would soon change with the arrival at Celtic Park of the genius Jock Stein. This man would be responsible for the assembling, and success, of the legendary Lisbon Lions, one of that number being Big John. One of the pride of Lions born in the Jungle at Paradise. How clearly I remember those years leading up to the glorious win in the Final of the European Cup in Lisbon in May 1967. It was show business at its best. Big Yogi would get the ball deep in his own half of the field and set off, in his own inimitable loping style, for the opponents' end, and the roar would start, eventually morphing into song:

Oh The Bear, The Bear,

The Bear Is Everywhere,

Feed The Bear, Feed The Bear!

At the sound of this, the Big Man's head would rise, and it seemed as if a goal was inevitable, and a lot of the time it was! From the bottom of my heart, thank you John Hughes, for the unforgettable moments I have witnessed over the years thanks to you. I'll never forget you.

Billy Connolly.

PROLOGUE
by BILLY HUGHES

John Hughes isn't just my brother; he's my hero.

You won't find a more enthusiastic fan than me of the player known fondly to the Celtic legions as Big Yogi. I am so proud of what my brother has achieved in life and in football and if anyone deserves legendary status it is him. I know what playing for Celtic in front of those magnificent followers meant to him. I am also very much aware what it means to him now to be part of that Celtic support. You better believe he is Celtic through and through.

John is almost six years older than me, but, in truth, he is the person I have always looked up to all of my life. He took care of me and was always there when I needed him most. If I required advice, he was the first person I went to. I've always felt safe with my brother around. He is the sort of guy who will go out of his way to do someone a good turn. No-one will ever hear about it. He'll just do it and that's the end of it. Putting this in print may even embarrass John, but I believe it must be said. A lot of people don't know the real John Hughes. He might even appear aloof, but nothing could be further from the truth. Simply put, he shuns publicity. He prefers to be out of the limelight. If he does something for someone, he won't shout about it from the rooftops. That's his style. He definitely won't thank me for saying this, but he is a genuine gentle giant.

On the exterior, he may look big and gruff. It's the inside that counts, though, isn't it? That's where the heart lives and no-one possesses a bigger heart than my brother.

One of my regrets in football was not being able to play alongside John - unless you count fifteen minutes at Sunderland. Yes, I did have the opportunity to join Celtic when I was about sixteen years old, but

I opted to go to England. I realised there would have been obvious comparisons with me and John and I thought it better to attempt to make a name for myself elsewhere. On the evening I told Jock Stein of my decision, he shook my hand, wished me good luck and said, 'I respect your decision. Ian McColl is going to be your manager. I've got more football knowledge in my pinky than he'll ever possess.' I wondered what I had let myself in for. Telling Big Jock was the easy part. When I broke the news to our dad I wasn't signing for Celtic, he went ballistic. He was so upset he refused to talk to me for about a year!

I had trained and played for the Celtic reserves when someone came up with a nickname for me. Well, if my brother was Yogi, I had to be Boo Boo, didn't I? I could live without that moniker.

Yes, it would have brilliant to have performed in the same team as my brother. I was eleven when he made his top team debut for Celtic. I watched him when he was only seventeen years old terrorising the Rangers defence in his first Old Firm game at Ibrox. I vividly remember their huge and sturdy centre-half, a bloke called Doug Baillie, being dragged along behind my brother as he clung desperately to his shirt. Celtic won 3-2 and John scored a truly memorable goal. What a great day that was.

One of my proudest moments while watching my brother was around the time I had just signed for Sunderland and Celtic had agreed to play a pre-season friendly at Roker Park. It was August 14 1965 and all the talk before the game was about Jim Baxter who had just joined the club from Rangers and was making his debut. After the game, all the talk was about John Hughes. What a devastating performance from my brother that glorious afternoon. Even I could hardly believe what I was witnessing. Around 10,000 Celtic fans were in the 35,000 crowd on a breathtaking, sunny day. It was the perfect setting and John was simply unstoppable. He ran amok as he scored two fabulous goals and Celtic won 5-0. I had to sit in the stand and keep quiet. I wanted to cheer every time Celtic scored. I wanted to applaud every time my brother was on the ball. At all times, though, I had to remember I was a Sunderland player. Not too sure how the Roker Park faithful would have accepted one of their team's youngsters going wild with delight every time the opposition scored a goal.

Sunderland had a Northern Ireland international right-back called John Parke in their team that day. My brother dismantled him. I think it took my new team-mate a couple of months to recover. Honestly, it was an unbelievable display from John. The Sunderland support had turned out to cheer Slim Jim, but they ended up applauding Big Yogi. Even Jim Baxter admitted after the game that he was in awe of my brother's performance. Sportingly, he said he was the most improved player he had seen in years. I know my brother's confidence received a massive boost four months or so beforehand when he picked up his first medal after Celtic had beaten Dunfermline 3-2 in the Scottish Cup Final. That may just have been the turning point for John. He had become a winner and, thankfully, there were more honours to follow.

I played only once for Scotland at full international level when I came on as a substitute for Graeme Souness in a 1-1 draw with Sweden in a friendly in Gothenburg in 1975. John's career at that level had ended six years earlier, so it looked as though we were fated never to be team-mates. Well, not on a football pitch, anyway. It was a crying shame that we were only brief colleagues at Sunderland when my brother arrived from Crystal Palace in January 1973. It just wasn't fair that John's playing career ended that day because he still had so much to offer. Some of his best days were still in front of him.

I never heard him complain. Not once. He took the blow and got on with it. But that's been the story of my big brother's life as you are about to discover. I hope, by the end, you will have a clearer insight into the personality of my hero...John Hughes, of Celtic Football Club.

Chapter 1

BIG JOCK, ME AND THE SECRET

In one startling revelation, I discovered two things about Jock Stein's single-minded attitude to life. One was the importance of Celtic Football Club to him as the manager. The other was his philosophy regarding the relevance of an individual to him and the club. After the discovery, I have to admit I felt shock, disbelief and, ultimately, betrayed. Trust me, I am not being overly melodramatic.

Back in 1966, Celtic embarked upon a month-long tour of Bermuda, The States and Canada. We kicked off in Bermuda on May 12 and completed the eleven-game jaunt in Los Angeles on June 12. My wife Mary was four-and-a-half months pregnant when I set out for the lengthy trek. If there had been any problems with the pregnancy, I wouldn't have hesitated in asking to be left out of the travelling squad. However, Mary had given birth to our first son Kevin two years earlier and had practically sailed through the antenatal stage and also the delivery.

So, I was as excited as my team-mates when we flew out for the trip of a lifetime. I was twenty-three years old and things were looking up on the personal and professional front. After seasons in the doldrums, Celtic had become winners. The previous year we had beaten Dunfermline 3-2 to lift the Scottish Cup - the club's first piece of silverware in eight years - and had followed that up with a truly wonderful League Championship success, our first title since 1954.

We had also thrown in a League Cup triumph, beating our oldest foes Rangers in the Final. And I was about to become a dad for the second time.

Unfortunately, on May 16, four days after Celtic's first game against a Bermudan Select, Mary was whisked into Bellshill Hospital after complications developed in the pregnancy. Regrettably, I was unaware of the change in her condition. Mary remained in hospital for a week during which time she miscarried. Again, I knew nothing about the disturbing situation. I was in America and I might as well have been on the moon. It was not the simple task it is today to lift a telephone, tap in a number and be connected immediately with another country. If that had been the case, I would have contacted Mary every day for a progress report.

I only discovered Mary had lost the baby when a reporter with a national newspaper was talking to me one day at training. He was a friend and, in fact, his wife got on very well with Mary and we had been on a couple of summer holidays together. He sidled up and said, 'Sorry to hear your news, Big Man.' You could say I was slightly taken aback. 'What news?' I asked, a little perturbed. It was my newspaper pal's turn to look surprised. Immediately, he realised I hadn't been told of the happenings back home. 'You don't know?' he queried, a frown on his face. 'What don't I know?' I replied, warily awaiting his response. 'Mary,' he just about spluttered, 'she's lost the baby.' I stared back at him. The sun was blazing in the Bermudan sky, but I was numb; absolutely stone cold. I've no idea how long I stood there trying to comprehend what he had just said. Then I heard the newsman say, 'I thought Jock would have told you.'

Once I had regained some sort of composure, I realised I had to go and see the manager. I couldn't believe he had known of the situation and not bothered to inform me. To me, that was unfathomable. The reporter must have got it wrong, I hoped. Deep down, though, I knew that would have been most unlikely. I met up with Jock to confront him. 'Did you know about Mary?' I asked. He didn't even blink. I could hardly believe my ears when he replied, 'Ach, what could you do about it, anyway? You're here and she's there. There's nothing else for it.' I was stunned; speechless. I waited for my head to clear before I said, 'You knew and you didn't think it was right to let me know? My wife losing a baby? Didn't you think that was important?' He said something along the lines, 'Oh, sort it out when you get home.' It was such a flippant, throwaway remark. We could have been talking about the weather. I glared at him for a moment, with all sorts of things flying around my head, before saying, 'Listen, Boss, I think that's ridiculous. You're bang out of order.'

I could see it wasn't any of his concern and the conversation was over. As I said, I felt a strange concoction of emotions. Shock. Anger. Betrayed. I had to think about Mary and how she was coping. I had to get to a telephone at the hotel and make a transatlantic call. It seemed to take forever before I got through. Thankfully, she was fine. Distraught, of course, at first, but she reassured me she would be well and I should concentrate on my football. There was never any discussion about flying home immediately. In any case, neither Jock nor the travelling directors made any offer for me to return to Scotland. The matter was over and done with, as far as they were concerned. I realise we all deal with grief in different ways, but surely there should have been a more compassionate way for someone at the club to deliver the news? I felt terribly let down by Big Jock and his complete lack of sympathy.

I returned to the training complex and sat on a bench and watched my team-mates having a kickabout, enjoying a laugh in the sunshine. Obviously, they hadn't heard my news. So, there I was, in one of the most beautiful islands on the universe, and I felt so alone. I watched my mates larking about and having a good time. I sighed, 'So, this is what they mean when they say, "Life goes on".'

Five years later, I was again on the receiving end of Jock's interpretation of the worth and value of a fellow-human being. I've never attempted to hide the fact I didn't want to leave Celtic.

However, once Big Jock had made up his mind, I realised it was time to clear my locker and get out. I was left with the overwhelming feeling I had served my purpose, as far as he was concerned. Celtic had seen the best of John Hughes, so it was time to vacate the premises.

It didn't matter I had given everything for the club since coming into the first team as an eager seventeen year old. It didn't matter that I was only twenty-eight years old and supposedly reaching my peak. It didn't matter that I was the sixth highest scorer in the club's history with 189 goals. It didn't matter that I had played my part in bringing six League titles, four League Cups and one Scottish Cup to Celtic. Nothing mattered. Suddenly, I was expendable; surplus to requirements and it was time to go.

I felt sick. Wouldn't you? My stomach was churning. I never even got the opportunity to wave farewell to those thousands of wonderful fans who used to chant, 'Feed The Bear' on matchday; a raucous chorus that used to propel me in the general direction of Cloud Nine. This may surprise you, but I never spoke again to Jock. I didn't receive a phone call or a letter. Nothing. Zilch. And, believe me, that hurt. One year I was good enough to play in a European Cup Final and the next I was heading for the Celtic Park exit. Goodbye and good riddance.

I accept that was Jock's manner. Players before me and after me always insisted he didn't get involved in popularity contests; he just didn't care what others thought of him. It was Celtic all the way and so long as they were winning then that was all that mattered. I'm a Celtic supporter and I can understand that. But there are ways of doing things and I thought Jock was just too savage and uncaring on certain occasions.

I will always believe he was unnecessarily brutal when he dealt with me in my last days as a Celtic player. I hadn't a clue the end was in sight when I trotted onto the field as a substitute in the 3-0 European Cup triumph over BK Copenhagen on Wednesday September 29 1971. I didn't realise I would never set foot on the Celtic Park playing surface again. Things were obviously going on behind my back and no-one thought to keep me informed. At the very least, I would have thought that would have been good manners. Twenty days after my appearance against the Danes I was a Crystal Palace player. I was caught up in a whirlwind that left my head in a spin. My eleven-year Celtic career seemed to evaporate in such an alarmingly short space of time. I may have been confused as the events unfolded, but one thing that wasn't in doubt was the fact I was no longer in Stein's plans. I was no longer wanted at Celtic.

Look, I understand football teams have to evolve. Celtic had quality youngsters such as Kenny Dalglish, Lou Macari, Victor Davidson and Paul Wilson challenging for places in the forward line. You would encourage such exciting protégés to push for places in the first team. That's a completely acceptable and expected development of a football team. I would have been part of that process eleven years earlier when stalwarts such as Neilly Mochan and Willie Fernie were being phased out. The legendary Charlie Tully had left just before I arrived. It's worth remembering these guys were in their thirties. Tully, in fact, was only five years short of his fortieth birthday before he quit to wind down his remarkable career at Cork Hibs. I was twenty-eight and, arguably, my best days were ahead of me. Or so I thought.

Jock had made up his mind and there was no point in arguing the case. I was left with the distinct feeling that I would be sitting in the stand every matchday if I didn't sign for Crystal Palace. Without win bonuses and appearance money, that would hit me hard financially. I was made well aware I wouldn't kick a ball in the first team again. What can you do in a situation like that? It was time to go and I'll never forget the day I walked through those front doors at Parkhead realising I wouldn't be back.

I scored against Falkirk in a league game at our place in a 4-0 win on March 27 1971. There wasn't anything special about it, but obviously I had no idea it was the last goal I would claim in front of my own fans at the place I truly believed was Paradise. My final goal for the club came in a League Cup-tie against Ayr United at Somerset Park on August 21 when we won 3-0. And, of course, my final farewell was the 3-0 triumph over BK Copenhagen. At least, I went out as a winner although I admit that is scant consolation.

Please don't run away with the idea it was all grunting and growling when Jock and I were sharing the same postcode. We could actually be in the same dressing room without an angry exchange. In fact, there is a lot I have to thank him for and I realise those words may surprise or even shock you. Back at the start of 1965, I genuinely thought my career might be elsewhere. I admit the possibility of asking for a transfer often occupied my thoughts. I couldn't help but wonder if a move might prove to be beneficial. There are always transfer rumours in football and I figured in more than a few.

By the time the chimes for 1965 were still fresh and another year had been welcomed, I had been playing first team football since the start of season 1960/61. I netted seventeen goals in my first campaign and followed that up with thirty-one. Then I hit a slump and claimed only twenty-two! I got eighteen the year after that bringing it to a total of eighty-eight goals in four campaigns. Not bad shooting for a rookie, even if I do say so myself.

And yet I wasn't guaranteed a first team place in a side that often struggled. Why? Sean Fallon simply didn't fancy me. Jimmy McGrory may have had the title of manager, but he didn't pick the team and we all knew it. Chairman Bob Kelly would take on that chore and he had the ear of Sean. We all realised, too, that Sean was Kelly's man. He fed him all the information and gossip from the dressing room. And, clearly, I didn't appear to be his idea of a footballer. It didn't matter that I was scoring goals every other game, my face didn't fit. He never bothered to tell me where he thought I was going wrong. I was left out of the team and I was too naive to ask for a reason. I doubt if I would have been given an explanation, anyway. I would probably have been shooed away into a corner like some errant schoolboy.

Frustrated? That would have been a massive understatement. Without warning, I would be chucked into the cauldron of an Old Firm confrontation and the next I was dropped and back in the reserves. I'm not exaggerating and facts will back me up. Look at season 1961/62, for instance. I scored seventeen goals in a sequence of twenty-five games. I was reasonably happy with that sort of form and, please remember, I was still a teenager. Then I hit two successive blanks and, you've guessed, was axed with Bobby Carroll taking my place for the next game against Raith Rovers which Celtic lost 1-0 at Parkhead. That was the way of things at the club pre-Stein. Sean Fallon had a lot of power in team matters and would even lock Jimmy McGrory out of the dressing on some occasions. Yes, I know that sounds absolutely ludicrous, but, believe me, it happened on a regular basis.

Before Big Jock walked back through that door in March 1965, I genuinely believed my future lay elsewhere. I wasn't alone. There were grumblings in the dressing room and we all knew Spurs wanted Billy McNeill. There were stories about Bobby Murdoch thinking about emigrating with his family to Australia. Falkirk were said to have taken a liking to Bobby Lennox and there was even speculation that Jimmy Johnstone was so fed up with his treatment that he was thinking of going back to the Juniors. Anyone who ever met Jinky will know that rumour may have not been too outrageous.

Jock was aware of my situation even while he was manager of Hibs. I bumped into him purely by coincidence at a midweek international at Hampden. Quietly, he took me aside. He whispered, 'I hear you're thinking about asking for a transfer. Is that right?' I nodded and said, 'I'm thinking about it.' He replied, 'Don't do anything.' I was a little puzzled. 'What do you mean?' I asked. 'Just what I say. Hold your decision for awhile. I want you to stay at Celtic. I know you can do a good job for the club. Give me time to get things sorted.' It was the first time I realised the rumour factory had got it absolutely right; Jock Stein was about to return to Celtic. I may have been astonished at the time, but it didn't take me long to discover that Jock had spies everywhere. He would have known as much of what was going on in the Celtic Park dressing room as the one at Easter Road. To this day, I still have no idea who would have alerted to him to the fact I had grown a little disenchanted with my situation regarding being in and out of the first team at Celtic, but, of course, his information was spot on.

Naturally, I was delighted to agree to remain at the club that was closest to my heart. I was excited by the news of Jock Stein coming back to Parkhead. Billy McNeill had insisted the club made a catastrophic error in allowing him to leave in the first place in 1960. Three years earlier, Jock's career had ended through the injury that left him with a limp for the rest of his life. He was thirty-five at the time and was put in charge of the reserve team. He made a huge impression on Billy, that much was obvious. Jock had been a centre-half in his playing days and he must have seen the potential in Caesar. It was only natural, I suppose, that he became a bit of a mentor. Yes, Billy was more than a little disappointed when Jock wasn't offered a step up in the management at Celtic and left to manage Dunfermline where, of course, he guided the Fifers to an unexpected 1961 Scottish Cup win over Celtic. Sadly, I have to admit I was centre-forward in that Celtic team. He had one year at Hibs before making the journey back to the east end of Glasgow.

I'll always recall Big Billy coming into the dressing room one morning and beaming with delight. 'Big Jock's coming back!' He stopped short at shouting 'Hallelujah!', but we could see our captain was more than overjoyed. 'Let's see what happens now.' I smiled because I had already been aware of the impending return of Jock, but had been sworn to secrecy. I believe Jock agreed to come back in January, but the move wasn't put in motion until March. That was in 1965. I was just as excited as Billy because, after years of uncertainty and a total lack of coaching or guidance from Sean Fallon or his other backroom staff, I knew there was a someone coming into the manager's job who appreciated me. Six years later, though, he had a change of mind and it was a case of 'Adios - and close the door behind you.' Yes, of course, I felt a great injustice. What had I done to deserve the brush off? I still ask myself that question today.

Of course, a lot has been made of a situation during half-time in a league game against St.Johnstone at Muirton Park in February 1971. That was a full eight months before I was shifted onto Crystal Palace. Would he have waited so long to push me out the door? Remember, there were no transfer windows at the time and Jock could have sold me any time he liked. So, was it something that occurred in that Perth dressing room that hastened my departure? I'll never know for sure.

What I do know is that the pitch in Perth that day was barely playable. It was just a sea of mud and, of course, defenders favour these sort of conditions a lot more than forwards. The big hard men at the back can launch themselves into slide tackles with reckless abandon. I took a sore one on the right shin that afternoon. By God did it hurt. I was on the ground when the blood began to flow. I pulled down my sock to be confronted by a horrible, ugly-looking gash. I wasn't wearing shinpads and a St.Johnstone player's studs had ripped through the sock and raked my leg. I was in agony. Was it an accident? Look, I know these things can happen on dodgy playing surfaces.

I didn't think there was a prayer of me completing the game. I hobbled around on the left wing until the interval arrived and I made my way to the dressing room to let the doctor inspect the damage. He wasn't too impressed. The doc inserted twelve stitches as an emergency procedure and I thought that was my involvement in the action over for the afternoon. Most people, I believe, would have thought that was a more than reasonable assumption. Stevie Chalmers was our substitute, so it wasn't like I was leaving the team a man short. Big Jock had other ideas, though. I was stunned when he asked me, 'Are you okay to go out for the second-half?' I pointed to my mangled right shin. 'Look at that mess, Boss. One touch and it will burst wide open.' He was neither convinced nor concerned. He said nothing more to me and told Stevie to get prepared to go on. Clearly, though, he wasn't happy with me. If there was a way I could have played on, I most certainly would have done. Everybody played through the pain barrier at one stage or another for Jock and Celtic. On this occasion, I couldn't take the very real chance of the wound turning poisonous. We lost 3-2 and Big Jock blamed me. I didn't think that accusation was fair. Needless to say, there was a bit of a frosty atmosphere on the team coach on the journey back from Perth to Glasgow. Not once did he ask me about the excruciating laceration. That was just Jock's manner, though.

The record books will show, by the way, that I was not fit enough to play a week later in a 1-1 Scottish Cup draw with Dunfermline, then I sat out the midweek 1-0 victory over the Fifers in the replay. There was still no-show from yours truly in a 4-1 win over Airdrie on February 20 and seven days later I was still in the stand for a 1-1 draw against Hearts. I came back after more than a month out to score a goal in a 5-1 win over Cowdenbeath on March 13. I had hardly been play-acting. I've still got a plainly visible scar to this day. And, only eleven days after my comeback against Cowdenbeath, the manager thought I had something to offer in one of the club's biggest games of the season; the second leg of a European Cup Quarter-Final encounter against the mighty Ajax, of Amsterdam, at Hampden. The game was switched to the national stadium to allow a crowd of 83,684 to attend while reconstruction at Celtic Park limited the number to 73,000.

I highlight this match because it underlined Big Jock couldn't have fallen out with me too badly after the St Johnstone incident. If there had been any sort of resentment on his part, I would not have played against the Dutch side. Those were the days when Celtic went into Europe's premier competition with real thoughts of winning the trophy. We were never just there to make up the numbers.

I missed the first game when all the team's good work disintegrated late in the second-half. The engrossing encounter was balanced at 0-0 when, suddenly, Johan Cruyff and his team-mates turned on the after-burners. They netted three efforts inside the last half-hour to leave Celtic walking a tightrope in Glasgow. I was given the nod to face the Dutchmen, but, first, there was another insight into how Big Jock's mind worked. Ajax had insisted on Celtic players wearing unfamiliar yellow tops and green shorts in the first game. They pointed out our green and white hoops, white shorts and white socks clashed with their iconic strip with the big red band down the front of their white top. However, they planned to wear their first team strip at Hampden. Apparently, in Amsterdam it clashed, but in Glasgow it didn't. Jock was far from impressed. He made certain they wore their change strip of blue shirts and shorts. They just didn't look like Ajax.

Wee Jinky netted in the twenty-seventh minute and their keeper, Heinz Stuy, looked rattled as we continued to take the game to the Dutch. I managed to slip the ball behind Stuy, but referee Concetto Lo Bello ruled it out for offside. Ironically, that was the same Italian match official who had been in charge in our European Cup Final the previous season against another Dutch side, Feyenoord. I'll talk about that particular confrontation elsewhere. Jinky's effort was the only valid goal of the evening and we went out. Ajax, on the other hand, went on to beat Greek side Panathinaikos, then managed by Real Madrid legend Ferenc Puskas, 2-0 at Wembley and they successfully defended for the next two years against the Italian double-act of Inter Milan (2-0) and Juventus (1-0). The margins between success and failure in top flight football are so tight.

We all had to accept that we had gone out 3-1 on aggregate to a superior team and, soon enough, everyone was talking about the likes of Johan Cruyff, Piet Keizer, Ruud Krol, Johan Neeskens, Wim Suurbier and Barry Hulshoff. Rinus Michels, their astute manager, had flooded the midfield and cut off the service to Jinky and me. We rarely got the opportunity to run at their full-backs. Jock didn't single out anyone for particular criticism after that match at Hampden. However, I recall receiving a ferocious verbal volley after a game against Hibs at Easter Road in January 1968. My offence? I went to offer my condolences to their right-back Bobby Duncan in their dressing room.

Unfortunately, Bobby had suffered a broken leg when I slid it to try to block the ball. His ankle got caught up in my outstretched leg and he collapsed to the turf in obvious pain. It was a complete accident, I hasten to add. The conditions were slippy that afternoon and we just collided with neither of us able to pull out. Unhappily, the defender had to be stretchered off and I felt sick. I never set out to injure an opponent; not once. Frankly, I wouldn't have known how to, but I did know some players who were well versed in the black arts. No names. No pack drills. No lawyer's letters! It just wasn't the right-back's day because he had also sliced a clearance into his net to give us a second minute lead. Bobby Lennox added a second shortly afterwards and it was game over. But the Hibs player's game, unfortunately, didn't last until the ninetieth minute and I headed for the home dressing room as soon as the referee blew for time-up. I was concerned for the player who, although he was a gritty campaigner, was never dirty.

I mixed with the Hibs players and told Bobby I genuinely hoped he would make a fast recovery. He accepted my good wishes and I thought that was the end of it. Suddenly, though, Colin Stein, who would later join Rangers, barged through his team-mates to have a go at me. He accused me of deliberately trying to injure Bobby. I wasn't having any of that and told him to get lost. I didn't stop to think I was actually in the Hibs dressing room. The usual pushing and shoving ensued before I was thrown out into the corridor. Jock wanted to know what all the commotion was about. I gave him my version of events and he blew up. 'What do you want to do that for?' he bellowed. 'It's bad enough the boy's got a broken leg, but you've got to go and make it worse!' I protested my innocence, by which time he was in full flow. 'What a daft thing to do.' And so on. I thought it had been a meaningful gesture from one professional to another, but Jock, clearly, disagreed. Sometimes you couldn't win with that man. And I should know.

As I have previously pointed out, I was the club's sixth top marksmen with 189 goals when I was moved on. An upstart called Henrik Larsson then came along, scored a mountain of goals, peaked at 242 and pushed me down to seventh. Actually, that's a phenomenal strike rate, but, then, Henrik was a phenomenal player. Yet I look at my tally and I know I could and should have scored so many more. Jock Stein always insisted on his players disguising their weaknesses and playing to their strengths. So, here's something that will undoubtedly surprise you. I may have been 6ft 2in, but I was utterly hopeless in the air. I don't know how many goals I scored with my head, but the total possibly didn't reach double figures. Funnily enough, I never once heard or read anyone saying it was a flaw in my game. However, I believed it was a massive Achilles Heel. Wee Jinky probably scored more goals with his napper than I did!

Of course, I wanted to do something about it. I volunteered for extra training and let it be known I would welcome coming back in the afternoons. I would have spent a couple of hours just running around in the penalty area with someone in goal and players battering over crosses from right and left. Heading a ball has got nothing to do with how tall you are. For me, it's all about timing. Denis Law was three inches short of six feet, but look at the goals he scored with flying headers. He had a prodigious leap, could almost hover in the air and when he made contact the ball came off his head like a cannonball. His timing was as close to perfect you will see for a penalty box operator in a congested area where you have very little room to manoeuvre. But that was all down to practice. Denis just didn't inherit that skill; he worked hard on it in training every day.

I wanted to improve that part of my game and I thought the only way to achieve that was extra training geared specifically to working on my aerial threat - or lack of it, to be more accurate. I put the suggestion to Big Jock. I was more than a little taken aback when he knocked the suggestion on the head. I could hardly believe it. I was giving up my spare time to put myself through punishing routines for the good of the team and my manager didn't want to know. As he would do so often, he simply waved me away with one his big shovel-like hands. 'Naw, naw, you don't need to be bothered with that. We score enough goals without you getting headers.' And that was that. I was completely mystified by the abrupt response, but, once more, there was little worth in debating the point.

If jock had permitted me a moment of his time, I could have underlined how many goals I would have scored coming in at the back post, running in from the left. We had guys in the team such as Wee Jinky, Bobby Murdoch and others who could hang up inch-perfect crosses and I've no doubt had I worked and polished that side of my game, then I would have scored a helluva lot more than 189 goals. It could have been a potent weapon for the club, but it was never utilised. Big Jock didn't want to know and his voice was the only one that mattered in the dressing room.

I scored one of the most crucial goals in Celtic history when I dived full-length in front of Jack Charlton to twist my head and flick an effort past Leeds United keeper Gary Sprake in that unforgettable European Cup semi-final second leg at Hampden in 1970. The Elland Road side had tied the game 1-1 on aggregate with a whizzbang effort from my wee mate Billy Bremner. That must have given them a powerful surge in confidence, but my goal took the wind out of their sails and, of course, Bobby Murdoch made sure we were in the Final with a quickfire second. Surely, the importance of that goal emphasised what I could offer when the ball was in the air in the opponents' penalty area. Jock still didn't want to know, though.

He was content when a rare headed goal came along because he was confident the likes of Bobby Lennox, Stevie Chalmers, Willie Wallace and Joe McBride would contribute more than enough in their direct fashion with the ball at their feet. And, of course, we had Billy McNeill for set-plays. Big Billy was magnificent in the air, just about unbeatable, so that contingency was catered for by our skipper.

Please don't get me wrong. This is not a Big Yogi versus Big Jack chapter in my life story. I just want the supporters to be aware of the facts. For a start, I think he did me an enormous favour by pushing me out from centre-forward to the left wing. I was happy enough in the central role, but Jock thought I could be more effective when I was taking passes on the half-turn. I would be off and running within seconds of the pass arriving at my feet. In the main striker's role, though, I would often have my back to goal. Controlling the ball in those circumstances would add vital seconds onto the manoeuvre. A centre-half could be breathing down my neck, forcing me to push the ball back for a midfielder. At outside-left, though, I could skin a right-back if he got too close. And once I was away, there was no stopping me.

Jinky used to like going back to beat the defender again. And then again. The steam used to come out of Big Jock's ears as he sat in the dug-out. Jinky, of course, was an entertainer and he responded to the crowds, who, rightly, adored him and urged him to go through his full repertoire. Jock didn't see it that way. He wanted the Wee Man to hit the byline and get crosses into the box. It took awhile for Jinky to understand the wisdom of his boss's train of thoughts. Until then, he would simply put on a show, skipping past tackles as only he could. That's not the way I performed. Once I was away from the bloke it was up to him to chase me and try to catch me. I was fast and had good ball control, so that was highly unlikely most of the time. It was Jock who noticed that in my play, so, of course, I will be forever grateful for that. But I still can't help wondering how many goals I would have had in my collection today if I had been allowed to work on my heading ability.

I'm sure it would have been an entirely different situation if I had signed for an English club long before I did. I used to watch a lot of English football on the television and it looked as though their style of play suited a big forward looking for the ball in the air. Liverpool had Tony Hateley, dad of former Rangers player Mark. I hope I'm not being too judgemental here, but I think it would be fair to say that Tony was just a little cumbersome on the deck. He did most of his good work in the air and he was actively encouraged to perform in this manner. West Ham had Geoff Hurst, who, to be fair, was a more skilled performer on the deck than he ever got credit for. Leeds United had Mick Jones, Spurs had Martin Chivers and West Brom had Jeff Astle. Then there was the Welsh pair of Wyn Davies, of Newcastle, and Ron Davies, of Southampton. They weren't related and the only thing they had in common in a football sense was that they were both terrific aerial artists. The old-fashioned Newcastle centre-forward was actually known as 'Wyn The Leap'.

To a lot of critics that may sound like 'Route One' tactics, the ball missing out the midfield players as a defender launches it straight down the pitch into the other team's penalty area. Yes, I've seen some teams simply adopt this so-called strategy, but, when it's done properly, it has its merits. Why not mix it up? Come at teams from all angles with a range of weaponry? Utilise the full skills your team? I don't see anything wrong with that way of thinking. The punters crave goals and they'll take them any way they can get them. And, after all these years, I fully realise I could have had those Celtic fans cheering a lot more times than my career total of eleven short of two hundred. Upon reflection, I must have been pretty good with the ball at my feet!

Being a one-time publican, I am well aware that sour grapes always provide the most bitter wines. I certainly don't want to come over as bitter as regards Jock Stein. As I have already outlined, there is a lot I have to thank him for. I've often been asked what were my feelings when Jock was nudged aside to allow Billy McNeill to take over as manager in 1978. I'm not sure what anyone expects me to say. Was I happy that he might have received some of his own medicine? No, I can say with utmost honesty that did not enter my head. Why would it? In genuine terms, it meant nothing to me. I had been out of football for over five years, so Big Jock leaving Celtic had no bearing whatsoever in my life. Did people expect me to gloat? Sorry, that's just not my style. I admit I didn't attend his funeral and some folk may interpret that as a lack of respect. That's not the case, either. I'm not a hypocrite. Jock Stein and I had no contact whatsoever following my departure from Celtic. We didn't speak at all, so that would have been at odds with me turning up to say farewell. He hurt me and I will never forget that, but that's the end of it.

I repeat I am not a bitter guy. Celtic Football Club, my team-mates and those wonderful supporters meant so much to me. When it ended so hastily, unexpectedly and painfully, I believe I was left in some sort of state of shock. I never saw myself as John Hughes of Crystal Palace. I was always John Hughes of Celtic. A huge chunk of my life and my passion had been taken away in what seemed an instant. That's difficult to overcome.

Let me also put the record straight here. It takes a big man to admit he has made a mistake and I've been called 'Big Man' goodness only knows how many times in my life. I have been quoted as saying Big Jock wrecked my career. After a lot of consideration and a bit of soul searching, I no longer believe that to be the case. Jock Stein did not wreck my career. However, I think he went a long way to shortening it. The injury I received in one of my first games as a Crystal Palace player meant I was forced to take a short cut to football's scrapheap before the age of thirty. However, that was all down to fate. I hope that clears up that point once and for all.

There is an old saying that goes along these lines, 'Good and true partnerships tumble out of heaven together.' It would appear Jock Stein and I became separated somewhere along the route to our different destinations.

Chapter 2

JINKY'S LASTING IMPRESSION

It was a fairly memorable occasion when I first clapped eyes on Jimmy Johnstone. I've still got the scars to prove it!

I was eleven years old and had been persuaded by a teacher by the name of Vincent Bradley to play for Coatbridge's St Augustine's Primary School football team. Until then, my main sporting pursuit had been running. I was equally fond of sprints and long-distance and considered myself to be an athlete. I worked on pace and stamina and at no stage did I even consider kicking a ball around for fun. As a matter of fact, I had a conversation with my teacher one day and I told him emphatically, 'I don't want to play football. I'm a runner.'

But Mr Bradley was so persistent I decided to give it a try, even if it was just to stop him nagging. I was tall and fairly well built for my age, so I was placed right up front in the middle of the attack and told to put the ball behind the opposition's goalkeeper as often as possible. I began banging them and I have to admit I was thoroughly enjoying my time on a football pitch. Running was soon put on hold.

I was making a bit of a name for myself, but so, too, was another youngster from Viewpark in Uddingston. Even at that age, Jimmy Johnstone was wowing audiences. His reputation was known to us and we were all looking forward with eager anticipation to a match between St Augustine's and St Columba, Jimmy's school, in Viewpark. We had a left-back by the name of Mick Connerty and we had been teasing him about what this little winger was about to do to him. Mick, though, had other ideas and actually trained hard for a week before the game. He probably quit smoking, too! On the Saturday morning, both teams turned up and I was amazed to see there was a fair crowd in attendance. Admittedly, the game had attracted a bit of local interest, but most of them would have been there to witness yet another display of trickery from the wee outside-right with a bouncing mop of bright red curls.

And that was the first time I ever saw the wee lad who was to become such a firm friend. Both teams went through the usual ritual before the kick-off. I always felt sorry for the goalkeepers at that point. Everyone wanted to leather the ball with all their might at goal. We were queuing up to batter shots at our guy and I took the opportunity to glance over in the direction of the character I came to know as Jinky. What was so special about this wee guy who looked just a shade taller than a Subutteo player? He was playing keepy-uppy with the ball and I was impressed. He looked so in control and so confident. 'We've a game on today,' said Mr Bradley by way of tactical nous.

When the action got underway, it was obvious Wee Jimmy had his personal fan club in attendance. His mother was among a clutch of noisy women who wildly cheered his every touch. Jinky played to the gallery, as he would at bigger and slightly more glamorous venues later in life. However, Mick Connerty was not quite ready to be made to look a fool. He stuck to his task, got his tackles in swiftly and accurately, read play well and wasn't too fussy about where he placed his clearances. Jinky was looking increasingly frustrated as our left-back refused to follow the script. At the other end, I was lucky enough to thump in the opener. Then I got another. Before the end I had completed my hat-trick. St Augustine's won 3-1 and my pals mobbed me as we celebrated at the final whistle.

Life couldn't have been better or sweeter as I came off the pitch. The next minute, though, I felt this terrible whack across the back of my head. I was startled and turned to face this lady with a rolled-up umbrella. It was Jimmy's mother. She was about to take another swing as she shouted, 'You big cheat. There's nae way you're under twelve. You look like you've been shaving for years.' I decided to revert back to my old sport and show her a clean pair of heels while some of her chums, flailing brollies and handbags at the ready, decided to join the throng. 'Save me, sir,' I cried as I raced past Mr Bradley. In a matter of moments, my teacher had just about caught up with me as we frantically dashed for the safety of the changing rooms. Yes, I do indeed remember the day I first met a certain Jimmy Johnstone. It would be extremely difficult to forget the experience. At least, later in life, I had a reasonable idea where Jinky inherited his fiery temperament.

Little did I know what lay ahead of me when I made my debut on the planet on April 3 1943, the first of three sons to James and Margaret Hughes with Patrick and Billy following in rapid succession. Home was a council house in Langloan, Coatbridge, and I remember we had fold-down beds because it was so cramped. Dad worked with the builders Mactaggart & Mickel before becoming a van salesman. He was a strict disciplinarian and, to my young mind, was overly-keen in his manner of chastising his children. Maybe that's just the way it was in those days. Mum made her living in a factory of some sort, but I haven't a clue what it manufactured. What I do recall, though, was that we had a family car and that was a rarity in our part of Coatbridge. My dad was a bit of a gambler and I remember the story of how he and two of his mates went over to Ireland to have a look at a greyhound they were interested in buying. They were so suitably impressed after seeing the dog that they shelled out £800 for it. Now that was a massive amount of money in those days, but, presumably, they saw it as an investment.

Anyway, the greyhound was packed up in the car and brought back to Scotland where it was put through a couple of solo trials. It smashed the track records at Coatbridge and Armadale and my dad and his pals thought it was only a matter of time before they were repaid their £800 and started coining in it with runaway victories at dog tracks up and down the country. They believed they had struck greyhound gold. Who could beat this rocket on four legs? Unfortunately, there was a slight snag. There was little doubt the dog was lightning quick and had the undoubted ability to break records everywhere. However, it wouldn't run with other dogs. It refused to race when it was put up against other mutts. Solo, it was unstoppable. At a track with dogs on either side, it just didn't want to shift. I wonder if the Irish guy who sold the greyhound knew about the flaw in the dog?

My first school, as I said earlier, was St Augustine's and, naturally enough, at the age of five you don't have a clue what's ahead. I was okay at arithmetic and English, but I was more interested in sports. I looked forward to the Physical Education classes and I was already beginning to fill out and stretch. While most of my school pals wanted to play football, I wanted to run. I was always the fastest kid on the block, even if I do say so myself. Some of my wee pals could hurry and scurry, but I always had the advantage because of the length of my stride. I didn't have any thoughts of figuring in track events or anything like that. I was simply doing something I really enjoyed. I would leave the Olympic gold medal to Allan Wells.

However, once the football bug bit I found it unshakeable. Suddenly, I was out on the street with my pals kicking a ball around day and night. Obviously, we couldn't always afford a full-sized football, so we made do with what was available. You could have about twenty kids chasing a tennis ball around for hours on end and you were lucky if you saw the bloody thing never mind got a kick at it. Older readers will recognise the term 'tanner ba' player'. I'll explain for the younger perusers of this tome. Before decimalisation, there was a coin known as a sixpence which was worth half-a-shilling, two-and-a-half pence in today's money. It was a small silver coin which was also known as a tanner. No-one was actually rich enough to boot money around the streets of Coatbridge, but because of the size of a tennis ball someone coined - no pun intended - the phrase and it stuck. For instance, Jimmy Johnstone was a classic 'tanner ba' player'. No-one appreciated it at the time, but it certainly honed your ball-playing skills. If you could trap, run and shoot with a tennis ball then it was a genuine bonus when you played for your school team and were given a full-sized ball to kick around.

I moved to St Patrick's Senior Secondary in Coatbridge and, happily, I continued to evolve and improve as a footballer. I was building up my levels of strength and I thought I always had the advantage when we were playing opposing teams. It was most unusual to come up against a centre-half so tall or of similar build. Around that time, Our Lady's High School in Motherwell had a good team and boasted players such as Billy McNeill, Bobby Murdoch, John Cushley and Benny Rooney. All four would become team-mates at Celtic in later years. I often reminded Bobby, John and Benny of the day I played against them and the three of them kicked lumps out of me. I can only think Billy wasn't playing that day!

I kept on thumping in goals and I was delighted to be called up to play for the Airdrie and Coatbridge Select. Willie Henderson, later to become a rival at Rangers, was also in the team at outside-right. One game I recall was against a very good Stirlingshire Select who had an exceptionally combative wee flame-haired player in midfield. There wasn't much of the guy, but he threw himself into every tackle and snarled his way through ninety minutes. I have to say I was really impressed by his commitment and desire to be a winner. His name was Billy Bremner, who, of course, went onto to captain Scotland and the hugely successful Leeds United side of the seventies. The Scottish Schoolboys versus their English counterparts at Wembley was coming up quickly on the horizon and the manager of the Airdrie and Coatbridge Select team took me aside and informed me, 'A half-decent performance from you today and you'll be certain to play for Scotland.'

So, I was on a high when we kicked off against Bremner and his mates. Despite Billy's efforts, we won 6-1 and I scored five. Frankly, I ran amok. 'Wembley, here I come,' I thought as I came off the pitch. My teacher and my team-mates were all convinced I would be playing against England. 'Score a goal for me, John,' they were saying. I had been told a half-decent performance would get me a place in the line-up to play at a ground I had only seen on the television when FA Cup or international games were being played. And now I was going to get the opportunity to play at that world famous ground. Or so I thought. When the squad was announced the name John Hughes was nowhere to be seen. My school teacher broke the news. I was shattered.

Mind you, it wasn't the only decision in football that would leave me more than a little bewildered, but more of that later. I was told a player called Nick Sharkey, who played for Helensburgh Schools, was going to be in the centre-forward position. Yes, Helensburgh, that hot bed of football. Sharkey did indeed go onto play in the senior game with Sunderland, Leicester City, Mansfield Town and Hartlepool United. He never got a sniff at playing for Scotland at full international level although, I believe, he picked up a couple of Under-23 caps. If I remember correctly, I might even have played alongside him against

England in 1964. One thing is certain, though; I'll never fathom why I was overlooked by the schoolboy selectors.

Thankfully, though, I was on Celtic's radar. A scout by the name of Jimmy Gribben liked what he saw and fixed up some training sessions at Celtic Park. I was fifteen years old and still hadn't left school. One day a member of the Celtic backroom staff asked, 'Are you okay to turn out for the third team on Wednesday afternoon?' 'No problem,' I fibbed. There was the little matter of attending school, but I wasn't going to allow such a trifling matter stand in my way of playing for my beloved Celtic. And at Parkhead, too. I went to school in the morning, but staged my disappearing act at the lunchtime break. I turned up at Celtic Park, was told I was playing at centre-forward and my little heart was beating away at a furious rate. I was actually going to pull on those green and white hoops. It didn't matter that it was a third team game. This was the big-time. I can't recall the opponents or the final score, but I thought I did reasonably well although I admit I found the pace a bit in the last half-hour or so. I was fit, but that was a gigantic step-up from schools football.

I was all smiles when I turned up at St Patrick's the following day. The geography teacher spotted me in assembly and called me over. 'Good morning, John,' he said in stern tones. 'I noticed you weren't at school yesterday afternoon. Any reason for that?'

'Sorry, sir,' I replied. 'I wasn't feeling too well and had to go home.'

'Really?' he asked with an arched eyebrow. 'Sorry to hear that, John. By the way, did you realise you have a double? I went over to Celtic Park yesterday for the second-half of the third team game. There was a young bloke playing at centre-forward for Celtic. He looked a lot like you.'

I stood there, slightly shame-faced. I had been rumbled. The teacher smiled, 'Get back to your class.' Then he added, 'I thought you did quite well.'

'Thank you, sir,' I answered before making a quick getaway. My secret was safe.

After I left school, my only ambition was to play for Celtic. To be honest, I never tried too hard at school and, to this day, that is something I regret. I made sure my children - Kevin, Martin, John and Joanna - went to fee-paying schools to get the education I never got and I have to say I am very proud of all four. Hindsight, as they say, offers twenty/twenty vision. I look back and know I should have done something entirely different. Fat lot of good years down the line to have that knowledge. Football and Celtic completely dominated my thoughts, though, and I had that inner confidence, that all-important self-belief in my ability that I had something to offer at that level. I wouldn't say I was optimistic because it was more like assured. That sounds cocky and I'm not that sort of character, but when you're fifteen years old and you've already played in the Celtic third team and you've been training on Tuesday and Thursday nights every week with the players, you do begin to think that it is all there in front of you. Take into consideration, too, that you can see young guys you know such as Billy McNeill and Bobby Murdoch getting ready to carve out a career in the game. It all seemed perfectly natural.

And so it proved. Eventually, manager Jimmy McGrory, one of the most modest of men it was ever my privilege to meet, asked me to sign proper forms. I had been farmed out to Junior club Shotts Bon Accord to get 'toughened up' and now I was about to become a full-time Celtic player. Naturally, I didn't have to be asked twice. I signed and agreed a weekly wage of £5.

I made my debut in a League Cup-tie against Third Lanark at the age of seventeen on August 13 1960 and marked my Celtic Park bow with a goal in a 2-0 victory. I'll never forget it. The game was goalless at the interval and, four minutes into the second-half, we won a corner-kick. John Divers, who would become a lifelong friend, took a short one to Bertie Peacock, a very clever Northern Ireland international. He swung a cross into the box and I threw myself at it. My heart skipped a beat as my headed effort soared past their keeper Jocky Robertson. Actually, that was a bit of a catchweight contest. Wee Jocky must have been one of the smallest netminders in history and stood at a mere 5ft 5-and-a-half inches. I towered over him!

After a few months, I had become a regular in the side and discovered the other first team players were earning £12 per week. I didn't think that was fair. I went to see Mr McGrory. I thought I was paying my way, I was scoring goals and getting the nod to play just about every week. Mr McGrory took a puff at his omnipresent pipe, shook his head and said, 'Yes, John, I see your point, but you must remember that you're still serving your apprenticeship. You're just a laddie.' I didn't know whether to laugh or cry. However, he did agree to give me a two quid hike. I was on £7 per week, a pound a day. Big money!

By the way, I received £250 when I put pen to paper on the formal signing papers with Celtic. Well, actually, say 'I received', but, in truth, I never saw a penny of that signing-on fee. I recall I used to wear a blue serge suit that was so worn and shiny that the backside of the trousers could have been used as a mirror. However, my hopes of much-needed new clobber were dashed. My dad probably spent it on another dud greyhound!

Chapter 3

ALL QUIET ON THE EAST END FRONT

I scored eighty-goals in my first four years in the Celtic first team and I can't remember manager Jimmy McGrory ever talking to me about football. Astonishing, isn't it?

Jimmy was more of a gentleman than a football man. You would have been forgiven if you believed it should have been the other way around when you look at his phenomenal goalscoring record with the club. He rattled in 410 goals in 408 league games. You don't have to be a mathematical genus to work out that averages more than a goal a game. In all, he claimed 550 goals in his fifteen years at Celtic. That's a British record and never likely to be broken. This guy, with the awesome, stocky build, used to terrorise defences, but when he quit the playing side of the game he reverted to his alter ego. Jimmy swapped his football gear for a three-piece suit, shirt and tie, a soft trilby hat and his trademark pipe. It was a remarkable transformation in the individual. I can only liken it to Superman turning into meek, mild Clark Kent!

This burly bloke, who looked as though he could knock over buses with a shoulder charge, had such a soft burr when he was speaking it really was difficult to fathom how he had gone about his business in packed penalty areas, grabbing so many goals, many with his head, in his utterly ruthless and courageous outlook. Remember, too, the old brown ball back then was like a cannonball. He was absolutely fearless and no-one messed with mighty Jimmy McGrory. Then he replaced his well-worn football boots for a pair of black brogues and was never seen in a football kit again.

How I would have loved to have had some advice from this prolific marksman, the most outstanding goalscorer in Celtic's history. I know you will find it hard to believe, but Mr McGrory - I could never call him Jimmy - never offered any help whatsoever. He never once took me aside to talk about my game. But please don't get the notion he was shunning or ignoring me. That would never have been in Mr McGrory's manner. Simply put, he never got involved in training sessions and there was a very good reason for that. He was never there. Incredible in this day and age of the tracksuited team boss, but that wasn't part of Mr McGrory's remit when he quit the playing side of the game. The role required so many clerical duties that he was often stuck behind a desk in his office. So, no offence was taken when he didn't suddenly appear at my side to coach me through the art of scoring goals.

I was seventeen years old when I came into the side. One minute I was playing schools football and the next I was rubbing shoulders with greats such as Neilly Mochan and Bertie Peacock. I have to say I wasn't intimidated playing in that environment. I had all the confidence of youth and I was used to scoring goals, no matter the level. But I was raw, no doubt about it.

My game was basically very simple. The defence would fire the ball down the pitch, I would hare after it and attempt to belt it on target. Such methods would be frowned on today, but I still see teams taking route one to goal. It may not be pretty or easy on the eye, but goals win games. Liverpool legend Bill Shankly once said, 'There is no such thing as a long pass or a short pass - it's all about a good pass.' When you consider what he achieved in the game, you have to respect his philosophy. Although I was getting on the scoresheet regularly, I knew I could do better. Maybe a lot of players would have been happy to claim my goal ratio, but I always wanted to push myself to the limit. If I scored one, I wanted two. If I got two, I wanted three. And so on. Jimmy McGrory would surely have identified with that because he once scored eight in one game against Dunfermline. I'm also reliably informed not one was from a trademark header and he was lethal when the ball was in the air. The record books also show he hammered in three in three minutes against Motherwell back in 1936. In today's game, it takes some so-called strikers about three months to score three goals.

So, when I signed for Celtic I thought I would be picking up all sorts of hints from this amazing penalty box performer. But, of course, I didn't know about the main duties Mr McGrory had to accept in his role as Celtic manager. So, the sought-after advice never came and that was not the fault of Celtic's most prolific goalscorer, but I still wonder about what I could have achieved in my early days at Celtic. Back then, though, so much of what was happening at the club was just a joke. Take the training, for instance. What training? Willie Johnstone was the club physiotherapist and he was in charge of all the routines. When I say 'all the routines' I mean running round the touchlines until you felt you had just lapped the globe. Sometimes it would be pitch black and Johnstone couldn't see that some of the players - notably goalkeeper Dick Beattie and centre-half John Jack - had nipped off to the back of the Jungle for a fly cigarette. They would stand up there and watch the rest of us go round and round in circles. Then Johnstone would signal there would be just one lap to go and they would put out their fags and join the rest of us. The physio never twigged.

Beattie, who played in Celtic's never-to-be-forgotten 7-1 League Cup Final win over Rangers in 1957, was a real character. In fact, neither Beattie nor Jack even bothered to get changed out of their daytime clothes when they turned up for training. When Johnstone wasn't looking, they just pulled on their tracksuits over their everyday gear safe in the knowledge they wouldn't be working up a sweat. Sometimes, if we were really lucky, we would get a ball to play with. Believe me, this was a rare occurrence and normally happened on a Friday, the day before the game. Obviously, it was thought useful to reacquaint the players with the instrument of their trade. Johnstone seemed more intent in turning Celtic Football Club into a squad of marathon runners than actual footballers. When I look back, it's easy to see why the club didn't figure too often in winning silverware. We might have been fit enough, with the exception of Messrs Beattie, Jack and the rest of the skiving smokers, to run from here to Borneo, but just don't ask us to do too much with that precious spherical object called a ball.

I might have expected some assistance, too, from one or two of the older hands when I was first introduced. I'm still waiting. They were too busy just getting by and concentrating on their own game to be concerned about a teenager. Trust me, I'm not saying this out of bitterness. Far from it. The guys who went before me would have all gone through the same routine. They didn't know any better. There was no-one there to guide them and so it went on down the line. I repeat, this is not intended to be any sort of criticism of Mr McGrory, who obviously was too busy with all sorts of other menial tasks. However, if we didn't see him at the park or Barrowfield, we made sure we caught up with him on a Tuesday. That was pay day and Mr McGrory used to pass out the wages in little brown envelopes. Another of his jobs was to look after matchday tickets. Can't imagine modern-day gaffers taking on that task, can you? Mr McGrory would be busy enough doing what was expected of him and didn't get round to matters pertaining to the football pitch. It was really amateurish.

Jimmy McGrory may have been the manager, but I soon got to know he wasn't in charge of picking the team. Mainly, that was down to chairman Bob Kelly with some input from assistant manager Sean Fallon. Yet they went through the farcical rigmarole every Thursday night of Mr McGrory submitting his line-up at the weekly board meeting. Bob Kelly would take the sheet of paper, thank Mr McGrory for his efforts and, with that, the manager was allowed to leave the building. Whether the team list on matchday bore any resemblance to the one selected by Mr McGrory is not up for debate. The chairman would make the changes he saw fit and that was the end of it. As far as I am aware, Mr McGrory never complained, not even once. I swiftly realised I should never take anything for granted in that sort of environment. I knew I could score a hat-trick in one game and be dropped the next. There was never any explanation and God forbid if you asked for one.

I played one of my first games against Rangers in an Old Firm League Cup-tie at Ibrox. I scored as we upset the odds with a 3-2 victory and I received a fabulous accolade in the Glasgow Herald. One of their top sportswriters wrote, 'Celtic have produced, almost from the playground, one big fellow of great potential. Hughes, who is only seventeen years old, caused havoc in the Rangers defence even when, for the greater part of the second-half, he was the only

Celtic forward in a position to threaten Rangers' goal, so committed to defence were his colleagues. The even bigger, heavier Doug Baillie, the home centre-half, was time and again confused as his much more nimble opponent beat him for speed and control of the ball.'

I have to say that guy certainly knew his onions! I've got another cutting from a newspaper at the time also describing my first Glasgow derby display. For reasons known only to the author of the piece, he decided to call me 'Johnny' Hughes. He wrote, 'It was asking a lot of a seventeen year old to throw him into the inferno of an Old Firm battle in his third Senior match, but young Johnny Hughes repaid the Celtic management in full for their faith in him. He won the battle of the 'Young Goliaths' with Rangers pivot Doug Baillie - and that pretty much decided the match.'

This obvious football-observing expert added, 'In a game packed with excitement and incident, Hughes gave Celts as much as any man with a wealth of experience - and the Rangers defence much more than they wished! Johnny assisted John Divers in scoring Celtic's second goal. He collected his own following a good Bobby Carroll run seconds before the interval. With any luck he might have added three more. In the first-half, Hughes gave us a slick display of footwork that baffled the four Rangers players surrounding him. Even the Ibrox followers were forced to show their appreciation.'

Aah, memories are made of that. I have to admit, though, I don't recall the Rangers fans cheering me that day. I'm sure that would have stuck in the memory bank.

Although I had scored and played reasonably well, there was no guarantee I would get the nod to keep my place in the top side. However, I am delighted to inform you I did keep my first team spot for the game against Third Lanark a week later at Cathkin Park where I netted twice as we won 3-1. So typical of Celtic at the time, that was our fourth tie in the old League Cup sections which was played on and home-and-away basis with four teams competing. We had also beaten Thirds 2-0 at Celtic Park and the only blip had been a 1-1 draw with Partick Thistle at Firhill. We were in a great position to qualify, but fell flat on our faces at the next two hurdles, both played at our place. Rangers and Thistle both beat us 2-1 and that particular dream of a trophy success evaporated all too quickly.

Of course, the Celtic supporters didn't have a clue what was happening inside the club. Back then, there were no press conferences, almost daily nowadays, it seems. The fans paid their money at the gate - we had very few season ticket holders in those days - cheered on their favourite club and left after ninety minutes, delighted with a win, disappointed with a defeat and somewhere in between with a draw. Sometimes we could really hit the heights and that would keep the fans happy for at least a week. In my first season, 1960/61, I recall scoring two in a 6-1 victory over a strong Clyde team. We were unstoppable that day. In the next home match we drew 1-1 with a fairly mediocre Raith Rovers team. Unpredictability was rife among our results and there appeared to be no rhyme or reason for our incredible highs and our dreadful lows. I suppose you could say, in fact, that the only thing consistent was our inconsistency! The loyal support appeared to accept such rollercoaster form. And worse, so, too, did some of the players. They knew they could make mistakes and no-one cared. But don't blame them for lack of ambition. Where was the motivation? If it was there, I never witnessed it.

Pre-Jock Stein, I never heard any of the players kicking off a new campaign believing we could actually win the Championship. We settled for the belief that our best chance of success was in a Cup knock-out tournament. Again, that wasn't the fault of the players. It just became an accepted fact that we were not as good as teams such as Rangers, Kilmarnock, Hibs or Hearts. In my debut season, Third Lanark finished third in the old First Division with forty-two points, three better off than us. Unbelievably, they conceded eighty goals and we lost a 'mere' forty-six from our thirty-four games. However, the now-defunct Thirds managed to rattle in exactly one hundred goals while our total was sixty-four. So, no need to look too far to discover where the deficiencies lay in our team. I knew I was in the side to score goals, but, despite netting seventeen in all competitions, it was obvious, at the age of seventeen, I needed support.

Of course, there were no such things as tactics in those dark, old days. Full-backs had to be able to tackle and hoof the ball as far down the field as possible. They were warned, too, about crossing the halfway line. That was a big no-no, especially with Sean Fallon, a former full-back, around. The centre-half was expected to win the ball in the air and on the ground and get rid of it as quickly as possible. Half-backs were there to support him and instructed to keep well away from the notion of attempting anything fancy. Inside-forwards were told to support the defence and the attack. Wingers were told to get down the line and thump over crosses for the centre-forward to try to score goals. And that was that. There seemed little room for improvisation. Veering from that formation was positively frowned upon. It was a case of 'just get on with the job and see what happens'.

I wasn't helped in my first couple of formative years when I was told Paddy Crerand didn't want me in the team. I'm the first to admit Paddy was a class act in the old right-half position and he was a master of a well-paced through pass. Mind you, I was faster than him running backwards with a piano strapped to my back! He was also a full Scotland international in 1961 and rated one of the best players in Scotland, possibly Britain. He was also four years older than me and would have known what I was going through because he made his first team debut as a youngster at the age of nineteen. Like me, he had been a Celtic supporter before joining the club. You might have thought we were kindred spirits. Nothing could be further from the truth, unfortunately.

Paddy just didn't like my style of play. No-one took the time to coach me on how to come back and accept a short pass to play in a team-mate. My game had always been about pace and power and I didn't know how to play in any other fashion. Paddy would say he got a bit frustrated when he looked up from his midfield berth and could only see the back of my head as I raced forward trying to get into a scoring position. He was frustrated? How do you think I felt? I believed I was utilising my build and speed to the best of my ability and then the ball would rarely arrive at my feet. If someone had taken me aside on the training field and talked me about the situation I'm sure we would have found a solution. That never happened.

I also heard via the dressing room grapevine that Paddy had actually gone to Jimmy McGrory and told him he wouldn't play in the same team as me. We were due to face Raith Rovers in a league game at Stark's Park two days before Christmas 1961 and I must have snapped Paddy's patience in my second season in the side. I'm not too sure what I had done to earn the scorn from my team-mate because I had actually scored in a 4-3 win over Hibs in the previous game. In fact, I had collected ten goals - including a hat-trick in a 5-0 triumph over Stirling Albion - in fifteen matches. I had been an ever-present since the start of the league campaign and I believed I was doing well enough, all things considered. But Paddy was insistent. He didn't want me in the team. When I heard the news it didn't do an awful lot for the confidence of an eighteen year old. Thankfully, though, whoever picked the team for the game in Fife didn't listen to Paddy's 'advice'. I was going to play and the ball was now in my mate's court. Would he refuse to turn out? Of course, not. We lined up together and we beat Raith 4-0. I would have loved to have scored that day, but, unfortunately, I drew a blank.

Paddy left the club for Manchester United in 1963 and was probably still moaning about my style of play. Obviously, he didn't rate my singing, either. Although Paddy had quit Celtic four years before we won the European Cup, he popped up while we were touring Dublin as we celebrated the 25th anniversary of our historic triumph. After a few drinks, it must be admitted, I was up on the stage singing with a female performer. I thought we were doing quite well. Had 'Wild Rover' and 'Oh, Danny Boy' ever sounded better? However, our impromptu duet was continually interrupted by one clearly unimpressed observer, Paddy Crerand. We meet at functions every now and again and I think the best I can say is that we tolerate each other. I suppose we've both mellowed in our seventies!

But, as you may have gathered by now, playing for Celtic in the early sixties was anything but a laughing matter. Thankfully, I'm no quitter and stuck with it. Happier days weren't too far away.

Chapter 4

AN OFFER I COULD REFUSE

John Hughes of Juventus. Doesn't sound right, does it? Yet that could have been the case at the start of sixties, remarkably only one year after I had broken into the Celtic first team.

Sounds far-fetched, I realise, but please believe me it is completely true. And I have to admit no-one was more amazed than myself when I first heard the news. One minute it seemed I was turning out in the harsh, grim world of the juniors for Shotts Bon Accord and the next I could have been playing in the glittering, glitzy top flight in Italy. You could only liken it to a bit-part actor getting jobbing roles at the Theatre Royal before being whisked off virtually overnight to star in a major movie production in Hollywood. Yes, these things can happen, but you just don't believe for a second they can happen to you.

I had made a bit of a name for myself by being promoted to the Celtic first team as a seventeen year old and, of course, had scored on my debut in a 2-0 League Cup victory over Third Lanark at Parkhead on August 13 1960. It was a nice way of introducing myself to the greatest fans in the world. I suppose the game that really caught the imagination was another League Cup-tie against Rangers at Ibrox a couple of weeks later. One newspaper report stated I had been 'unstoppable' and I have to say I had one of those games where everything fell into place. I was playing up front directly against Doug Baillie, who had just been signed for something like £12,500 from

Airdrie in the summer. That was a lot of money back then. He was a man-mountain centre-half, a no-frills defender, but I was hardly intimidated. I had scored a lot of goals for Shotts the previous year and I simply thought I could do it at a higher level. Maybe that was just the confidence of a youngster, but that was my firm belief. I couldn't wait for that Rangers game. I scored a good goal and we won 3-2. My performance and that result sent reverberations around the football world. I thought I had arrived!

A national newspaper journalist by the name of Jim Rodger caught me coming out of Celtic Park one day. He had worked for the Daily Record before moving to the Daily Express and he was known to everyone as 'Scoop'. I've since been told he couldn't write his name, but his contacts in the football world were second to none. He wasn't expected to write flowery features for his newspapers, but his remit was to go out and simply uncover exclusive football stories and pass the facts on to someone else to put in a readable form. He sidled up to me and said, 'Son, I've been watching you and I've been impressed. Aye, I think you've got it, son.' I thanked him for his very kind words and was about to walk past him and go to get my bus to take me home to Coatbridge. He took my arm and pulled me closer to me and said very surreptitiously, 'Son, there's a very big club looking at you.'

I smiled at the newspaperman. 'I'm perfectly happy, Mr Rodger,' I informed him. Let's face it, I was only a teenager not long out of school and was still a big, raw laddie. I was content just to get near the first team dressing room at Celtic. I also knew I had so much to learn. The journalist leaned forward and said the words I'll never forget. 'Juventus, son,' he whispered. 'Have you heard of them?'

Well, of course, I had heard of them. They were one of the biggest and richest teams in the world and, as far as I was concerned, operated on a different stratosphere. Apart from their obvious reputation, I knew very little else about them. I couldn't have told you they played in Turin, for instance. Frankly, I wasn't one bit interested; I was living the dream playing for Celtic. 'Think about it, son,' said Jim Rodger. 'I'll speak to you again.' To be honest, I thought nothing more about it. I wasn't even interested enough to ask what kind of cash they might be offering. Back then, that never even came close to entering the equation. I was a Celtic player and I was very happy being a Celtic player. What could have been better for a young lad who grew up supporting the club?

What I didn't realise, of course, was that Juventus were already searching for a possible replacement for Welsh international John Charles who had joined the club from Leeds United in 1957. He was a big, burly player who became known to the Italian supporters as 'Il Gigante Buono' - The Gentle Giant. Maybe they saw me as 'Il Gigante Bouno Mark Two'! Charles cost £65,000 when he switched from England to Italy which was by far a British record transfer fee at the time. He was extremely popular with the Juventus fans and little wonder when you take a quick look at his record. He was top scorer at the club in his first season with twenty-eight goals, an almost unheard-of strike total in the ultra-defensive Italian league. He was with the Turin outfit for five years in total and claimed ninety-three goals in 155 games. Juventus triumphed three times in the league championship and lifted the Italian Cup twice. He also had the distinction of winning the country's Player of the Year in his first campaign. He may just have been a hard act to follow!

Someone must have mentioned yours truly to the Italians and they set the ball rolling through Jim Rodger. That wasn't an unusual ploy back then and is possibly still the case today. Clubs couldn't be seen to be 'tapping', as it was known, another club's players. That was beyond the rules. The powers-that-be frowned on that sort of thing and the penalties could be severe. It was a lot safer to get in touch with a trusted newspaperman who would make the initial contact. Now it must be said here that Jim Rodger was an excellent fact-finding professional and I have been reliably informed he never took a single penny for any of the many stories he broke in his long and distinguished career. He did it simply for the exclusive story. He was behind such transfers as Alan Gilzean leaving Dundee for Spurs, Ian Ure moving to Arsenal from the Dens Park side and Dave Mackay joining Spurs from Hearts. Those were all massive headline-grabbing stories of their day.

I also found out later that Jim Rodger was very friendly with an Italian agent by the name of Gigi Peronace. Like the newspaperman, he had his finger in a lot of pies and was involved in an awful lot of wheeling and dealing in players coming and going. Remember, too, these were the days when there were only a handful of football agents operating throughout the world of football. Changed days with some current players having an army of advisers on their payroll. Anyway, I was more than a little surprised when I saw Jim Rodger waiting for me outside Celtic Park a couple of days later. He shuffled up beside me and once again took me aside. 'Have you given it any thought, son?' he said from the corner of his mouth. I had forgotten what he had said by the time I got home after our original meeting. 'Oh, Juventus?' I said, shaking my head. 'No, Mr Rodger, I'm not interested.'

The newspaperman could see a potential back page splash story disappearing over the horizon. 'I can introduce you to a friend of mine,' he added. 'He'll be able to outline a few of the financial matters.' I am now aware he would have been referring to Gigi Peronace. As Marlon Brando would say in *The Godfather* movies a few years later, 'Make him an offer he can't refuse.' Once again, I shook my head. 'There's no point,' I insisted. 'I'm not leaving Celtic.' He could see that I meant it, too. The journalist shrugged his shoulders under the big heavy coat he always wore and sighed, 'Okay, son, that's your decision. Good luck with your career at Celtic.' And with that he walked off.

Later that year Denis Law, who was to become a Scotland international team-mate, moved from Manchester City to Torino for £110,000, a mind-boggling fee for a footballer. The same club bought Hibs forward Joe Baker for £75,000. It was clear the Italians saw Britain as being a suitable market for fresh footballing talent. No doubt Juventus would have been more than delighted with their purchase of John Charles four years earlier. And I believe Jim Rodger was sincere when he made that original overture.

Mind you, it should be pointed out that both Law and Baker hated their time in Italy and couldn't wait to get home after only a year. Denis, in fact, went AWOL before Torino reluctantly allowed him to Join Manchester United for a fee of £115,000. And do you want to take a guess who was behind that move? Yes, none other than Jim Rodger in tow with Gigi Peronace. And I'm sure the same double-act had something to do with Baker's £70,000 shift to Arsenal around the same time.

But John Hughes of Juventus? No, I have got to admit I have always much preferred John Hughes of Celtic!

Chapter 5

OLD FIRM AND
THE GREAT ESCAPE

I should have been ordered off against Rangers in a particularly bruising League Cup-tie at Celtic Park in 1969. My crime? Well, the newspapers described it as 'an ugly incident'. I hold my hands up all these years later and readily admit I should have been banished and, if that had been the case, I accept I couldn't have offered a valid argument. I was guilty and I knew it. I was prepared to accept the consequences which, of course, would have included facing the full wrath of a furious Jock Stein. And that, trust me, was never a pleasant experience.

That inevitable repercussion never even entered my thoughts that fateful evening in the midst of a typically explosive and aggressive Old Firm encounter. Tackles were flying in all over the place, elbows were working overtime and all sorts of threats were being issued. It was all part and parcel of a Glasgow derby and, of course, I had been through it all before. On this occasion, though, I blew a gasket. I'm ashamed to admit it, but I reacted violently to a crude insult from Rangers forward Willie Johnston, a feisty wee character at the best of times.

Johnston picked the wrong moment to verbally abuse me at the height of the battle. As I recall, we were winning 1-0 through a rare Tommy Gemmell headed goal and our oldest foes were desperately trying to get back into the game. I was tracking back as they mounted another attack and I was aware of Johnston's presence close by. Now,

I had been booked in the first-half and I fully realised that another caution would see me sent packing. So, I was on my best behaviour until Johnston let fly with a hardly-articulated vocal slur.

It went along the lines of 'You big ------ bastard' - I'll let your imagination fill in the missing word - and I just saw red. Maybe the Rangers winger had just got caught up in the heat of the battle and sanity can often depart the scene in those circumstances. I'm sorry for what happened next, but I couldn't help myself. I accept what I did was inexcusable. We confronted each other and I don't know if Johnston thought I was some sort of coward, but he had this smirk on his face that drove commonsense out of the equation. I pulled up my right knee and connected with a very delicate part of his anatomy. If it had landed with more accuracy he might have been walking and talking funny for the rest of his life. Unsurprisingly, he went down as though he had been shot.

The referee, Jim Callaghan, had his back to the incident, but the linesman on the Jungle side saw everything. He waved his flag furiously to attract the attention of the match official, who was blissfully unaware of what had just happened outwith his view. Sure enough, Callaghan detected his assistant's flag, stopped play and went over for a confab. I stood there for a moment and thought to myself, 'What the hell have I done?' Then I turned away to start the long walk back to the dressing room. I believed it was inevitable that I would be sent off. It didn't matter that I had been cautioned earlier because I knew what I had done merited a straight expulsion from the field of play. Listen, anyone who knows me will tell you I am no thug. As is often the case, the sinned-against are punished when they get a bit tired of continually turning the other cheek. That's what happened that particular evening. Anyway, as I headed for the tunnel, I was amazed when I was called back by the referee. I was even more astonished when I realised he wasn't about to tell me to get packing.

I've been asked about this incident countless times and people have queried why I wasn't ordered off. To this day I can only give the same answer. 'I don't know.' I have been told Jim Callaghan might have heard Johnston's unacceptable remark and taken a lenient approach. Maybe he reacted sympathetically to the vulgar and offensive comment. I haven't a clue. What I do know is that he restarted the game with a free-kick to Rangers and I was let off with a stern warning. I sighed with relief, but, as you might expect, the Rangers hierarchy went potty afterwards, especially as we held onto our one-goal advantage and eventually qualified from the section - we had lost 2-1 at Ibrox in the earlier match - by one point. Rubbing salt into the Ibrox wounds, we went on to lift the League Cup by beating St.Johnstone 1-0 in the Final with a second-minute goal from Bertie Auld as I added to my medal collection.

That wasn't the end of the situation, sadly. Rangers sent an official letter of complaint to the Scottish Football Association and the Scottish League. We all knew the Scottish football bosses were notoriously slow in reacting to any sort of objection from one of their member clubs. Not in this case, though. The game took place on August 20 and inside a month Jim Callaghan had been suspended for eight weeks. It was remarkably swift action from the SFA and League supremos. Indecent haste, you may even observe. Let's make this clear. Jim Callaghan was a first-rate referee and had even been in charge of the Scottish Cup Final the previous season when, coincidentally, Celtic thumped Rangers 4-0. Not even the Ibrox side could grumble after that one-sided affair that saw us three goals ahead by the interval. Jim Callaghan was also on the FIFA referees' list and was a well-respected international match official.

However, the SFA effectively ended his career when they slapped a two-month suspension on him. They must have been pretty upset that I wasn't removed from proceedings that particular evening. Yes, as I've already admitted, I was culpable and should have been expelled from the field of play. I could never argue with that. But that ban on the referee was ridiculously harsh and only served to demonstrate the influence Rangers yielded over Scottish football at the time. Read into that what you will. I don't think Jim Callaghan was ever put in charge of another game. I don't know if he was so disgusted he quit the game of his own volition or was told he was as good as finished. Either way, he was removed from the Scottish football scene. And all because of one incident.

As you will discover as you read on, there was a lot that went on during Old Firm collisions that owed more to the Marquis of Queensbury Rules that those of the Football Association. Believe me, I know what I'm talking about because I have come off the pitch after more than a few of those brutal confrontations with black and blue marks all over my rib cage. By the way, the SFA obviously missed a great chance to chastise me for my part in the so-called 'ugly incident'. They could have taken action retrospectively, but they passed up that opportunity. Possibly they were too busy concentrating on making a scapegoat of poor Jim Callaghan.

Yes, meetings with Rangers could often produce fireworks. I will never forget my first league appearance in these fraught fixtures on an unforgettable - for all the wrong reasons - Saturday afternoon on September 10 1960. I was seventeen years old and had already played against the Ibrox side on two occasions in the League Cup earlier in the season which I will talk about later in this chapter. I was absolutely bursting with anticipation before the confrontation and manager Jimmy McGrory didn't have to fire me up for the occasion. Which was just as well because, as you will have undoubtedly gathered by now, he was a man of few words. I ran out onto the park to be greeted with a packed crowd, one half green and white, the other predominantly blue. That's the way they did it in those days. Rangers got half of Celtic Park for their supporters and we had a similar arrangement for our fans at Ibrox. I have to admit it was an extremely strange occurrence when one team scored and one half went doolally with delight and the other was cloaked in silence.

On that particular day, I looked around the Celtic dressing room and saw colleagues such as Dunky Mackay, a superb right-back who was ahead of his time. He liked to push forward, but that was frowned upon by the less-than-gifted backroom staff who were hardly blessed with tactical genius. God help the full-back who dared to venture across the halfway line. Paddy Crerand, already a Scottish international, was in the right-half berth while the celebrated Northern Ireland captain Bertie Peacock was on the left. A bloke called John Kurila - nicknamed 'Gorilla' - was in between them at centre-half. He did his best to live up to his nom-de-plum. Stevie Chalmers, pacy, direct and alert, was in attack alongside John Divers, a player who was completely under-rated at the club. I'll talk about JD elsewhere. I found myself lining up at outside-left.

I knew all about the Rangers right-back and skipper Bobby Shearer. He was known as 'Captain Cutlass' and I don't think that was a testimony to his elegant footballing skills. He was the type of defender who could pass the ball about one hundred yards. I was soon to find out that he would try to reach the same distance with an opposing winger. Bobby was a lovely guy off the field, all very friendly and suchlike. On the pitch, he was an animal. The Ibrox stalwart would sidle up to me and whisper in my ear, 'Try that again, kid, and I'll break your fuckin' leg.' Nice to meet you, too, Mr Cutlass.

However, it wasn't Rangers' stocky wee right-back who made the biggest impact on me that afternoon. That honour fell to Harold Davis, a lump of granite masquerading as a right-half. He was known as 'a real Rangers man'. I reckoned that meant he would kick lumps out of his granny in the Ibrox side's cause. It must be said that Davis had such limited footballing ability that he never won a single Scotland cap and those were the days when it seemed you just had to walk through the front door at Ibrox to have international reckoning thrust upon you. My goodness, even the pedestrian Shearer represented his country four times. Mind you, one of those occasions was the 9-3 defeat from England at Wembley in 1961, so that might tell you all you need to know. (We'll overlook the fact that Celtic's Frank Haffey was in goal that afternoon.)

Davis was seen by some as a war hero after fighting in the Black Watch Regiment during the Korean War in the early fifties. He was injured after being hit by shrapnel and was hospitalised for about two years. Apparently, his disability pension was still valid while he was turning out every week for Rangers. Interesting, that. Anyway, he was twenty-seven years old when I faced up to him in the east end of Glasgow that September afternoon and it seemed to me that he believed it might be a good idea if yours truly ended up in casualty for a lengthy spell. It breaks my heart to recall that game, but Rangers trounced us 5-1. As a matter of fact, Stevie Chalmers got our consolation goal in the last minute to prevent that reverse being our biggest loss to the Ibrox side in the Twentieth Century. I wouldn't have wanted that stain on my CV.

I was reminded how painful such an emphatic Old Firm defeat can be, physically as well as mentally, at one stage during the second-half. Sadly, it was a one-way procession towards John Fallon and it appeared the likes of Ralph Brand, Jimmy Millar and Davie Wilson were queuing up to take pot shots at our exposed goalkeeper. Rangers were leading 4-0 when someone managed to get the ball out of our half. I turned to chase it when I suddenly felt this sharp pain in the pit of my stomach. Harold Davis had just delivered a punch to my solar plexus that Floyd Paterson, the world heavyweight boxing champion at the time, would have been proud to claim as one of his own. It wasn't an elbow or a shoulder charge or even a push; it was a sneaky punch delivered as hard as possible by the Korean war 'hero'. I went down in a heap, the wind completely taken out of me. The referee either didn't see it or didn't think it warranted a foul on our behalf and took no action. Possibly Celtic should have complained to higher authorities.

So, that was my first meeting with Harold Davis, an individual who was fighting in Korea while I was still at my Coatbridge primary school. I didn't look for any special dispensation or consideration while playing for Celtic as a raw youngster, but neither did I expect a belt in the guts from a so-called model professional. I learned there and then that you had to grow up very swiftly in this no-punches-pulled - literally - environment. The Rangers player would never have realised it, but he did me a massive favour with his pathetic and devious act. It made me understand I would always have to stand up and be counted in the frantic, hell-for-leather atmosphere of a Glasgow derby, where, clearly, no favour was asked or given. Lesson learned.

Davis was nowhere to be seen when we played Rangers in the 1962/63 Scottish Cup Final. By that time a youthful John Greig had taken his place and the man who would go on to captain and manage the club looked as though he had picked up a hint or two from his old team-mate. The first game ended 1-1 where our goalkeeper Frank Haffey was clearly the Man of the Match. Big Frank was one of the most unpredictable footballers I have ever witnessed. He would make a spectacular save and you had to rub your eyes to make sure it was Frank in goal. In the same game, he could make a mess of a harmless passback.

At Hampden, though, on this May day he answered all our SOS calls. He was magnificent. So, too, was a wee lad on the right wing by the name of Jimmy Johnstone. He was utterly fearless as he tormented David Provan throughout the game. We all thought he was outstanding. I played through the middle of that encounter with Ronnie McKinnon as my direct opponent. I thought I had done reasonably well and Bobby Murdoch got our goal after Ralph Brand had somehow nicked one past Haffey.

However, as we prepared for the replay the following Wednesday, chairman Bob Kelly made one of the inexplicable decisions that permeated around the club at the time. Wee Jimmy was dropped and Bobby Craig, signed the previous year from Blackburn Rovers, was handed the right wing berth. Just as bewildering, I was told I was being moved to outside-left with Stevie Chalmers coming in to lead the attack as Frank Brogan, a very fast and direct winger, made his way to sit in the Hampden stand beside Wee Jimmy. It was all very puzzling and I won't dwell on this game that ended with Rangers dominating proceedings throughout.

Jim Baxter strutted around like he owned the place and there was little we could do by way of resistance. The Ibrox side won 3-0, but it was over before the interval. The eccentric Haffey failed to cut out a low right wing cross in the opening minutes and Ralph Brand tucked the ball in from virtually under the crossbar. Davie Wilson netted another before half-time and this time Haffey couldn't be blamed. However, he was lamentably slow in diving for a half-hit twenty-five-yard effort from Brand and the ball crept in at the post for their third. There were still nineteen minutes to go and that was the signal for most of our fans to get out of Hampden. Frankly, they couldn't stomach any more and it was a painful experience for the players, too. It was also the club's fourth consecutive Scottish Cup Final defeat since 1955.

I've got nothing against Bobby Craig, but he had a stinker. Big David Provan must have been the most overjoyed Rangers player BEFORE the kick-off when he was told Jimmy Johnstone had been removed from the first team. Maybe he thought the Wee Man was injured. I can tell you he was fit and raring to go. And as mystified as the rest of us to why he wasn't lining up that evening. By the way, that was Craig's last game for the club before he was offloaded to St.Johnstone in the summer. That was the Celtic way at the time. One minute you were important enough to play in a crucial Scottish Cup Final and the next you were out the door. Crazy!

Another Old Firm game embedded in my memory bank for all the wrong reasons is the 1966 Scottish Cup Final replay. By the way, Celtic fans, there are a lot of exceptionally joyous tales still to come, so let's get these ones out of the way. I always love a happy ending! Celtic were overwhelming bookies' favourites to lift the silverware for the second successive season after our 3-2 triumph over Dunfermline in the previous campaign. It was easy to fathom the reckoning of our Rolls-Royce-driving friends. We had annihilated Rangers 5-1 at Parkhead in the traditional New Year fixture and had also beaten them 2-1 in the League Cup Final where I netted two penalty-kicks.

The first game ended goalless and was a huge disappointment as far as spectacles go. The nearest to a goal came when Billy McNeill sent in a typical effort after getting his head to a Charlie Gallagher corner-kick. The ball whipped over the hands of Billy Ritchie, but, unfortunately for us, clattered off the face of the crossbar and was hastily booted to safety by a desperate Rangers defender. Dame Fortune continued to snarl at us in the replay the following Wednesday. Midway through the first-half I got clear and picked out Joe McBride, normally so lethal with his head in the penalty box. Joe's timing was perfect as he got in before the hesitant Ronnie McKinnon, but his direction was just off. Ritchie was helpless, but the ball agonisingly swept just inches wide of his right-hand upright.

Worse was to follow in the seventieth minute. Rangers built a move on the left before Willie Johnston sent over a low cross. George McLean missed it completely smack in front of goal about six yards out. If he had connected our opponents would surely have scored - and I would have escaped a rollicking from Jock Stein. Let's continue, though. The ball ran to Willie Henderson who was also unguarded on our left and his drive was scrambled clear by Ronnie Simpson and our defenders. The ball could have gone anywhere, but, unfortunately for Celtic and me, it went straight to the feet of their right-back Kai Johansen. It sat up perfectly to be hit and he walloped in a screamer from twenty-five yards. Ronnie didn't stand an earthly as the effort flew over his left shoulder. We were all disconsolate and I knew I would have some explaining to do to The Boss, who could be very unforgiving in these circumstances. I was always instructed to get into defence to mark the opposing right-back when he came forward. Normally, I would have done so, but the truth of the matter is I was struggling with an injury knock that night.

I informed the backroom staff at half-time I could feel my hamstring and, clearly, all was not well. Those were the days before substitutes. If they had been around in 1966 I have no doubt Big Jock would have taken me off and put on a replacement. Alas, we didn't have that luxury back then. So, I went out for the second-half and was told to disguise my injury. That was something that was drummed into us. We were continually told to never let our opponents know we were hampered in any way. I did my best, but I'm sure Johansen must have had an inkling I was not firing on all cylinders. I had destroyed him in the New Year game, but, on this occasion, I could hardly get away from him. I just couldn't get into my stride and, possibly, that was why he ventured so far forward at that crucial moment.

The Danish defender seemed to score as often as there was a sighting of Haley's Comet. In fact, the record books show his ratio was a goal in each year of his five seasons at Rangers and it was just my luck that one came along that evening to pinch silverware away from Celtic. Such is football.

But even after he scored, no-one wearing green-and-white at Hampden that evening thought the game was over and the Cup was lost. No chance. We still had twenty minutes to play and that was plenty of time for Celtic to turn this game on its head. Only minutes after Johansen's strike, I did manage to clip over a ball from the left and once again Joe McBride was there to snap in a header. It looked a goal all the way until it hit the Rangers keeper on the shoulder, flicked up, ran along the top of the crossbar and then dropped onto the top of the net. In moments like that you could be forgiven for believing your name is not on the Cup. And so it proved. I explained everything to the manager afterwards and fitness tests backed up everything I said, but Big Jock just let it be known he thought I had let down the team. There was no point in arguing.

Interestingly, that was Rangers' last trophy success for over four years and they were knocked out of the Scottish Cup the following season at the first hurdle when they were beaten 1-0 by little Berwick Rangers at Shielfield. Surely it would be churlish of me to even suggest they used up all their good fortune against us in that Cup Final replay? Also, we played them in the Glasgow Cup the following August at their place and gubbed them 4-0. Just thought I would mention it!

Of course, it was an entirely different outcome only three months prior to our Hampden disappointment. The traditional New Year game was due to be played at Parkhead - in fact, it was January 3 after we had beaten Clyde 3-1 on the first day of 1966 at Shawfield. I have to say the playing surface was treacherous that afternoon. It was flint-hard and there was a silvery glow under the floodlights. We didn't possess such a luxury of undersoil heating in those unenlightened times. The ground staff used to spread bundles of hay all over the place in an effort to protect the pitch. They would sweep it off as close to kick-off as possible. Then they put down what seemed like a few tons of sand. To be honest, it wasn't very satisfactory for a footballer. There was absolutely no give on the rock-hard surface under your feet. If you tried to turn swiftly in these conditions there was every chance you would end up skidding around on your backside. Actually, it could often become a bit farcical with players resembling giraffes on ice as they fought for their balance. Dignity went right out of the window.

In many people's eyes, Pele was the greatest player on the planet at that time. Make no mistake about it, even the legendary Brazilian would have struggled on these surfaces. In South America, many youngsters honed their skills performing on the Copacabana and other beaches. When they moved up a grade, they played on pitches where the grass was deliberately left a little longer. That allowed players to ping the ball around with amazing accuracy. They could hit a fifty to sixty-yard pass and the ball would simply settle on the grass. Goodness knows what they would have thought of Scotland's pitches in the dead of winter.

In fact, Jock Stein tried a little experiment in the summer of 1965 when he brought over four Brazilians to the club on trial. They were unknowns - certainly not at the Pele or Garrincha level - named Ayrton Ignacio, Marco Di Sousa, Jorge Farah and Fernando Consul. It was novelty value, of course, but they attracted a fabulous crowd, around 20,000, to a reserve game at Parkhead where Ignacio scored two goals in a 3-1 win over Motherwell. Three of them left for the sunnier climes of their homeland after only a month or so, but Igancio signed a short-term deal with Clydebank. I had to laugh at a report in a national newspaper when the Bankies took on Albion Rovers at Cliftonhill. It was another freezing, cold evening in Coatbridge and the reporter actually wrote, 'It was so cold Ignacio was turning blue with the cold.' I'm no racist, but the player in question was as black as two minutes past midnight. Unsurprisingly, Ignacio caught up with his team-mates shortly afterwards.

Anyway, back to our first Old Firm meeting of 1966. It was due for a 2pm kick-off, but there was a further problem with fog beginning to settle on the east end of Glasgow. Celtic were top of the league and Big Jock was determined to get the game played to increase our lead over our main rivals. He was confident of a victory and it was so important to show who were the new masters of Scottish football. We were all sick to the back teeth of getting Rangers rammed down our throats and, although we had won a Scottish Cup and a League Cup in the previous eight months or so, the league crown was the one we wanted. That was the priority target. It was preposterous to accept the club had last lifted the championship in season 1953/54. During that grim period Rangers won the flag on six occasions. We knew our time was coming, but even the most optimistic among those at Celtic would never have believed we would be victorious in 1966 and win it on another eight successive occasions.

Jock, as was his normal pre-match routine, walked onto the pitch with referee Tom Wharton, a massive match official who, at 6ft 4in was actually two inches taller than me. So, naturally, he was known as Tiny. At this stage, possibly about half-an-hour before the kick-off, the game must have been in doubt. The Celtic manager was nothing if not persuasive. He must have got to work on the ref. I can almost hear him say, 'Och, there's nothing to worry about, it'll clear in a few minutes.' Anyway, Tiny agreed and he declared the game on.

However, Jock must have wondered if his compelling and forceful argument to play the fixture might just have backfired on him. Rangers left-winger Davie Wilson was a tricky, little customer. It was often said he could win the Ibrox men a penalty-kick when he was fouled on the halfway line. Listen, Wee Davie could get our old foes a spot-kick at Aberdeen when he stubbed his toe getting on the team coach at Ibrox! A bit far-fetched, but you get the drift.

Having said that, he was a superb goalscorer for the club, especially for a player normally operating in a wide position. He demonstrated that against us inside ninety seconds of that particular confrontation. He mastered the tricky conditions better than our defenders, collected a rebound and slammed a low left-foot drive away from Ronnie Simpson. The man known to us all as 'Faither' was blameless as the ball squeezed in at the far post. It was a blow, no argument, but I doubt if there was a single team-mate on the park that day who didn't believe we could turn it around. Although it must be admitted it's never clever to give Rangers a goal of a start.

We began to turn the screw and pummelled their defence for just about the entire remainder of the first-half. They were defending frantically and I must admit I wasn't getting too much joy out of my immediate opponent Kai Johansen. I had made life difficult for him in the League Cup success at Hampden in October. Actually, to be fair, that was Johansen's first Glasgow derby after he arrived in the summer from Morton and I'm sure the 107,000 crowd would easily be the biggest attendance he had ever performed in front of and that can be more than a little daunting. Still, I was certain I could replicate my good form of the previous encounter. Johansen was a lot quicker than my old sparring partner Bobby Shearer and was turning quite well on the frosty and problematic conditions. I was pushing the ball past him and chasing after it, but he was doing a very reasonable job of getting back to put in tackles. It was frustrating, to say the least.

As ever, Big Jock had something to say in the seclusion of our dressing room at the interval. Like the rest of us, he was not happy. 'This is more important than a Cup Final,' he observed. 'This is the league championship. Win this and they'll never catch us. Get out there and get the job done.'

We had forty-five minutes to change things around. I spotted a pair of discarded white training shoes lying in the corner. They had suction pads and were used for training indoors. I think they were Billy McNeill's gear, I'm not sure. I had been wearing rubber studs in the first-half and they were as useful as a chocolate fireguard. I decided to give them a try and, thankfully, they fitted. What had I to lose? Johansen, I realised, would have been more than delighted with his performance up to that point. I had to give him something else to think about. I discarded my normal boots and put on the shoes. Could they make a difference? We would find out soon enough.

The game was merely four minutes into the second-half when I combined with Tommy Gemmell and our left-back sent a dangerous low cross skidding into the Rangers penalty area. Joe McBride dummied the ball and that was just perfect for someone of the speed and courage of Stevie Chalmers. He darted into the danger area and turned the ball past Billy Ritchie. Game on!

I was beginning to get into my stride on the left wing. The shoes were doing their job and definitely helped me maintain my poise and balance when I was running with the ball. Suddenly I was leaving Johansen in my slipstream. My pace was beginning to tell and he was mistiming his tackles. Thirteen minutes after the equaliser, we were ahead. It was Stevie again with a header from a left-wing corner-kick. Rangers were on the ropes and we knew it. So, too, did they. Time to go for the jugular and finish them off.

Seven minutes later, I got away from Johansen again and saw Charlie Gallagher taking up a great position about twenty-five yards out. Charlie could strike a beautiful ball, that was undoubtedly his forte. He wasn't a tackler and Big Jock always insisted we had to let our opponents know we were on the field. 'Win the battle and you'll win the war,' he would say often enough. Charlie had other strengths, though. He was a lovely passer of the ball to unlock the meanest of defences, but he could hit a shot with a lot of venom, too. I beat another couple of defenders before looking up to make sure Charlie was still unmarked and slipped the ball as expertly as I could in front of him. Charlie simply lashed an unstoppable drive in the direction of Ritchie's goal. The ball exploded against the underside of the crossbar before bouncing down over the line. The Rangers keeper didn't move a muscle.

The fourth goal in the seventy-ninth from Bobby Murdoch was a collector's item. Not because of the awesome power and flawless accuracy from our midfielder; he displayed both of those qualities often enough in his exceptional career. No, it was the role referee Tiny Wharton played in it. Jimmy Johnstone and Gallagher combined on the right before Charlie sent the ball across the Rangers defence about twenty-five yards out. The pass was actually heading for Tiny when he suddenly opened his legs and let the ball go through them. It was a consummate dummy any pro footballer would have been proud to claim. Bobby read it perfectly and hit a devastating left-foot drive that almost took the net away. I have watched a video rerun of that game and I was hugely impressed by Billy Ritchie. He was left lying on the turf, beaten for the fourth time, the game lost and, staggeringly, he got to his knees and applauded Murdoch. That didn't often happen in the heat of an Old Firm duel, but it did display the keeper's unbelievable sportsmanship.

It was all over for the Ibrox side when I moved the ball over from the left, Wee Jinky got involved and the ball dropped perfectly for

Stevie to launch a low drive past Ritchie. It was the end of a perfect day played in hellish conditions. The fog continued to descend and about an hour after the game, you could hardly see a hand in front of your face. The Rangers contingent in the 65,000 crowd must have hoped it had fallen earlier in the afternoon. It's interesting to note that we had another seventeen league games to play and we lost only three. One was at Aberdeen, another was at Hearts and the last came, rather bizarrely, at Stirling Albion.

Of course, I was delighted at the end of that unforgettable match. Stevie claimed a hat-trick, but I got most of the headlines. One newspaper emblazoned this across their back page: 'JOHN SHOES THE HERO'. A terrible pun, but I liked it all the same. By the way, it's almost stupefying to realise that Stevie's three-goal blast was the last trio claimed by a player in an Old Firm league game. Harry Hood hit three in the League Cup semi-final in 1973 and Ally McCoist knocked in a hat-trick for Rangers in the Final of the same tournament a decade later. Bobby Lennox and McCoist notched three in Glasgow Cup-ties. Celtic players such as Willie Wallace, Charlie Nicholas, Brian McClair, Lubomir Moravcik and Henrik Larsson all smacked in doubles in league games against the team from Govan, but, remarkably, Stevie's record stood right up to the Ibrox side went into liquidation in 2012. You could argue Stevie's feat will now never be emulated as it was against the old Rangers and not the so-called Newco. He continues to deserve the applause. Just so long as he remembers the part I played in it!

I had been involved in the League Cup Final a year earlier and was bitterly disappointed to be on the wrong side of a 2-1 scoreline. We knew who the dangerman was - Jim Forrest. The quick and stocky striker was on fire in the tournament and had scored an amazing sixteen goals in nine games leading up to the Final. He collected a double as Rangers dumped Dundee United in the semi-final. I think Forrest enjoyed the tournament because he had smashed in four in a 5-0 triumph over Morton the previous season's Final. So, we knew we had our work cut out to keep him quiet.

So - surprise! surprise! - we were two goals adrift just after the hour mark. Who scored them? No prizes for guessing Jim Forrest. And yet we had started brightly enough. I skinned David Provan, playing at right-back that afternoon, to whip over a cross, but it was just out of Bobby Murdoch's reach with the goal gaping. A few minutes later, Eric Caldow headed an effort from John Divers off the line. The game turned in the sixty-fourth minute when Forrest waltzed through the heart of our defence and plonked the ball wide of the advancing John Fallon.

There was a moment of high controversy minutes later when Murdoch hammered in a powerful shot. Billy Ritchie fumbled the effort, it crept under his body and the keeper had to swivel on his stomach to claw the ball back from the line. Was it over? Half of the 91,000 crowd thought so as did eleven players in green and white. Referee Hugh Phillips wasn't swayed by our appeals and waved play on. To be fair, photographs in the following day's newspapers appeared to indicate Ritchie had just prevented the whole of the ball from rolling over the line.

That was all Rangers needed to motivate themselves into storming back at us and Jim Baxter slipped the ball through for Forrest to score almost an exact replica of the first goal. Jimmy Johnstone pulled one back with twenty minutes still to play, but, agonisingly, it wasn't to be our day once more against our rivals from across the Clyde.

As I've already stated, the League Cup Final only a few months before the 5-1 New Year drubbing was a lot more enjoyable. I believe that was the first time I had come up against Kai Johansen. He had played for Morton for a year after they signed him from Danish team OB Odense. I have to say I didn't know that much about the style of the player, but Rangers manager Scot Symon had paid £20,000 for him and that was a fairly hefty fee in those days.

I had left for Hampden with two wishes in mind - to gain revenge for the previous season. And for Celtic not to be awarded a penalty-kick! Let me hastily explain before you get the wrong impression. I was the designated spot-kick taker at the club and I realised the immense pressure on me if we got an award. It was difficult enough in an ordinary league game, but in a Cup Final against Rangers at a packed Hampden Park would have been awesome. Please remember I was only twenty-two years old at the time. To get two in the same game was unthinkable. Mind you, I wasn't grumbling by time-up after I had placed two shots in the Rangers net and we avenged the defeat of twelve months earlier with an identical 2-1 scoreline.

Both penalties were given in the first-half and I don't think even the biggest Bluenose could have a complaint. The first came when Ronnie McKinnon handled needlessly as a long ball was going out of play. Referee Hugh Phillips pointed to the spot and I realised I had a golden opportunity to put us on our way. All sorts of things go through your mind at that point. You want to look cool and in control. There must be no trace of nerves. I placed the ball, moved back, the match official blew his whistle and I stepped forward to hit it practically down the middle of the goal. Thankfully, Billy Ritchie had anticipated a shot to his right and took off in that direction. Boy, was I relieved when I saw that net rippling behind him.

Not too long afterwards, Jimmy Johnstone was bought crashing to the turf after a badly-timed challenge from David Provan. Once again, the ref had no hesitation in pointing to the spot. 'Oh hell,' I thought, 'where do I place this one?' Once again, you have to give the impression you haven't a care in the world. I went through the same routine and hit the ball to the keeper's right. I figured he might have believed he would have more luck going to his left on that occasion. Thankfully, I hit it with enough force to see the effort come off his right hand and the ball strangle itself in the net.

I wasn't playing too badly, even if I do say so myself, and I was having a lot of success running at Kai Johansen. It was an October afternoon, but the playing surface at the national stadium was in excellent condition. The two goals gave me an incredible surge in confidence and I would have happily have taken a third penalty-kick!

Ian Young, our right-back, was unfortunate enough to put through his own goal with about seven minutes left, but it was too late for Rangers to change the scoreline. It was their turn to go to the silent dressing room of the defeated we had occupied so often in the past. No less than such an esteemed newspaper organ as the London Times noted, 'Hughes, the Celtic left winger, exerted such a mastery over Johansen, Rangers' Danish full-back, that the score might have risen.'

Who am I to argue with that acclamation?

Chapter 6

DRIVEN TO DRINK

The pressure of playing for Celtic drove me to drink. Quite literally! I was twenty-two years old when I first tasted alcohol and I have to say it was an experience I will never forget. To be honest, though, I didn't remember too much about it at the time.

Champagne corks, with reckless and frenzied abandon, were whizzing around the Hampden dressing room after we had overcome Dunfermline 3-2 in an enthralling, nerve-shredding Scottish Cup Final on the Saturday afternoon of April 24 1965. Celtic had actually won a trophy at a stadium that was so often the graveyard of our hopes, a ground that, unfortunately, had become synonymous with failure.

I had been in the same sporting arena exactly six months earlier and once again had been presented with a runners-up medal after we had been dumped 2-1 by Rangers in the League Cup Final. Two years earlier I was left in tears when we were walloped 3-0 by our Ibrox foes in the Scottish Cup Final replay. I was beginning to hate Hampden.

The run from hell kicked off on April 22 1961. I had celebrated my eighteenth birthday only nineteen days before our Scottish Cup Final meeting with overwhelming underdogs Dunfermline. We were huge favourites to end the silverware famine that had engulfed the club since the remarkable 7-1 victory over Rangers in the 1957 League Cup Final. It had been four long years since the Celtic supporters had enjoyed a trophy success and it looked odds-on the agonising interruption in our history was over.

Me? I was on a high. I believed this was to be the start of something wonderful and the medals, the accolades and the glory would surely follow in full flow. Ah, the exuberance and optimism of youth. It wasn't a question of would we win. Supporters were excitedly talking about the winning margin. Dunfermline, we were assured, were merely cannonfodder and the green and white ribbons were as good as already on the national trophy. Football doesn't quite work like that, unfortunately.

However, back then, there was genuine reason for optimism in our ranks. Three weeks beforehand we had annihilated a sturdy, workmanlike Airdrie side 4-0 in our semi-final. They had an exceptional goalkeeper in Lawrie Leslie, who moved to West Ham and made a name for himself south of the border. In fact, he signed at the end of that season for the princely sum of £14,000 and, believe it or not, that was a massive transfer deal in those days. He was also the Broomfield team's club captain and that, too, was a bit of an honour for a goalie. Leslie was unfortunate in winning only five Scottish international caps because he was in competition with such a fine and consistent performer as Bill Brown, shotstopper of that excellent Spurs team in the sixties. So, when I faced up to Leslie I was well aware that it would take something exceptional to get the ball past him. Luckily enough, I managed it twice and, once the cheers had died down, we were booked on our passage to the Hampden Final.

On the same day, Dunfermline toiled in their semi against St. Mirren at Tynecastle. It ended in a dour, goalless stalemate and they had to do it all again in a replay at the same ground four days later. This time the Fifers squeezed through 1-0. At that stage, I have to confess the warning signs were not flashing. There was no evidence of thin ice or banana skins. We had scored nineteen goals in six ties in reaching Hampden and I had helped myself to five of them. I was just a big raw laddie and I was living the dream. 'Celtic for the Cup,' was the cry en route to Mount Florida as our team bus crawled through the crowds heading for the game. It was all so exciting. What could go wrong? Well, everything.

Dunfermline, of course, lay in wait and we had no doubt that a certain Jock Stein, who had left his post as reserve team coach at Celtic to become manager of the Fifers the previous year, would have something up his sleeve. He still had many admirers among our ranks, including, of course, our centre-half Billy McNeill, who had worked closely with Stein since arriving at the club in 1957. But we didn't believe for a split-second that there was anything Jock could conjure up to derail us on our quest for football treasure.

In goal for the Fifers that season was a smallish keeper by the name of Eddie Connachan, who was about the 5ft 9in mark. He had just given up his job as a miner to concentrate full-time on football. He wasn't exactly a clean sheet specialist, either. Connachan had conceded five goals in the opening three ties, including three against Aberdeen at Pittodrie where he was bailed out by his forwards who scored six. By the end of the league campaign, he had shipped eighty-one goals in thirty-four games, joint worst record in the division along with Ayr United who were relegated. So, the scene was set for not just a Celtic victory, but an overwhelming Celtic victory as we trotted out on Cup Final day.

Incredibly, we just could not get that damn ball behind Connachan that afternoon. He proved to be unbeatable. He twisted and turned every which way to defy us. I remember getting my head to a deflected shot from Paddy Crerand. The ball spun in my direction and I instinctively thrust myself forward and diverted it towards goal. It looked an absolute certainty, but somehow Connachan performed an acrobatic back-flip to claw the effort away from under the bar. I stood there open-mouthed for a moment as I could hardly believe what I had just witnessed.

Thanks to the heroics of the Dunfermline keeper the game finished scoreless. He undoubtedly deserved the accolades that came his way in the following day's newspapers and I, for one, didn't begrudge him his moment in the sun. However, like the rest of the lads, I was determined to make him suffer in the replay the following Wednesday. Surely he couldn't emulate that breathtaking performance? As a matter of fact, he didn't - he surpassed it. Amazingly, Connachan followed the game of his life with an even better display, if that's possible. As I said, he wasn't the tallest custodian, but he was coming for all our crossballs and holding them confidently. Shots on target were being repelled as he sprawled all over the Hampden mud in one of the most defiant showings I have ever seen from a keeper. He was playing like a man possessed.

For me, the turning point of the confrontation came midway through the second-half with the scoreline still blank. Alec Byrne, a tricky outside-left, sent me on my way with a neat through ball that carved open their defence. I latched on to it, took a touch inside a defender and decided to batter it with all my might with my right foot at their goal. Connachan, from about ten yards, managed to get his hands to the ball, but couldn't hold it and it rebounded straight to the onrushing Stevie Chalmers. He thumped it first time past the keeper, but it was bundled off the line by a desperate defender.

There was a cry for a handball and, as they say nowadays, I've seen them given. I thought the player almost juggled with the ball before it was pushed past the post. However, referee Hugh Phillips, who I always thought was a fair match official, didn't get a good view of the incident. He looked across for a flag from his linesman, but, to our dismay, there was none. We hardly had time to protest as Willie Fernie took a quick corner-kick on the left and that was the flashpoint episode over and done with. There were no TV action replays back then and no fevered inquisition, but you could imagine a panel of so-called experts pouring over the occurrence these days. The commentator simply said something along the lines of, 'Oh, was that handball? The referee hasn't given it. Corner-kick for Celtic.' Can you imagine what would happen in today's game? The poor match official would be chased round the track for about five minutes!

But in such moments games - and trophies - are won and lost. And so it proved on this occasion. They opened the scoring through a header from Davie Thomson in the sixty-seventh minute with virtually their first attack over the two games. I'm not being unsporting in saying that, but our keeper, Frank Haffey, hardly had to get his knees dirty until that moment. Normal service was resumed as we took the action down to the other half of the field, but no matter how much we tried, Connachan just wouldn't be beaten. The one-man barrier of resistance kept us at bay and, as so often happens with the minutes ticking away and with Celtic surging forward, our opponents sneaked upfield to hit us with a classic sucker-punch.

It was well known that Haffey was unpredictable as well as eccentric. He made a hash of coming off his line to pick up a simple bouncing ball into our penalty area and it fell perfectly for Charlie Dickson, a bald, battering-ram of an old-fashioned centre-forward, and he just walked past our crestfallen keeper and plonked an effort into the unguarded net.

Back then, the beaten team had to wait on the pitch while the victors went up the famous Hampden steps to accept the trophy. All you want to do in those circumstances is disappear up the tunnel and get out of sight. However, the Scottish Football Association, in their infinite wisdom, insisted on the protocol of the triumphant team being handed the silverware while the poor beaten wretches were forced to look on and listen to the cheers of the opponents' delirious supporters. Not a very pleasant feeling, I can tell you.

Our own fans were left so disappointed. Some stayed behind to politely applaud us as we were handed our runners-up medals and that didn't help matters. We had promised so much and, in the end, delivered nothing. All these years later I can inform them of this; if they were hurting, they wouldn't have wanted to experience what was happening under my particular green and white hooped shirt. I was devastated. It's a gut-wrenching feeling realising you have let down so many loyal followers. We gave it our best shot, but, on the day, it just wasn't good enough to beat a goalkeeper named Eddie Connachan. I doubt if he ever replicated those two performances against us. I'm sure if he had, Real Madrid might have been beating down his door with a lucrative contract to whisk him off to play for the European champions. Let's be fair, though, he deserved his place in Fife folklore although I have to admit I wasn't feeling so benevolent or charitable on the evening of April 25 1961.

And so to the afternoon of May 4 1963 and the chance to atone. I've talked about that particular Scottish Cup Final against Rangers elsewhere, so I won't dwell on it. We did well to get a 1-1 draw in the first game and then crazy decisions were made concerning the team selection and formation for the replay. Jimmy Johnstone, excellent in the first game, was out, Bobby Craig was in and we were hammered 3-0. Another evening to forget at our national stadium, another unwanted runners-up medal.

The Hughes Collection of Unwelcome Medals received another addition after our 2-1 League Cup Final loss against our age-age old rivals on October 24 1964. A hat-trick of misery and I hope I could be forgiven for believing there was some sort of hoodoo hanging over me any time I ventured in the general vicinity of the south side of

Glasgow. It appeared I had my own personal black cloud awaiting me in that part of the city.

Things changed, though, on a glorious April afternoon in 1965. And I had the pulverising headache the following morning to prove it. Dunfermline were actually favourites to lift the Scottish Cup on that occasion. Let's face it, they had been an awful lot more consistent than us in the league that season. In fact, they finished third in the table on forty-nine points, only one adrift of joint-top Kilmarnock and Hearts. While we were beating the Fifers in Glasgow, Killie were doing likewise against the Edinburgh team at Tynecastle to lift the championship on goal average, as it was then. We weren't at the races in the league campaign and finished a dreadful eighth, a full twelve points behind the East End Park outfit in the days when you got two points for a win.

Alarmingly, we lost thirteen of our thirty-four First Division encounters. It was a wretched record and, once again, our best bet to win anything was in a Cup competition. No-one could have blamed the Celtic fans for thinking, 'Is there another disappointment waiting for us at Hampden?' After three Cup Finals defeats on the bounce at the start of the sixties, it looked as though we were beginning to develop the loser's habit. Sometimes that is difficult to shrug off. It's a heavy burden, believe me. At the age of twenty-two and after five years in the Celtic first team squad I had had nothing to celebrate with regards to silverware. Until that wonderful, fateful day.

Dunfermline, who had replaced Jock Stein as their manager with Irishman Willie Cunningham, had already proved they could beat us in Glasgow that season when they triumphed 2-1 in the league at our place. Possibly, they thought they had nothing to fear on this occasion. But they came up against a different Celtic team that day. Big Jock had arrived from Hibs in March and he brought with him a winning mentality; a drive and a force. He installed belief in the players. The bookies backed Dunfermline, but you wouldn't have known that if you had been in the Celtic dressing room that afternoon.

Actually, I believe we might have started to have faith in ourselves after the quarter-final tie against Kilmarnock at Parkhead. That game was played on Saturday March 6 1965 which was, technically, four days before Jock Stein took over the running of the team. That managerial debut is often given as the league match against Airdrie at

Broomfield where Bertie Auld scored five goals as we overwhelmed our opponents 6-0. All modesty aside, I gave Wee Bertie a helping hand by getting the first goal that night! You can be sure, though, the presence of Big Jock was around Parkhead the day of the Cup confrontation against the Ayrshire side. He might not have been sitting in the dug-out, but all the players got the distinct impression this was HIS team and not one selected by chairman Bob Kelly. Times they were a-changin'.

Kilmarnock were league leaders when they arrived in the east end of Glasgow for the Cup-tie and must have been fairly confident of reaching the semi. Our form was erratic, to say the least. We could wipe the floor with some opposition when we clicked into gear and then fail miserably a couple of weeks later. Here's a perfect illustration. I scored five goals in an 8-0 demolition of Aberdeen at Parkhead on January 30, but four games later we lost 1-0 to lowly St.Johnstone at our place. Inconsistency like that would drive anyone to strong drink. But I'll come to that in a moment.

So, we were well up for the challenge from Killie. They had a very strong squad at the time and had two excellent goalkeepers in Campbell Forsyth and Bobby Ferguson and both would later play for Scotland. They had a stuffy right-back in Andy King, two good central defenders in Jackie McGrory and Frank Beattie, a wily little inside-left in Davie Sneddon and tricky wingers in Brian McIlroy and Tommy McLean, later to become a rival at Rangers. There was also a tall, rangy frontman called Jackie McInally who just happened to have a son called Alan who would play for Celtic in the Eighties. You might know him better as Rambo.

Anyway, it was our belief that they should worry about us and they must have realised we could clobber any opposition when we got into our stride. Bobby Lennox got the ball rolling that day with a close-range header early on and it remained that way as the contest edged towards the hour mark. Then calamity as they equalised through McInally, a player who was always difficult to handle. However, within a minute, our fans were cheering wildly again as Bertie Auld forced us in the lead once more. Killie attempted to come back at us, displaying a lot of resilience it must be admitted, but I'm delighted to say I had the final say. I recall the pitch that day was exceptionally muddy and in those energy-sapping conditions I was more than happy with my strength and build. I zipped in a shot that eluded Forsyth in the sixty-seventh minute. I knew we wouldn't lose after that strike. As ever, though, we made life difficult for ourselves by allowing McInally to score a second for our visitors about five minutes later.

We held on for a superb triumph against strong opposition, a team that would go on to win the title and we might have thought our name was on the Cup after that result. I had long since discounted that theory. If we were going to win silverware, we were going to have to earn it.

My old friend Joe McBride was a real pain in the back four when we faced up to Motherwell in the semi-final. The likeable and courageous striker may have been well known to have an allegiance to all things Celtic, but he never let that interfere with his professionalism on the park and he displayed that as he rifled two goals beyond John Fallon. We got two ourselves courtesy of Bobby Lennox and Bertie Auld to force a replay the following Wednesday and this time there was no faltering. We won 3-0 with goals from yours truly, Stevie Chalmers and Lennox again. By the way, the next time I met up with Joe McBride at Hampden I was playing alongside him after he had joined us in the summer for £22,000 - Big Jock's first signing for Celtic. We enjoyed a 2-1 League Cup victory over Rangers on that occasion.

While Joe was making life awkward for us, Dunfermline were seeing off Hibs 2-0 in their semi-final and I can tell you Jock Stein was mightily relieved. He really didn't fancy taking us into the Final against the team he had left only a couple of months beforehand. Mind you, the way the Fifers started against us, he might have wished his old side were providing the opposition. Harry Melrose, who had played against us in the 1961 upset, opened the scoring after our defence got in a fankle and couldn't clear the ball. Possibly, in days gone by, we might have let our spirits slip, but not on this occasion. There was a genuine growl and a snarl when we replaced the ball to kick off.

Bertie Auld got the equaliser after a Charlie Gallagher screamer had thudded off the crossbar and rebounded about twelve feet in the air. Goalkeeper Jim Herriot was on the deck after failing to stop Charlie's long-range effort and Bertie was poised under the bar. Right-back Willie Callaghan raced in to clear, but Bertie was having none of it. He took to the air and, almost on the goal-line, nodded the ball in to the delirium of his team-mates and, so it seemed, the whole of

Hampden.

Once again, though, we shot ourselves spectacularly in the foot by gifting Dunfermline the advantage again just before the interval. Now I've never played in goal and I know it is all too easy to blame the last line of defence. Having said that, I thought John Fallon might have done better after our opponents had worked a clever one-two at a free-kick about twenty-five yards out. John McLaughlin blasted an attempt goalwards and to me, at least, our keeper appeared to move at the very last moment for a ball that had travelled a helluva distance. It didn't bend, swerve or dip - the old balls were far too heavy - and it went in straight as an arrow as Fallon eventually moved to his right. Too late, the ball was nestling in the back of the net and we were a goal adrift at the interval.

I thought Big Jock was remarkably laidback in the dressing room at half-time. Maybe he was still feeling his way with the players because he swiftly developed an acid tongue in these situations in years to come. On this occasion, though, he simply had a word in our ear, an arm over an individual's shoulder, cajoling us to go out and 'get an early goal and the Scottish Cup is ours'. I got the feeling the players were already pumped up for the challenge, in any case. We knew exactly what was in front of us, what we had to achieve and we had forty-five minutes in which to turn things around. There was a good spirit within the group, I was aware of that.

Seven minutes after the break the tie was level. There was a good move down the left with Tommy Gemmell and Bobby Lennox combining and the man known as the Buzz Bomb took off at lightning speed before lashing a low cross into the danger zone. I couldn't get a touch as it was a couple of yards in front of me, but, thankfully, Bertie was following up to first time the ball beyond the stranded Herriot. There was a crowd of 108,800 at the game that day and they all seemed to rise to acclaim that equaliser. It was nothing to the din that swept over the stadium with nine minutes to go.

With his usual precision, Charlie Gallagher breezed in a left wing corner-kick and Billy McNeill's timing in the air, as ever, was impeccable. As their keeper hesitated, Big Billy - or Caesar, as he was known - launched himself into orbit to make a flawless connection and the ball flew straight and true into the net. I chased after our skipper to congratulate him and then wondered how long there was still to go in the Final. Surely, nothing could wrench the trophy away from Celtic? I had been involved in two Scottish Cup Final defeats and, in fact, the club had lost four consecutive Finals after winning it in 1954 when we beat Aberdeen 2-1. Sean Fallon, our assistant manager in 1965, scored the winner that day. But there had been back-to-back Hampden woe when the club lost 1-0 to Clyde in a replay the following year and then Hearts 3-1 the season after that.

So, when you take all that into consideration, was it any wonder we all went doolally at the final whistle? We cavorted around the pitch like schoolkids and matchwinner Billy McNeill, waving the Cup, was joyously lifted aloft the shoulders of Stevie Chalmers and Bertie Auld. Suddenly, Hampden had been transformed into paradise. The supporters danced with delight on the old terracings in the vast bowl of the national stadium and there was a great sense of pride that we had, after too many setbacks, delivered the goods for those so special people.

The Cup was passed around in the dressing room and I tasted champagne for the first time in my life. I only got a sip before the trophy was whisked off to someone else. However, it was after our team coach dropped the squad off at the Vesuvio, an upmarket Italian restaurant in St Vincent Street in Glasgow city centre, that I really got involved with the celebratory bevvy. See what I mean about being driven to drink!

We were all just so happy and I never gave a thought to what I was guzzling; it was such a fabulous feeling to be a winner. I had never got involved in pub culture, so drinking wasn't a natural progress for me. I left school and immediately went to Celtic where I was training to get fitter to make me a better player. Going on a booze cruise with my mates just didn't hold too much appeal. To be honest, I didn't see the sense in it. All that went out of the window at the Vesuvio!

Let's face it, Billy McNeill, John Clark, Charlie Gallagher, Stevie Chalmers and I had all sampled the misery of losing a Scottish Cup Final against Dunfermline in 1961. Billy, Stevie and I had all been given the runaround in the replay against Rangers in 1963. We went into the match against the Fifers well aware we could have the dubious distinction of being three-time losers in the competition. No thanks!

By the time we piled out of the restaurant, I was zooming towards Jupiter. A lot of us headed over to Stevie's house in Bishopbriggs where we continued to attempt to drink the country dry. I was feeling sensations totally alien to me. Basically, I was as drunk as a skunk. The boys didn't help much, either. I was asking them for water and they, helpfully, supplied me with vodka. In my condition I didn't know the difference. I did the following day. I had heard people talking about hangovers and I didn't really have a clue what they were talking about.

Unfortunately, I did after that never-to-be-forgotten Scottish Cup victory in 1965. Yes, I was the Bear with a sore head. Well worth it, though.

Chapter 7

BEWILDERED IN BUDAPEST

There was some fairly ludicrous decision-making at Celtic in the early sixties. But I don't think there was anything crazier than our pre-match briefing as we prepared to play MTK Budapest in the second leg of our European Cup-Winners' Cup semi-final at the Nep Stadium on April 28 1964. We were 3-0 ahead from the first game at Parkhead and were a mere ninety minutes away from achieving the honour of playing in a prestigious European Final. What an awesome prospect for a young team performing at this level for only their second year.

Okay, you don't need to be blessed with an IQ of genius proportions to work out what should have happened next. We're three goals ahead, on the brink of making club history and even the dejected fans of the Hungarian team have conceded defeat with only 10,000 tickets sold for the game in a ground that could comfortably house over 100,000. So, you're going to defend your lead, aren't you? Keep it tight for the first twenty minutes or so, take the sting out of their initial attacks, maintain possession and look to take advantage on the break. Frustrate their players right from the kick-off and leave them simply going through the motions long before the referee blows for time-up and puts them out of their misery. That looks like a game plan, doesn't it? Well, that's the strategy just about every other team in the world would have adopted. Not Celtic, though. Not while chairman Robert Kelly was calling the shots. Nope, we were told to play in the

'Celtic way' and to continue taking the game to the opposition.

Kelly addressed the players and I'll always remember his words. 'We beat them in Glasgow fair and square and I believe we can beat them here in the same manner. That's the Celtic way.' Naive? Tactics like that were simply preposterous, absolutely suicidal, completely irrational, totally absurd. We were sitting in our dressing room in the world famous stadium and looking for guidance. We had a very youthful team. There were two twenty year olds - Jimmy Johnstone and Bobby Murdoch - while Ian Young, Tommy Gemmell and I were a year older. Billy McNeill, John Divers and goalkeeper John Fallon were twenty-four. We listened intently at what our chairman had to say and we blinked in combined astonishment. Jaws bounced off the floor. 'Did he say ATTACK them?' we thought in unison. That European tie predated the movie *One Flew Over The Cuckoo's Nest* by eleven years or else I would have been looking around to see if Jack Nicholson was in the room. Manager Jimmy McGrory, of course, said very little, maybe something along the lines of, 'Enjoy the game, boys.'

The entire Celtic party had been invited to an official reception at the British Embassy in Budapest the night before the game and you couldn't help but wonder if some of our directors had been drinking something a little stronger than tea. How else was it possible to justify such bizarre thinking? In fact, the entire couple of days in Budapest had an unreal feel. The players were all presented with massive bouquets of flowers when we first arrived in the city. Maybe someone at MTK thought it would be a nice touch and there was the possibility of some members of the Glasgow Royal Horticultural Society among our number. Most of us wouldn't have known one end of a weed from another.

So, with all that in mind, we took to the field that night with orders to be on the offensive. None of this 'shutting up shop' nonsense for Celtic Football Club. We had earned the right to be overwhelming favourites to earn the right to become the second Scottish club to take their place in the Final of the competition, second only to the European Cup in importance. Rangers played in the first in 1961 when it was a two-legged affair and they had lost home and away to Italian side Fiorentina on a 4-1 aggregate. UEFA changed it to a one-off Final the year before we met MTK and that wonderful Spurs team of the era, with Dave Mackay, Jimmy Greaves, John White and Bill Brown in the line-up, demonstrated what could be achieved at this level with an excellent 5-1 triumph over Atletico Madrid in Rotterdam. Brussels was earmarked for the Final in 1964. Was it too much to hope that we could emulate the White Hart Lane outfit? Yes, we dared to dream, especially after our three-goal trouncing of MTK Budapest in Glasgow.

However, let's go right back to the start of that eventful campaign and to far happier memories. We were drawn against Swiss side Basle in the opening round and I marked my European debut on September 17 1963 by becoming the first Celtic player to score a hat-trick in a European tie. And away from home, too. We thumped the Swiss 5-1 on their home ground and no doubt Robert Kelly would have been satisfied that we had won in the 'Celtic way'. My mate John Divers got our opener midway through the first-half and I netted my first European goal two minutes from the interval. Thirty-six minutes later I had claimed a treble. Bobby Lennox hit our third about ten minutes after the turnaround and I helped pile on the agony for our opponents with a fourth shortly after the hour mark. To be honest, the thought of becoming the first player in Celtic's history to score a hat-trick in Europe never occurred to me. You tend not to think about these things when you're out on the field. I was playing through the middle that night with Frank Brogan, a real speed merchant, on the left wing. Basle had no answer to our forceful play and my big moment arrived in the seventy-eighth minute when I was presented with an opportunity smack in front of goal. I duly whacked it past the keeper and put myself straight into the record books. The miserable Swiss beggars refused to give me the match ball which was the norm for a player hitting a hat-trick. 'SWISS ROLL FOR CELTIC' was the headline in most newspapers the following day. And, ball or no ball, it had been a fairly satisfying experience.

The second leg, as you could imagine, was a stroll, but it wasn't without the usual baffling decision from our chairman. After scoring three goals away from home and shaking up their central defence all evening, he switched me to outside-left with Stevie Chalmers leading the attack. Go figure, as they say in America. It didn't matter a jot in the end as two goals from John Divers and singles from Stevie, Jimmy Johnstone and Bobby Murdoch made it an overwhelming 10-1 aggregate scoreline. Dinamo Zagreb were next up and everyone at the club had to admit we had very little knowledge of our opponents, their players or their style of play. The goings-on in Communist Eastern Europe at the time were a mystery to the rest of the world, so there was little chance of us getting the lowdown on a football team. What we did know, though, was that Dinamo had got through on the toss of a coin after drawing 1-1 on aggregate following their two matches against the Austrians of LASK Linz. It was a 1-1 stalemate in the replay and the Slavs called it right to make the next stage.

The first leg against the Slavs on December 4 turned into a bit of a canter which surprised us, I must say. We expected sterner opposition. We realised they were a defensive-minded outfit, but we dismantled them with a fair degree of ease. I netted my fourth goal of the campaign and Stevie popped in another two. We were three goals ahead and surely that would be enough of a margin for any team to progress through to the next stage. On this occasion, I'm only too delighted to inform you, dear reader, that it was more than adequate. Bobby Murdoch walloped in a powerful drive just before the interval and Zagreb found themselves requiring five goals in forty-five minutes to progress in the tournament. Even this Celtic team wasn't that naive. The Slavs got two in the last twenty-five minutes, but there was no way back. The game itself wasn't particularly memorable, but Zagreb does have a special place in my nightmares. John Divers and I got lost in the mountains around the city the night before the match and I was convinced someone was shooting at us! Let me explain.

This may surprise you, but, despite flying to just about every corner of the earth, I don't like air travel. It's something I have never been comfortable with. Of course, I still zoom here, there and everywhere on holiday and it's something I simply get on with, sometimes through gritted teeth. But there is another mode of transport in which I will NEVER travel for the rest of the life. I'm talking about cable cars. I experienced them in Zagreb. Now that was a scary encounter and I wouldn't wish it on anyone. The day before the game in Yugoslavia, our hosts thought it would be a good idea to take the Celtic officials and players to view Mount Sljeme, a 3,000ft-high peak on the edge of the city. It probably looked very picturesque in a postcard, but I didn't really appreciate a close-up view. We didn't know what lay ahead of us as the Zagreb officials arranged a trip for us up to the mountains. It was there that I was introduced to my very first cable car ride - and my second last. We were ushered into these death traps to apparently enjoy the mountainous terrain of this bleak, foreboding part of the world.

I felt sick as we dangled in mid-air, the cable car swinging wildly from side to side. Eventually, after what felt like a lifetime, we reached our destination on a cliff top. I looked down which wasn't my best initiative. It was pitch black, a huge uninviting hole. I gulped with relief when my feet reached terra firma once again. 'We leave in an hour,' one of our guides informed our party. 'There's no way I'm going back on that bloody thing,' was my retort. 'I'll walk down.' I told Sean Fallon and, thankfully, he accepted there was no way I would change my mind. He could have threatened to drop me from the team and it wouldn't have bothered me. I was more concerned about being dropped into the menacing canyons below. I had made up my mind. Cable car trips were for the skiing fraternity as far as I was concerned and I didn't mix with that set. John Divers agreed to walk down the mountainside with me which was much appreciated. The natural light was fine when we set out, but all too quickly darkness descended. Obviously, neither JD nor I had bothered to pack a flashlight, so we gingerly paced our way down the slopes, hoping to come upon a dirt road somewhere on our trek.

After about an hour or so, as we wandered around in the murkiness, clattering into all sorts of rock formations and shrubbery, I looked up in the gloom and saw the fully-lit cable car with my team-mates making its way back to its station. I might just have cursed. But banging about in the shadows was still better than getting back into one of those contraptions. JD and I kept on walking down the mountainside. Suddenly, I heard a loud bang. And then another. 'What the hell is that, JD?' I asked, fairly frantically. 'Don't know, Yogi,' he replied, a fair bit of trepidation in his tones. 'Definitely sounded like gunfire, didn't it? Couldn't be a car backfiring up here, could it?' 'Don't think so,' I said. Before I could speak again, there was another crack, a sharp noise reverberating around the still surroundings. 'That definitely sounded like a shot,' I observed. After another couple of minutes, there was a bright orange flash and another sharp crack in the distance. Then another. And another. Suddenly there were booms and bursts of light going off all over the place. 'What the hell are they shooting at?' asked JD. 'Hope it's not us,' I exclaimed, more than a little alarmed. I realised Dinamo Zagreb were desperate to get through to the quarter-final of the Cup-Winners' Cup, but I hoped they weren't quite THAT desperate!

My companion and I continued our descent into the twilight zone, slipping and sliding down the slope to the accompaniment of a cacophony of gunfire. We still had no idea who or what these guys were shooting at. We were well aware of the Soviet Secret Police's presence in the country and we wondered if they had taken an unfortunate defector up for some target practice! That wasn't our concerned as we fumbled our way towards safety. At one stage, I took a tumble and went flying. I ripped my club trousers, skinned an elbow and covered my blazer in mud. I realised that may take some explaining to those who counted the pennies at the club. We kept going until we reached some sort of patched-up road and, lo and behold, we spotted a pair of car lights. What a welcoming sight. JD and I raced towards it, yelling and waving our hands. The car came to a halt and out stepped two armed policemen.

'Oh, shit,' said JD. 'Oh, shit,' I echoed. The policemen removed their revolvers from their holsters as they walked slowly towards us. I pointed to the Celtic club badge on my mud-spattered blazer. JD did likewise. There are times when you are totally grateful that Celtic are such a famous football club. This was one of them. A policeman, still holding his gun in his right hand, stepped forward to look at my badge. 'Ah, Celtic,' he exclaimed, recognising the name. 'Glasgow Celtic.' He said something in the local dialect to his colleague. They both nodded their heads and I was fairly relieved to witness them reholstering their pistols. They motioned for us to follow them to their patrol car. They managed to find a track and my heart plummeted when I realised they were taking us back up the mountainside. We were heading for the bloody cable cars!

Even more terrifyingly, they pulled their vehicle over at one point as they checked directions. Once again, I thought it would be a good idea to look out of the window. It wasn't an inspirational thought. I peered down into the inky void and quickly realised the cop had parked the car right on the edge of the cliffside. The tyres must have been touching the very rim of the precipice. I almost passed out! Eventually, we reached the cable car platform and JD and I were escorted back into a brightly-lit compartment. Once more I took a sharp intake of breath. I looked at the policemen and they were all smiles. They thought they were doing us a favour. They even saluted. I tried to grin, but it was probably more of a grimace.

I exited as quickly as possible once we reached the bottom of the mountain. I was relieved to see our team bus was still waiting for us. Mind you, our colleagues weren't too happy - they had been stuck on the coach for two hours. Their mood wouldn't have been enhanced by the fact there was no form of heating on the bus. I told Robert Kelly about our ordeal and the rifle shots. He informed me, 'I'm not surprised. It's their bear-hunting season.' I was just a little startled. Sean Fallon might have passed on the information before I decided to clamber down the mountainside. Anyway, JD composed himself well enough before saying, 'Hey, Yogi, how lucky are you that those guys with the rifles didn't know your nickname?' I just growled.

Zagreb had been a fairly drab, grey old Iron Curtain country, so, it goes without saying, no-one was celebrating when we were paired with Slovan Bratislava, of Czechoslovakia, in the quarter-final. We were going into the unknown once more, but there was one thing that was certain - our opponents were a class act. Their nation had reached the World Cup Final only two years previously when they lost 3-1 to Brazil in Chile after taking the lead through Josef Masopust, who played for Dukla Prague against Celtic in the 1967 European Cup semi-final. Slovan were clearly no mugs and they had a top notch keeper in Villiam Schroif while defenders Jan Popluhar and Svatopluk Pluskal had even represented the Rest of the World against England at Wembley in the FA's centenary year celebrations in 1963. So, we went into the first leg at our place on February 26 in the full knowledge we would have to battle for everything.

It was a bruising encounter as we pummelled them right from the start. I was back on the left wing with Stevie Chalmers continuing to lead the attack. They repelled raid after raid until a vital moment after the break. Stevie burst through and was in the act of taking the ball round the keeper when Schroif brought him crashing to the ground. A stonewall penalty-kick and, of course, these days would have earned the Czech No.1 a straight red card. Not back then, though, and Schroif remained on the pitch to face the spot-kick. He might as well have been sitting in the dressing room. Bobby Murdoch took it with consummate ease and fired it in at the keeper's right as he went to his left. That was the end of the scoring and we wondered if we had done enough as we prepared for the return leg. The Czechs didn't seem too despondent to have lost by only a single goal in Glasgow.

After my experience in Zagreb, I made certain I didn't go anywhere near a cable car in Bratislava. It really wasn't much of a sight-seeing paradise, that's for sure. It looked a dull old place and most of the people looked poor as they scurried around going about their business. Strangely, though, we were placed in a fairly opulent hotel with marble floors and walls. There was also a piano player at the reception who seemed to play for twenty-four hours without stop. I hoped they paid him well.

As we got ready to go out for the action, I couldn't have imagined that I would score one of the greatest goals of my life. The game was tight in the first-half and I remember Billy McNeill was holding things together in the middle of the defence. Jinky was roaming around on the right wing and Bobby Murdoch was putting in another assured performance. No prizes for guessing we were urged to take the game to the Czechs after the interval. And that's when my magical moment arrived. It was one of those virtuoso inspirational flashes for which you cannot possible legislate. It was completely off the cuff and might have surprised me as much as it did the opponents.

I was just inside our own half when I accepted a pass from Jim Kennedy. Normally, the man known as Pres would sling the ball as far downfield as possible and expect the likes of me, Stevie and Jinky to chase after it. On this occasion, thankfully, he thought better of it and slipped a short pass in front of me. I gathered the ball and looked up to spy my options. There wasn't a lot on, so I decided to amble forward. I hugged the left touchline as one of their players came out to confront me. I slipped the ball past him and, gathering a bit of momentum, I kept going as I came inside. Another defender came out to put in a challenge, but I dodged him and, suddenly, there was the possibility of driving at goal. There were a couple of other Slovan players in front of me and I knew in an instant I had thrown them into a bit of disarray. One of the defenders stepped forward and he could do two things; he could try to jockey me while his defence regrouped or he could go straight in and try to win a tackle. He decided on the latter. The Czech moved quickly, but I moved just a little more slickly and, before he could rethink his strategy, I was away from him with the ball fully under control. These are the moments where you pick up a full head of steam. I now had one man between me and their keeper. I decided to arrow in on him. He hesitated and I left him for dead. I was clean through on Schroif who had been left totally exposed. He dashed from his line, but I had already made up my mind where I would stick the ball in the net. I made clean contact and the world-class shotstopper hadn't an earthly. The ball flew straight and true towards its destination in the back of the net. I was overjoyed. I'm no big head, but it was a superb goal. The main thing, though, was that it gave us a 2-0 lead on aggregate and we held onto it until the final whistle.

Next up was another visit to a bleak and mysterious land as we were drawn against MTK Budapest. The ballot hadn't been particularly kind to us again. Every team prefers to play their first leg away from home as it gives the players the knowledge of what they have to do in front of their own fans to reach the next stage. For a third successive occasion, Celtic were pulled out of the hat to play the opening game in Glasgow allowing for the possibility of a dangerous second leg in enemy territory. However, I have to say not one single Celtic player was looking ahead with trepidation to the match in Hungary. Could you blame us? We were three goals to the good and the supporters even called for a lap of honour at the end. We were already getting out of our kit in the dressing room when Sean Fallon came in to say, 'You better get some gear back on because the fans are refusing to leave until you go out there.' The players grabbed at the assorted discarded kit and, with many of us bare-footed, went back out to take a bow. The supporters clearly thought we were heading for a date in Brussels. In truth, so, too, did the players.

We had played extremely well against the Hungarians and were a goal ahead in the thirty-fifth minute, an effort that owed everything to the bravery and speed of thought of Wee Jinky. I touched a pass inside to the Pres, again lining up at left-half, and the ball was worked across to John Clark. It was rare to see Luggy, who was playing in the old right-half role, venturing into the other team's territory. In fact, he scored only three goals in 318 games for the club, so I think it would be fair to say striking wasn't his strong point. Undeterred, though, he smashed a low shot at goal and the MTK keeper went down to scoop the ball into his arms. However, he fumbled his attempt and that was all Jinky needed to race in and bundle an effort into the net.

Stevie hit the second with a sweet left foot drive from about sixteen yards in the sixty-fifth minute. This time the keeper didn't have the ghost of a chance as the ball sped low into his left hand corner. And it was Stevie again on target with around ten minutes remaining. I passed inside to Bobby Murdoch and he picked out our centre-forward with an exquisite cross into the box. Stevie made a perfect connection and once more the MTK goalie could do nothing as the net bulged behind him for the third time. We all danced a jig of joy as the referee blew for time-up and we genuinely believed we were on the verge of something special with glory beckoning in Budapest. Then came the instructions that shredded all our good work. I still can't believe how we were asked to perform in that second leg. The chairman always got what the chairman wanted and that led to our downfall. No-one argued in the dressing room that evening. We were told what was expected and, of course, we would do our best to carry out those orders.

MTK couldn't believe their good fortune. Why weren't we attempting to stifle them? Why weren't we retreating into defence? They may have been a little puzzled with our unusual formation at the start, but it didn't take them long to realise they were onto a good thing. Our clueless system was there for the taking. After just over an hour we were hurtling out of the competition. They pulled one back in the eleventh minute through Istvan Kuti, but we still didn't respond to the flashing danger signals. Jinky put the ball in their net, but Austrian referee Dimitrus Wlachojanus ruled it for offside. I suffered the same fate before the interval and, once again, it came into the doubtful category. Everything seemed to be going for our opponents.

Very little was said in the dressing room at half-time. There was no reorganisation and no revamp of our thinking. We were a tactically unsophisticated bunch and we would be punished for such unworldliness. Two minutes after the break, our advantage was cut to one. Mihaly Vasas was the guy who did the damage with a penalty-kick after Tommy Gemmell had punched an effort off the line with John Fallon absent. John, by the way, was called Peter by the rest of his team-mates. There was a TV programme at the time called 'The Invisible Man' and its main character was called Peter Brady. Hence, when our keeper went walkabout, we labelled him Peter. He still answers to it! Karoly Sandor, who had been thundering up and down their right wing all night, rifled in a third and that was our lead well and truly obliterated. The agony was complete when Kuti got No.4 nineteen minutes from the end.

Believe it or not, as soon as they were ahead in the tie, MTK dropped into a defensive shell. They were going to hold what they had. If only we had adopted the same sensible thinking when we were three goals in front. After such a resounding failure and horrible disappointment we might have expected nooses to be knotted and gallows to be erected. A firing squad might have been summoned. Not a word was said. There was no criticism from above. No fingers were pointed. No scapegoats were sought. After all, we had lost in 'the Celtic way'. And that, sadly, seemed to be all that mattered.

We were guileless innocents abroad and we paid a heavy price for our gullibility. We were manipulated all the way to oblivion. And no-one seemed too upset. In time, we would learn from this folly.

Chapter 8

ANGUISH AT ANFIELD

I was doing a fair impersonation of the Incredible Hulk on the night Celtic were robbed of the opportunity of winning a European trophy a full year before we managed the historic feat in Lisbon. A refereeing howler prevented us from reaching the Cup-Winners' Cup Final which was due to be played at Hampden Park in 1966 and I would have put my house on Celtic beating any team in the world in such circumstances.

I could hardly contain my rage in the Anfield dressing room, absolutely shattered along with my mud-spattered, exhausted team-mates following our 2-0 second leg defeat from Liverpool. I felt as though we had been cheated. I'm not saying the match official had been nobbled, but he made a crazy and inexplicable decision in the fading moments of the game that killed stone dead our hopes of getting to that Final.

Picture the scene. We had won 1-0 through a Bobby Lennox goal in the first game at Parkhead. In fact, it was 1-0 going on 5-0, but I'll talk about that later. It was goalless at Anfield for about an hour before they levelled the tie with a deflected free-kick. Five minutes later, a player who shouldn't even have been on the pitch scored their second. With the clock ticking down, Joe McBride turned Ron Yeats, their colossus of a centre-half who would never become famous for his nimble feet or quick movement, and hared towards their goal.

Bobby Lennox was about five or six yards behind Joe when he started his run. Joe squared the ball across and Bobby tucked it beyond goalkeeper Tommy Lawrence and their left-back Gerry Byrne, who was on the goal-line. What was wrong with any of that? Our guy couldn't possibly have been offside, but that's the way the Belgian referee Josef Hannet called it. He wiped out the effort that would have most assuredly booked us a place at Scotland's national stadium the following month.

Wee Bobby's strike would have tied the score at 2-2 and we would have been through because of the goals away counting double rule. UEFA had just introduced the directive the previous year in the hope that an away team might think it was worthwhile to open up a little on their travels. With a goal away from home counting as two if both ties were level on aggregate, it may just entice some managers to change their mind about defend-at-all-costs methods that were ruining the European game. Some teams looked as though they had no intention of leaving their own half of the field if they were a goal ahead from the first leg and they had something to protect.

Just to rub salt into our wounds, referee Hannet admitted he got it wrong after he had seen the incident on television. Belgium doesn't appear to be famous for anything and that must also go for their football match officials.

Yet it could have been an entirely different story as we prepared for the first game in Glasgow on Thursday, April 14. Liverpool were running away with the English First Division and, as well as former Dundee United defender Ron Yeats, they had other Scots in goalkeeper Tommy Lawrence - imaginatively nicknamed 'The Flying Pig' which, presumably, had something to do with his bulk - Billy Stevenston, a former Rangers half-back, and Ian St John, a wily little striker they had signed from Motherwell in 1961. We reckoned their biggest threat to us would come from their swift wingers Ian Callaghan and Peter Thompson, both England internationals. The media had entitled it 'The Battle of Britain', but there was no need for hype to sell out this encounter. Fans queued for hours outside Celtic Park the previous Sunday to get their hands on the precious tickets with a stand seat costing thirty shillings (£1.50p). A crowd of 76,446 crammed into the ground and the place was rocking by the time East German referee Rudi Glockner blew his whistle bang on 8pm to get the action underway.

I had been an ever-present on the six-game surge to the semi-final and had operated on the left wing for the games against the wonderfully-named Dutch side Go Ahead Deventer, the Danes of AGF Aarhus and the tough Soviets of Kiev Dynamo. We had won five out of the six - drawing away to Kiev - and I was looking forward to the visit of the much-vaunted Merseyside outfit. I thrived on these so-called clashes of the giants. But I was left feeling sick when I failed a late fitness test. I had been forced to sit out five games through a leg injury, but had come back for a 5-0 win over St.Mirren five days before the Liverpool tie. Something, though, wasn't quite right and Jock Stein changed things around with Bobby Lennox being asked to play wider on the left. Bertie Auld may have had the No.11 on his shorts, but he took his usual place in midfield beside Bobby Murdoch. It was very much a fearless, attacking formation with Jimmy Johnstone on the right and Joe McBride and Stevie Chalmers operating through the centre.

I recall there was a stiff breeze whipping around the east end of Glasgow that evening and Celtic kicked into the wind in the first-half. My team-mates could have been facing a full-blown hurricane, it wouldn't have stopped them from just about camping in the Liverpool half for the entire forty-five minutes. We came close to the perfect start when a through ball from Bertie was dummied by Wee Bobby and ran straight into the path of Joe. In normal circumstances, our prolific frontman would have rattled the net, but his effort was just too close to Lawrence and the beefy custodian managed to save. Very quickly, we had put down our marker. Liverpool were obviously wary of Wee Jinky and that was underlined when St.John came racing back into defence to upend his fellow-Scot and go straight into the referee's black book as a consequence. It was one-way traffic, but Bill Shankly's side were holding firm. They were exceptionally lucky to escape a strong penalty claim before the interval. Tommy Smith was wearing the No.10 jersey, but was being deployed as a sweeper behind Yeats and Stevenston. He sent Lennox tumbling in the box with a crude challenge, but, astonishingly, Herr Glockner waved play on. I wondered if players had to lose a limb before a spot-kick was awarded in East Germany.

Jock, as you might have expected, was reasonably pleased at the interval. However, it's always a bit worrying when you have so much possession and have nothing to show for it. With the considerable gusts at our backs, we were certain we could get the breakthrough. Some players fail to annex the advantage of having the wind as an ally, but Bobby Murdoch and Bertie Auld were two midfielders with the craft and guile to utilise it perfectly. And it was Bobby who helped to change the complexion of the contest only seven minutes after the turnaround. With Gerry Byrne concentrating on keep tabs on Jinky, Bobby sneaked into a great position on the right and picked out Stevie, hovering near Lawrence's left hand post. With a neat back heel, he bamboozled the Liverpool defence and Wee Bobby stormed in to first-time a close-range drive into the net.

I sat back in my seat in the stand and awaited the deluge. Liverpool were being decimated and very little had been seen of their wingers Callaghan, on the right, and Thompson, on the other flank. Tommy Gemmell was getting forward as often as possible and Callaghan was being forced to back-track which, I'm sure, would have been something alien to him in the English game. Lawrence's goal lived a charmed existence as we hammered away. Wee Bobby slashed one wide of the upright, Stevie, with a clear sight of goal, put one over the bar, Joe missed after being presented with a great close-in heading opportunity. And so it went on all the way to the final whistle. Tommy Smith, who had put his weight about all night, was eventually booked near the end for one foul too many on Stevie. So, we had to be content with a one-goal advantage to take to Anfield where the return was due the following Tuesday. UEFA obviously believed in quick turnarounds in those days.

We were based at Southport and travelled down on the Monday, only forty-eight hours after drawing 0-0 with Hibs at Easter Road. We were astounded when hundreds of Celtic fans turned up at Central Station to cheer us off. I felt fully recovered and had lasted the ninety minutes in Edinburgh against a strong and robust Hibs side. After another precautionary inspection, I was given the go-ahead and Big Jock put me at outside-left for the Tuesday night encounter, our third important match in only six days. I wonder how today's pampered superstars would cope with that sort of hectic schedule!

Jock might have been tempted to alter the team's tactics. He could have thought about putting Charlie Gallagher into midfield beside

Bobby and Bertie to shore up that part of the line-up. Jim Brogan, only twenty-two, had made several first team appearances since the arrival of the manager the previous year and was earning the reputation as a tough-tackling left-back or wing-half. There was also the ever-reliable Willie O'Neill to consider. His defensive qualities were well known. In the end, though, Jock left out Jinky, but still went with an adventurous formation with Joe, Stevie and Wee Bobby sharing the load up front with me on the left. Many may not have been too surprised at the non-appearance of our world class outside-right. The Anfield pitch was a quagmire and the game was played in monsoon conditions throughout. Personally, though, I would have played Wee Jinky because I was always convinced he could perform in ANY elements. And he demonstrated that so consistently throughout the rest of his glittering career.

Would he have made a difference at Anfield? Who knows? But for a dreadful refereeing blunder, Celtic would have taken their place in the European Cup-Winners' Cup Final against Borussia Dortmund at Hampden on May 5 and I don't think too many people would have been complaining. Alas, it was not to be. It sounds unsporting, after all these years, but Celtic were by far the better team than Liverpool over the two legs. There was just no justice whatsoever in losing 2-1 on aggregate to the team that went on to win the English First Division Championship that campaign. I lined up at outside-left that horrible evening on Merseyside with around 10,000 of our fans boosting the gate to 54.208. We kept things tight, but we did get a scare in the first-half when a long-range drive rattled our crossbar with Ronnie Simpson helpless.

Ten or so minutes into the second-half, we were still doing our job. I was up against Chris Lawler and the Liverpool right-back was their answer to Tommy Gemmell. He liked to bomb forward at every opportunity and I had to make sure I tracked his sorties into our territory. At the same time, my remit was to get the ball and race into their half to keep them occupied at the back. In stamina-sapping conditions that is quite a task, but I was built for it. On the hour mark, though, disaster struck. Our friend in black, Monsieur Hannet, deemed I had fouled Tommy Smith as he broke forward. Smith was known as the 'Aintree Iron Man' and there were reports he shaved with a blow torch. This so-called tough guy went down like a sack of spuds when I merely touched him. It was an obvious dive and, unfortunately, the match official bought it.

The free-kick was about thirty yards out and, in normal circumstances, a player would have been wasting his time having a direct shot at our goal from such a distance because of the competence and quality of our keeper. Sadly, these were anything like normal circumstances. The wind was howling and the teeming rain was coming down in torrents right into Ronnie's line of vision. Smith lined it up and struck his shot low into our defensive wall. It took a nick off someone and even our keeper could do little as the ball was diverted past him low at his right hand post. What a sickener. All our good work over two-and-a-half hours of football disappeared in a flash. It didn't get much better five minutes later.

Geoff Strong was called in after Roger Hunt had to withdraw through injury just before the game. Strong's main asset was his ability in the air whereas you would have had difficulty getting a sheet of paper under Hunt's studs when he jumped for the ball. As luck would have it, Strong was perfectly placed as Ian Callaghan slung over a cross from the right. The Liverpool striker actually hovered above Billy McNeill - no mean feat in itself - to get his head to the ball and Ronnie had no chance as his effort slithered in at his left hand post. The game had turned itself on its head in such a short space of time. However, we didn't waste any time feeling sorry for ourselves. We still had twenty-five minutes to get ourselves back into the fray and that's exactly what we did. We had them on the run and we were out of luck again when an effort from Stevie rattled the woodwork.

They were living dangerously and it looked as though they had blown it when Bobby Murdoch picked out Joe who placed the ball neatly inside for Wee Bobby to ram a ferocious drive into the net. There were only seconds to go and we believed we were through. Then came the controversial decision from the referee. Unfortunately, our supporters were every bit as angry as the players and bottles hurtled down from the terracings behind Lawrence's goal. You can never condone such actions, but, at the same time, you have to understand their feelings at that exact moment. The missiles rained down until Neilly Mochan and Bob Rooney appealed for them to halt. Thankfully, order was restored.

But let's be clear about this. The Celtic supporters did not begin the bottle-throwing that evening. I know what I'm talking about because I was almost clattered by projectile lobbed by one of the Kop fans. They chucked bottles onto the field after Tommy Gemmell had brought down Callaghan. The tricky winger was giving our defender a hard time and Tommy had connected with some sturdy challenges. On this occasion, the Liverpool forward went sprawling and the home support decided to show their disapproval. I was standing on the left wing beside Tommy when a full can of beer sailed past my right ear. If we had been Vienna Rapid circa Parkhead 1984, the pitch would have been littered with 'injured' players.

Moments later the bungling Belgian blew for time-up. As I walked off the field, I overheard a remark from one Liverpool to another. 'Thank Christ we don't have to play that lot every week,' was his observation. The referee not only gifted them a 'Get Out Of Jail' card, he had also booked them a place in the Hampden Final. As ever, once you've calmed down, you have to seek that little shaft of light amid the darkness. It was provided by a relieved Bill Shankly after the game. He and Jock were the greatest of buddies and, of course, had both started their working lives as miners. Back in the sixties, you could collect something like 3d (about one pence today) on the return of an empty bottle. Shankly said to our manager in his porridge-thick accent, 'Dae ye want the gate money just noo or will we just send up the empties?' Ha bloody ha!

I wonder if Shanks was still cracking the one-liners after the Final? A crowd of only 41,657 bothered to attend at Hampden whereas a sell-out 130,000 would have been guaranteed if we had had a rub of the green on Merseyside. They must have thought their name was on the trophy that season. They went a goal behind when Sigi Held scored just after the hour mark. However, they equalised shortly afterwards when another debatable decision went their way. Peter Thompson whipped over a ball from the left and Roger Hunt smashed it into the net. The linesman waved frantically to signal the ball had gone out of play before Thompson sent over his cross. French referee Pierre Schwinte was having none of it and awarded the goal to Liverpool.

But eventually you cannot rely on the gods continually smiling upon you. That was underlined in extra-time when Borussia Dortmund got the winning goal. Tommy Lawrence was forced into a quick clearance and a tricky little winger by the name of Reinhard Libuda latched onto the ball and lobbed a thirty-five yard effort at goal. The keeper was stranded as Ron Yeats raced back in an effort to clear. The ball struck the inside of a post, rebounded against the centre-half and then bounced into the net. Liverpool had finally run out of luck.

We were laughing, though, when the competition kicked off on September 29 in Holland against Go Ahead Deventer, who, by the way, never got the chance to go ahead. Bobby Lennox followed my example and became the second Celtic player to score a hat-trick away from home in a European tie. I added a single to my collection and Wee Jinky claimed a double. To be honest, we coasted from the first minute until the last. The fans who couldn't get to the away game must have thought they were in for a storm of goals at Parkhead in the return leg the following week. We triumphed 1-0 and the tie was notable for two things. Joe McBride, signed in the summer from Motherwell, marked his first appearance in Europe with the only goal and a tall, rangy guy came in at right-back for his debut. His name was Jim Craig and, of course, he would pick up a European Cup medal the following season.

And it was Joe on target again in the Second Round as we beat AGF Aarhus 1-0 in Denmark. We doubled that scoreline when we met the Danes at our place on November 17. Jinky and Big Billy were on the scoresheet on this occasion and the only thing that was remarkable about those two ties was the displays of their goalkeeper Bent Martin. He was tall, blond and athletic and Big Jock was looking to add competition in this department to Ronnie and John Fallon. There was a three-month delay before his transfer went through, but, once again, Jock wasn't entirely satisfied with the goalie. Bent played in one game, a Glasgow Cup-tie, before he was sold to Dunfermline for £3,500 in December later that year. Jock must have wished he had left the keeper in Denmark because he put up the shutters in a Scottish Cup-tie against us at Parkhead in the opening round in 1968 as the Fifers won 2-0. He won a Cup medal that season as his new team beat Hearts 3-1 at Hampden.

We had reached the quarter-finals of the competition without conceding a goal and, in truth, had hardly being extended. But we knew we were in for a real test when we were drawn against Kiev Dynamo. The USSR had relented and had allowed their teams to play in European competition for the first time. The opening leg was at

Parkhead and the order from the manager was simple, 'Pile on the goals and make it easy for yourselves over there.' We didn't know too much about our opponents from the Soviet Union, but we were told their goalkeeper, a bloke called Viktor Bannikov, was the best the country had produced since Lev Yashin. We hoped he didn't live up to his reputation against us. Our only problem before the game was the fact that Big Billy was struggling with injury. He failed a fitness test and John Cushley took over in the middle of the defence. A crowd of 64,000 - our highest in Europe at that point - turned out to roar us on.

Tommy Gemmell beat the highly-acclaimed Bannikov with a twenty-five yard effort around the half-hour mark and we had to be content with that until Bobby Murdoch sizzled in a second in the sixty-fourth minute. And it was Bobby who beat the Bannikov barrier again five minutes from the end. Thank goodness for those whizzbang efforts from Tommy and Bobby. Strangely, despite his excellent reputation, Bannikov didn't play for Kiev when they returned to Glasgow in our first defence of the European Cup in September 1967. His coach thought he might be too traumatised by what had happened to him in his earlier visit and brought in a giant by the name of Yevhen Rudakov. The ploy worked, unfortunately, but that's another story.

With a three-goal lead we were relatively confident in completing the job in Kiev. Remember, air travel was still relatively knew to most of us in the mid-sixties. It's not like it is today with affordable flights to every corner of the globe. It was mainly the privileged who could utilise this form of transport, so footballers enjoyed the fact they were among the exclusive ranks when we took to the air. Playing in the Soviet Union presented obvious problems, though. For a start, the annual snowfall in Kiev had been at its harshest and the tie had to be switched from the Ukraine to Tblisi in Georgia. Kiev had been gripped in the winter and the city came close to a standstill. One thing was certain - there was no chance of a football game taking place in these severe conditions. When we did eventually kick off in Tblisi, Jock had decided to go with a joint central defensive partnership of Big Billy and John Cushley with John Clark sweeping up around them.

However, our defence was breached in the twenty-second minute with a goal from their skipper Josef Sabo and they increased the tempo as they strived to get another before half-time. Tommy Gemmell, having scored his first-ever European goal in the first leg, decided to have another go from distance in the thirty-first minute and once again he was successful. Our hosts had been reasonably sporting up until that point. They must have worked out they now had to score four goals to knock us out and they must also have realised that was highly unlikely. They decided to put the boot in. It all got a bit untidy and reached a crescendo when Jim Craig got involved in a fracas with one of their players and both were sent off. Poor Jim had to be escorted to the dressing room by soldiers from the Red Army. I wasn't surprised he didn't hang around to argue with the referee. It ended 1-1 and we progressed 4-1 on aggregate.

Actually, the game against the Soviets was a stroll in the park compared to our efforts to get back to Scotland. The atrocious weather conditions had caught up with Tblisi and our plans to fly back the morning after the game were well and truly scuppered. We were marooned in the city and were hit by delay after delay. Eventually, we managed to get a flight to Moscow and that took us onto Stockholm. We disembarked and, an hour or so later, were told to get back on board. Then we were ordered off again. A combination of the freezing weather and technical problems with the aircraft meant we would have to stay the evening in the Swedish capital before attempting to get home on Friday, a day before we were due to play Hearts at Tynecastle. Surely someone at the SFA would postpone the game? Aye, and pigs might fly - and I'm not referring to Tommy Lawrence, the Liverpool goalkeeper.

We eventually got to Prestwick Airport late on Friday evening and I, and the rest of my team-mates, thought we could head off home for much-needed sleep. We were all astounded when Big Jock informed us we were going to Parkhead for a training session. The club had asked again for the powers-that-be at the SFA to reschedule our league game against Hearts, but, once again, they made the ludicrous decision of telling us the match must go ahead on the Saturday with a 3pm kick-off. We were knackered and just about out on our feet when we arrived at Celtic Park to be put through our paces. The floodlights were switched on, which must have disturbed the sleep of most of the nearby residents of the east end of Glasgow, and we trained until around 3am. Twelve hours later we played at Tynecastle and lost 3-2. Joe McBride and I scored our goals while Big Billy was fielded at right-back instead of the errant Craig. My future Celtic and Crystal Palace team-mate Willie Wallace scored two for the Edinburgh side and Don Kerrigan got the winner twenty minutes from the end. Amazingly, no-one in the Celtic team had to be treated for exhaustion afterwards. I had to smile when Hearts claimed they, too, had been away from home for a midweek fixture. Where were they? All the way over in Valencia where they drew 2-2 with Real Zaragoza. Spain or the Soviet Union? Did anyone at Hearts really believe there was any comparison? For their sanity, you have got to hope they didn't.

It had been a bewildering decision by the SFA to ignore the club's pleas to rearrange the fixture. We were on business on behalf of our country and trying to enhance Scotland's reputation and standing in Europe. You might have thought we would have been rewarded for our efforts instead of being punished. No matter. We still won the league title, anyway.

Then came the epic encounters against Liverpool. I'm not going to labour the point. When we lost to MTK Budapest in the 1964 European Cup-Winners'Cup semi-final we deserved all we got. It was a different story against Liverpool at the same stage of the tournament two years later. I will never change my mind.

Chapter 9

LAMENT IN LISBON

'I am sorry, Yogi, there's no way you can play. In fact, I don't think you should even get on the airplane.'

Two simple little sentences, twenty-two words in all, and they left me feeling as though I had been hit by a wrecking ball. The words were delivered in a typical matter-of-fact manner by Celtic club doctor John Fitzimons and, after finally digesting them, I was utterly devastated. There was no point in asking Fitz for a second opinion because, deep in my heart, I knew his prognosis was accurate. 'Sorry, Yogi,' repeated Fitz and this time there was genuine warmth and feeling in his tone. He left the room as I sat on the treatment table. For a moment, I was left alone with my thoughts. Slowly it dawned on me. I would not be fit for selection for Celtic's biggest game in their history, the European Cup Final against Inter Milan in Lisbon on May 25 1967.

My thoughts were in a swirl. How on earth could this happen? A simple kick on the ankle in the Scottish Cup semi-final against Clyde at the start of April and, almost six weeks later, a dream had been obliterated. Don't get me wrong, I never thought for a second I would be an automatic choice to play against the Italians. With Jock Stein around, you never took anything for granted. I had played in the 3-1 triumph over Dukla Prague in the first leg of our semi-final at Parkhead, but that would have meant nothing to Jock. Nor would it have mattered that I had performed in five of the eight ties leading up to Lisbon. So, there was every possibility, even if I had been fully fit, the manager might have gone with the selection that got a goalless draw in Prague to book the historic European spot and then go on and take their deserved place in club folklore.

So, at long last, I've got the opportunity to answer the question I have been asked so many times while dismissing some of the nonsense that has cropped up over the years. First up, the query that has followed me around for decades. 'How did you feel when Jock Stein dropped you from the team to play Inter Milan in Lisbon?' I wasn't dropped. I wasn't up for selection in the first place. End of story. Jock didn't have to work too hard on that decision. I couldn't have played even if my life had depended on it. And let's nail this piece of rubbish. I've been asked if I regret owning up to the injury and that I may have been able to disguise it and play while only half-fit. Honestly, that is just so stupid. It goes beyond comprehension. Disguise the injury? I could barely walk! And Fitz was so concerned it would flare up in the pressurised atmosphere of an aircraft cabin that his advice was to stay at home. Believe me, that was never going to happen. I would have hobbled all the way to the Portuguese capital to cheer on the team. Remember, I wasn't just a Celtic player, I was also a Celtic supporter.

Yes, I admit I felt as though I had been stabbed in the heart when I heard those chilling words from Fitz. And, yes, I felt like an outsider when Celtic conquered Europe. I'm not going to lie about that. I was so desperate to be involved, to be out on that lush pitch at the Nacional Stadium and to be playing my part as my team Celtic became the first British club to be acclaimed as the best in Europe. I wanted to be in the side that followed in the wake of legends such as Real Madrid, Benfica and the two Milan clubs, AC and Inter, previous winners of the fabulous silverware, rulers of all they surveyed, masters of the beautiful game. How much would that have meant to a guy from Coatbridge who had to be persuaded to take up football by a primary school teacher? Well, in a word, everything. How would it have felt to have been on the pitch when the referee blew his whistle for time-up in Lisbon with the scoreline reading: Celtic 2, Inter Milan 1? It goes beyond description.

Even today, when the players meet for anniversaries and celebrations of Lisbon, I don't really feel a part of it. I didn't play in that game and that, of course, is the difference. Had I been on that pitch, I would still be talking about it. You would need a gag to get me to shut up. But I was in the stand that memorable day when I ached to be out on the field with my pals, playing my part in turning over Inter Milan. Of course, I was overjoyed for my team-mates at the end and we whooped it up big-style, but I couldn't help thinking of what-might-have-been. I suppose that's only natural.

However, back at Celtic Park when Fitz dropped the bombshell news a week or so before the game, I felt sick. I looked at my ankle and I thought of the game against Clyde on April 1. How appropriate is that date? April Fool's Day. Ten of the eleven who started that Cup-tie would line up against Inter Milan. I was the odd man out. Bobby Murdoch was injured and Willie Wallace took his place on the right-hand side of the midfield. When Bobby was fit, he, as expected, went straight back into the side with Willie pushing forward and I dropped out. The semi-final against the stuffy Shawfield outfit will hardly be remembered by even the most fanatical among the Celtic support. It ended in a goalless draw and I actually remained on the pitch for the entire ninety minutes. I had taken a knock, painful upon impact, but it had settled down as the game wore on. That sort of thing happened all the time. The old expression is 'running off an injury' and that was true that afternoon at the national stadium.

However, these sort of injuries have a horrible habit of manifesting themselves the following day. I awoke and my ankle had ballooned to three times its normal size. That wasn't an unusual occurrence, either, and I wasn't overly-anxious. I rested it all Sunday because I knew the Cup replay against Clyde was due on Wednesday and I didn't want to take any risks. Back at training on Monday, I realised I couldn't put my full weight on the foot and the ankle was still giving me jip. The swelling was beginning to relent, but it was still uncomfortable. Bob Rooney, our physiotherapist, and Dr Fitz got to work on it that afternoon. We had reached a crucial part of our campaign and I didn't want to miss out on the run-in. We looked as though we were about to retain our League Championship although Rangers were pushing us all the way. I had picked up a League Cup winners' medal after we had beaten our Ibrox rivals 1-0 at Hampden and, at that stage, had played in four of our six European Cup games and we were due to play Dukla Prague in the semi-final. Exciting times lay ahead. If only I had possessed a crystal ball.

'How's the ankle, Yogi?' asked Big Jock on Tuesday morning. I told him the truth. 'Still feeling a little bit of discomfort, boss.' He thought for a moment and said, 'Okay, take it easy today.' I went through a light routine, a bit of running, twisting and turning and striking the ball. There were twinges, but I was sure I could play at a push. Jock, though, rarely took risks with a player's fitness. When he named his line-up, I found I was on the substitutes' bench. Fair enough. There was the possibility I couldn't have gone full pelt for ninety minutes so it made sense. Remember, too, teams could only name one player on stand-by back then. Maybe, as in the present day, if the manager had an entire platoon at the ready with three being allowed to get the nod, things may have been different and Jock may have been tempted to take a chance. Doubt it, though. He was a real stickler for full fitness throughout his team. Anyway, Jock brought in Charlie Gallagher to the midfield and pushed Bertie Auld slightly wider on the left. It worked, too, with Bertie scoring one of the goals that helped the club ease to a 2-0 win over Clyde. I came on in the second-half to test my ankle. By the way, that was a very good result because the Shawfield side had an excellent season in 1966/67 and finished third in the league behind ourselves and Rangers. So Jock was absolutely right to make sure his team was firing on all cylinders that night.

A week after the Scottish Cup win over Clyde, there was the very different challenge of Dukla Prague to contend with in the first leg of our European Cup semi-final at Parkhead. Veteran midfield playmaker Josef Masopust was by far their most recognisable name. He had been Czechoslovakia's captain when they reached the World Cup Final against Brazil in Santiagio, Chile, in 1962. Masopust, who won the European Footballer of the Year that same season, actually scored the first goal of the encounter before the South Americans came back to win 3-1. He may have been thirty-six years old by the time the Czechs reached the last four of the most prestigious tournament in club football, but we knew he could still play a bit. Dukla had got their campaign underway with a 6-0 saunter against the Danish part-timers of Esbjerg. They threw their hat into the ring for the silverware in the next two rounds. They thrashed a very strong Anderlecht side 6-2 on aggregate, beating them home and away with Masopust scoring in the first leg in the vast and charmless Juliska Stadium where Celtic history would be made later that season.

Europe really took notice of their next result. Ajax had produced the sensation of the previous round when they annihilated Liverpool 5-1 in the first leg of their confrontation in Amsterdam. Legendary boss Bill Shankly claimed the result was 'a complete fluke' and his side would turn it around at Anfield. Johan Cruyff wasn't listening and netted the opener on Merseyside as the Dutch eventually cemented a 7-3 passage to the quarter-finals. They were being tipped as outsiders to win the tournament. This was at a time before anyone had a clue what 'Total Football' was all about. The Dutch had invented the system and it was good enough to get Ajax to the European Cup Final in 1969 where they lost 4-1 to AC Milan. Obviously, though, they perfected it by the time the seventies rolled round and Feyenoord beat us 2-1 in Milan and then Cruyff and Co racked up a memorable hat-trick in the following years. Back in 1967, however, they were still seen as a bit of an unknown quantity. Any team who had taken seven off the English champions deserved respect, though. Dukla beat them 3-2 on aggregate and earned the right to their trip to the east end of Glasgow. We understood completely that only our best would be good enough against this lot.

Willie Wallace, signed for something in the region of £30,000 from Hearts just before the turn of the year, should have made his European Cup debut against the Slavs of Vojvodina Novi Sad in the quarter-final, but some sort of administrative blunder meant he was forced to watch the action from the stands. Apparently, he hadn't been registered in time which is a bit strange when you consider he had been at Celtic for two full months before the Vojvodina game. Anyway, he was primed and ready to go by the time Dukla turned up. I had played at outside-right in our 2-0 win over Motherwell the previous Saturday. That was classic Jock Stein. He knew only too well that the Czechs would have a spy at Parkhead that afternoon and he liked to bamboozle the opposition. He was into mind games long before the current batch of bosses came on the scene. I had played in Wee Jinky's position a couple of times earlier that season, so it wasn't exactly a new role for me. The Dukla scout would have returned to camp with the news that the guy who normally plays on the left had switched wings. It was all part of the game for Big Jock. He always liked to keep the opposition on the back foot.

I felt 100 per cent fit when I was told I would be back on the left wing for the tie against Masopust and his men on the Wednesday. Jock, in fact, held back announcing his line-up until the last possible minute after he had a final check on the ground conditions. He paced around the pitch about an hour before kick-off and it looked like a straight choice between me and Bobby Lennox. I was given the green light. Jinky was back in his normal place on the right. Ronnie Simpson was in goal while Jim Craig and Tommy Gemmell were on the defensive flanks. Billy McNeill and John Clark completed the back four and Bobby Murdoch and Bertie Auld dovetailed in the middle of the park. With Jinky and I on the touchlines, Jock gave the main striking roles to Stevie Chalmers and Willie Wallace. Once again, there were ten players on the pitch that evening who would perform in Lisbon. Do you need to guess who missed out?

I realise I am not the first person to say this and I doubt if I'll be the last, but European nights at Celtic Park were something else altogether. You had to witness these electrifying spectacles first hand to totally appreciate them. The stadium would rock for hours before kick-off and the din the fans created as you come out the tunnel was ferocious. We would trot out onto the pitch and every now and again I would sneak a quick look at the opposition. I could see some faces draining of colour and knew they had never encountered anything like this in their life. The decrepit Jungle, a vast area that resembled an enormous rusting farmyard shed, housed the noisiest of the fans. The racket ricocheted around the corrugated iron surroundings and, genuinely, you could feel the hairs standing up on the back of your neck. It was orchestrated bedlam as they raised the roof. 'CEL-TIC...CEL-TIC' were the words that tumbled down from the packed terracings and if that couldn't inspire a footballer to the heights of his ability then I haven't a clue what could. I would go over to the left wing and when you were smack in front of the Jungle you couldn't help but feel elevated. I really mean that. The sheer fanaticism of those supporters let you know how much the club meant to them. How could you let down these guys?

They were at their most raucous on the evening of April 12 as we prepared for the challenge of the Czechs. There were 74,406 in attendance, but I'm fairly certain you could add another 5,000 or so to that total. The constabulary and stewards couldn't keep these guys out of the ground. Not having a ticket was a mere irrelevance to so many. They would have parachuted in if need be. Tunnelled up from Melbourne. You get the picture.

Jock had stressed the need for patience. He warned us they were a neat, compact side who liked to keep possession and piled forward in numbers on the break. He also told us they had a very dangerous centre-forward who was good in the air. No wonder! I took a look at this guy called Stanislav Strunc and he towered over me. I would guess he was about 6ft 6in and wasn't unlike Peter Crouch in height and build. He proved to be a nuisance most of the night when Dukla broke forward. The referee stifled the cheers of the vast support when he ruled out a Stevie Chalmers headed 'goal' early on. The Portuguese match official indicated Jinky's foot was high when he went into a challenge just before he sent over the cross for Stevie. We didn't argue as we single-mindedly went about our business.

But the Wee Man responded by plonking one in the net that stood just before the half-hour mark. It was a race between Jinky and the sturdy Ivo Viktor, the Czech international goalkeeper who was rated one of the best in the world. If he thought our diminutive winger might pull out when confronted by his massive frame, then he was in for a surprise. Jinky had the heart of a lion. People could kick him all over the place and he kept coming back for more. Nothing intimidated this wee guy. Jinky got there just before the goalie and lofted the ball sweetly over his head and into the net. We were looking good at this stage and I was more or less hugging the left wing while Jinky did a bit of roving around over on the right. However, disaster struck just on the half-time whistle when they levelled and it was a real sickener. It was a goal that could have been avoided ten times over. Our defence just couldn't get rid of a bouncing ball on the edge of the penalty area. A player would slash at it, miss, it would hit someone else, come back into the mix and boots and bodies were flying everywhere as we tried to clear our lines. As luck would have it, it took one rebound too many and fell right into the tracks of the gangly Strunc. He dragged it wide and then slid a right foot drive across Ronnie into the far corner. I've never heard Celtic Park so silent. Not even in training back at the start of the sixties when we ran round the park in the dark. It was eerie.

Losing a goal at any time is never a good feeling, but when you concede one just before the interval it leaves you more than a little deflated. We trudged towards the tunnel while their players were still congratulating each other, looking as though they had already turned the game around. Someone should have informed them that a game at Celtic Park lasted ninety minutes and the only time opponents earned the right to look smug came with the final peep from the referee's whistle. Jock was always good value during half-time pep talks. He would notice all sorts of things during the opening period, where we could exploit their defence, areas we could dominate and how to curb their threats when they came forward. No-one was hitting a panic button in our dressing room as we prepared to take the field for the next forty-five minutes. Once again, we got a real lift by the rousing, ear-shattering welcome from our support. They let us know they were solidly behind us no matter what. I can tell them here and now it was always most appreciated. They were our twelfth man and they played their part. They did so again on that April evening.

Masopust wore No.9, but certainly didn't play like a centre-forward while Strunc had No.7 on his shirt, but I doubt if he went anywhere near the right touchline all night. So, there was a little bit of kidology from our Czech opponents, too. It made little difference to us. We began to dictate the pace of the game as we forced them back. Masopust was less influential and Strunc was becoming isolated, a lone figure in attack. Bobby and Bertie got a grip of the midfield and they refused to let go. Stevie was challenging for everything and Wispy was drifting to the right with Jinky coming inside. I remained on the left and was told to hit the by-line and get balls across, high or low. We got the breakthrough goal just before the hour mark and it was as simple as you like. No intricate footwork was required as Tommy hammered the ball out of defence. It caught the Dukla back lot out of position and Wispy chased after it and connected perfectly with the outside of the right foot. The ball simply sailed high past the astonished Viktor. Tommy later claimed it was a pass. I'll take his word for it.

Six minutes later Celtic Park was in uproar when we got a third, a goal straight from our training ground at Barrowfield. Jock always wanted to be inventive with set-pieces and would urge the players to attempt something different to catch our opponents off guard. We were awarded a free-kick after one of their panicking defenders punched away a pass from Bobby Murdoch. It was about twenty-five yards out and fairly central. We all took our positions as Bertie strolled forward to take it. He hesitated and then motioned to re-centre the ball. Their defensive wall must have taken a collective breather for a split second and that was all our crafty midfielder needed. He touched the ball sideways to his right and Wispy came thundering in to first-time an unstoppable drive through the wall and past a static Viktor. What a way to celebrate your first-ever European Cup-tie. And it might have been even more memorable for Wispy. He could have claimed a hat-trick, but struck the top of the crossbar with a clipped drive after great work from Stevie as we piled forward looking for a killer fourth. That, surely, would have put the tie to bed and make absolutely certain there would be no repeats of the bungling in Budapest three years earlier.

Bobby sent a left-foot twenty-yarder just over the top and then followed that up with another drive from a similar range that whipped past the upright. Stevie almost scored from under the crossbar, but the keeper somehow managed to scramble the ball to safety. And where was I while all this was taking place? I remained wide on the left to stretch their back line. The right-back had rarely strayed from my side since the kick-off and when I received a pass I heard him barking orders for someone to come and play behind him to offer cover. That suited me fine. If I was on the ball and effectively taking two of their players out of the game, then that was leaving room for my mates to exploit in other areas of the pitch. If I am being brutally honest, I would say I didn't play as well as I would have hoped. However, I did take great exception to a match report in one of the national newspapers that stated, 'Celtic had ten professionals on the field. And John Hughes.' That was way over the top.

No, I hadn't put in an eye-catching performance and I will readily admit that. But to say I wasn't professional was unacceptable, possibly even a bit vindictive from a scribe I didn't rate in the first place. Anyway, I still managed to keep the right-back occupied throughout the night and that was important. Mainly, we got it right against Dukla on the night, but we left Celtic Park talking about some of the missed opportunities that would have brought a vital fourth goal. They were on the ropes for the remaining twenty-five minutes of the game and were there for the taking while we bombarded their goal. Most clubs would have been satisfied with a 3-1 advantage, but strange things could happen on your travels in Europe. If any team knew that, it was Celtic. What I didn't realise, though, was that I had kicked my last ball in the European Cup for the season.

A few days before the return leg in Prague, my ankle had started to act up and I was forced to sit it out as Celtic drew 0-0 against Aberdeen at Parkhead. Amazingly, it was the first time we had failed to score a solitary goal at our place during the campaign. It may surprise you even more to learn the team that drew a blank was the same side that won the European Cup.

Maybe Jock thought it was the ideal dress rehearsal for the meeting with Dukla because he ordered a blanket defence for this tie. I had never before heard our manager urging the team to adopt negative tactics. He wanted to smother the Czechs and give them no space whatsoever on their own massive pitch. I've heard it said that Dukla were so good they pushed Celtic back for the entire ninety minutes and it wasn't part of Jock's game plan. That's nonsense. Just ask Stevie Chalmers and he'll verify that. Stevie was given the lone role up front and was told to chase everything that dropped anywhere near him. His team-mates were instructed to play their passes into channels for Stevie to run into, utilising his fabulous speed. Stevie was another who was as brave as they come. He was a warrior on that football field and his display that afternoon in the Czech capital was absolutely awesome. He was here, there and everywhere as he chased lost causes. On the rare occasion he actually got the ball to his feet, he would take it down the line towards the corner flag, inviting defenders to tackle and give away a throw-in. And, of course, we wouldn't be in too much of a hurry to take the shy.

I think that's the one and only time anyone could ever say Celtic were spoilers. That just wasn't our style, but Jock was absolutely determined to guide the club to Lisbon and he was going to do it in whichever manner he believed would be necessary and, ultimately, successful. The razzmatazz could wait until May 25, as far he was concerned. It was a very disciplined display from our players and Ronnie Simpson was immaculate in everything he did. I recall our old friend Strunc blitzed in an early shot, but Faither was equal to it and pushed the ball over the bar. That was a rare attempt on target by the Czechs that day. Billy McNeill played a real captain's part and there was the utterly astonishing sight of Jinky and Bobby Lennox almost playing as auxiliary full-backs alongside Jim and Tommy.

I was in the stand alongside Charlie Gallagher, Willie O'Neill and Joe McBride, three players who had contributed in getting the club to this stage. Joe, of course, had been so unlucky with injuries and, in fact, had marked his debut in the competition with the second and clinching goal against FC Zurich in the first leg away back in September 28 which, coincidentally, was just a few days before Jock's forty-fourth birthday. Willie had played in the first two rounds against the Swiss and French outfit Nantes before the manager switched Tommy Gemmell from right to left-back and brought in Jim Craig at No.2. Charlie's last touch in the competition was to send over the inviting corner-kick for Billy McNeill to bullet in the last-minute winner against Vojvodina Novi Sad in the quarter-final. What a way to sign off!

It wasn't pretty in Prague, but no-one cared. Celtic were through to the European Cup Final, the first British club to achieve such a feat, and we felt like partying. Strict teetotaller Jock, though, had other ideas and was swift to remind the players we had a wee game to look forward to on the Saturday - the Scottish Cup Final against Aberdeen. 'There's plenty time to enjoy yourselves at the end of the season,' he said. 'Not long to go now then you can all let your hair down. Ach, I don't know why you bother with that stuff, anyway.' Unfortunately, I was in the stand again when two goals from Willie Wallace gave us a 2-0 win over Aberdeen at Hampden. My ankle was still a problem and Bob Rooney and Fitz seemed concerned that it hadn't healed completely. Celtic didn't need my services on the day as they dominated the Cup Final against what we thought would be dangerous opponents. Wispy sidefooted in the opener in the first-half and lashed in the second after the turnaround. I have to say the team looked more like Celtic as they surged forward at every opportunity. Thankfully, the tactics in Prague were never repeated.

My problem was now obvious. I hadn't played a full game since the 3-1 triumph over Dukla in Glasgow and, as I've said, Jock would never contemplate choosing anyone he believed wasn't completely matchfit. To be fair, he put me in the team for the league match against Dundee United at Parkhead on May 3, a full twenty-two days before Lisbon. I had played against the Tayside outfit when they had shocked us 3-2 at Tannadice on Hogmanay. They were still the only

Scottish club to have beaten us when they came to our place with only three league games remaining. There was no talk of revenge among the players. Simply put, we were within touching distance of a second successive championship and a victory was the only thing that occupied our minds.

United were no dummies. They proved that by dismissing Barcelona 4-1 in the old Fairs Cup, now the Europa League, winning home and away. The club had also embarked on a Scandinavian signing spree and had brought in talented players such as Finn Dossing, Lennart Wing, Mogens Berg, Finn Seamann and Orjan Persson, who later joined Rangers and was promptly nicknamed 'Orange Person'. Who said the Ibrox support didn't have a sense of humour? Anyway, the player who did the damage to us that night was a bloke from exotic Alloa called Dennis Gillespie. He played in their midfield and, at that stage of his career, could hardly have been termed a goal threat. Yet, he had scored against us at Tannadice and, unfortunately, he repeated the feat at Parkhead. We were coasting at 2-1 ahead after goals from Tommy Gemmell, with another blaster of a penalty-kick, and Wispy. I think there were only about ten minutes to go when they equalised and worse was to follow when they got the winner. Amazingly, they had beaten us 3-2 once more. Only two teams turned us over that season - United and Vojvodina. And the Tannadice side managed it twice. Strange game, football.

Once more I took my place in the stand for the following game. It was against Rangers at Ibrox and we knew a point would be enough to retain the title. Rangers, naturally, were determined to make sure there would be no flag celebrations in Govan that afternoon. The rain poured from the heavens all day and the playing surface became a quagmire. Yet Wee Jinky found superhuman reserves of strength to torture and torment their defence for most of the ninety minutes. They scored first with a pulverising long-range drive from Sandy Jardine, but Jinky swiftly levelled before putting us ahead in the second-half. That is still one of the best goals I have ever witnessed. David Provan, their overworked left-back, must have thought he had won a watch when our Wee Man decided to take the ball inside. Provan had been getting turned inside out for most of the game as Jinky tore straight at him, shimmied one way and went another on his way along the touchline. On this occasion, he decided to come inside and Provan believed it was now someone else's problem to pick up our player. However, before anyone could react, Jinky took aim and let fly with a left foot drive from about twenty-five yards that almost tore a hole in the roof of the net. Norrie Martin, their keeper, was still leaping for it while Jinky and his team-mates were celebrating. Roger Hynd equalised late on, but it made no difference. The trophy was heading back to its rightful resting place where it would remain for another seven wonderful years.

Not too far from me in the Ibrox stand that day was Helenio Herrera, the famed manager of Inter Milan. I have to say he looked fairly grim at the end. A reporter asked for his immediate observations, but he wasn't too forthcoming. 'Celtic? Very fast,' he said. And Jimmy Johnstone? 'Very fast.' The rest of the team? 'All very fast.' It sounded a bit like a brush off, but when he returned to Italy he had a press conference with the local media and continued to repeat the same observation. The forward line against Rangers was Jimmy Johnstone, Willie Wallace, Stevie Chalmers, Bobby Lennox and Bertie Auld - the same five who would face Inter in Lisbon. Herrera had done his homework. 'They are very fast because they have all played as wingers at some stage in their career,' he pointed out accurately. 'Auld now plays in midfield, but I know he was once an outside-left when he started at Celtic. He also played in that role with Birmingham City in England. Wallace plays as a centre-forward now, but I know he played on the right wing earlier in his career.' I had to admit Herrera was thorough.

Sadly, I was struggling. My ankle refused to respond to treatment. Fitz worked on it, but it had him baffled. It had me fairly frustrated, I can tell you. I continued to train and do some ball work, but it just didn't feel right. We were edging ever closer to Lisbon and I was desperate to be involved. Jock, as ever, kept his thoughts to himself. He refused to even hint at his line-up for the most important game in the club's history. The last league match of the campaign was switched to Monday May 15 to give Celtic extended time to prepare for Lisbon. I realised at that stage I had to be involved against Kilmarnock at Parkhead to have any sort of chance of playing in the European Cup Final. A couple of days before that encounter, Dr Fitzimons delivered his calamitous news. 'I am sorry, Yogi, there's no way you can play.' Those words will live with me forever.

All these years later, I can understand the confusion among the Celtic support about my exclusion from the Lisbon line-up. No-one could blame them. Big Jock ordered a complete clampdown on any news coming out of Celtic Park. There was no way he was going to show his hand to Herrera. Why should he? Jock realised the Inter boss had an encyclopedic knowledge of the players his team would face in the European Cup pinnacle. If he knew Bertie had played outside-left at Birmingham City in the early sixties, you had to ask what he didn't know. Jock wanted to keep him guessing. Herrera would have been well aware I could play at centre-forward as well as on either flank. I was an entirely different proposition to Stevie and Wispy coming through the middle. Would he consider tinkering with his defence to deal with that sort of threat? It was all very hush-hush, but twelve days before the game in the Portuguese capital I had to accept the nearest I would get to the pitch would be a place in the stand. Yes, it was heart-breaking, especially when well-meaning supporters asked me for my thoughts on the rundown to the game. 'Stick one in the pokey for me, Big Man,' they would say. I could only smile and reply, 'I'll do my best, mate.' And all the time I had to accept I wouldn't be out there in the thick of the action in the most momentous encounter in Celtic's history.

So, Big Jock continued to perform his psychological games in an effort for his one-upmanship over Herrera when we played Kilmarnock and he knew only too well the Inter Milan supremo had a couple of spies at Parkhead that night. Billy McNeill lined up with the No.8 on his shorts, but even Caesar would be the first to admit he was no midfield player. John Cushley played his only game of the season at centre-half. West Ham manager Ron Greenwood was looking for a rugged, no-nonsense central defender to play alongside England's World Cup-winning captain Bobby Moore in the heart of the London team's rearguard. Jock told him to have a look at Cushley and fielded him against Killie. My old mate must have done quite well - we won 2-0 with goals from Willie Wallace and Bobby Lennox - because the West Ham gaffer agreed a fee of around £25,000 for his services shortly after the game. Cush, however, remained a Celtic player until after Lisbon. Jock wasn't even going to allow that snippet of news to filter through to Herrera. John Fallon also played in goal that evening, his only appearance in the top side during the campaign.

Yes, Jock enjoyed his manipulations and strategies. But there was still no place for yours truly. That hurt and I couldn't tell anyone. Even newspaper reporters I was friendly with were kept in the dark. I had to maintain the great pretence right up until kick-off time. Then, and only then, could the truth come out. Understandably, though, it was swept into the mists of time in the glorious aftermath of Lisbon. So, all these years down the line, I have at last been able to set the record straight. There is every possibility I might not have been in Jock's plans in any case, but I wasn't fit to play even if I had been.

On the flight to Lisbon I could feel the ankle begin to swell. Fitz was right and there was clearly a reaction to the pressurised atmosphere inside the aircraft. By the time we reached our hotel in Estoril I was wondering if I could remove my footwear. I was rooming with John Cushley and he helped me ease my foot out of the shoe. I took off my sock and, at that very moment, liquid spurted out of my ankle. Unfortunately, the injury had become poisonous and the four hours or so on the plane brought everything to a climax. Cush managed to find some tissue paper to stem the flow. We called in Fitz and he took a look at my ankle. He didn't waste too much time in summing up the situation. 'Complete rest throughout the summer,' he said. 'Don't even think about kicking a ball.'

My season was finished. But a new era for Celtic was just beginning. It would be fair to say I had mixed emotions. Alas, there was a little bit of grief amidst the glory. It was a very different tale, however, at the beginning of that remarkable campaign. We may have been novices in the European Cup - that was out first time in the competition at a time when you had to be champions of your country - but people shouldn't have forgotten that we managed to reach the semi-finals in the European Cup-Winners' Cup on two occasions, losing out only by the odd goal both times. So, we did possess some sort of pedigree although, to be absolutely truthful, I never heard any of my team-mates actually saying we could go on to win the trophy when we were preparing for the campaign. We were a fairly confident bunch, but that would have been stretching it a bit too far. I'm willing to bet that none of my mates even knew where the European Cup Final was to take place that season. Actually, John Clark might have had an inkling because he used to devour football magazines and World Soccer was a must every month for our knowledge-seeking sweeper. The rest of us, though, wouldn't have been looking that far ahead.

The draw paired us with FC Zurich and the first game was in Glasgow. Funnily enough, I recall Jock telling us we would probably get it easier against them in Switzerland than we would at our place. He reckoned we would get more space on their pitch and so it proved. Zurich upset us a little at Parkhead. It was clear they were an accomplished outfit and had a few performers in their line-up who had played for their country in the World Cup Finals in England the previous year. Surprisingly, they weren't slow to put the boot in, either. I had never associated Swiss teams as being tough guys, but these blokes were quite happy to mix it in Glasgow. I was pitched in at outside-left with Joe McBride and Stevie Chalmers the main strikers. The first-half came and went with little of note. As ever, Jock stressed the need to remain calm, keep possession and continue plugging away. 'Something has got to give,' he would often say. Thankfully, the Swiss surrendered on the sixty-fourth minute just when it looked as though we might be grinding to a goalless stalemate. They were well drilled in defence and we weren't getting much joy in breaking them down. Enter Tommy Gemmell.

It was obvious the terrifying shooting power of our full-back hadn't filtered through to the land of the cuckoo clocks. John Clark, with his usual minimum of fuss, broke up a Swiss raid and lobbed the ball out to Tommy, playing at right-back with the ever-dependable Willie O'Neill behind me. Tommy was never shy at letting fly from any range or angle. He nodded the ball down in front of him as the Swiss retreated into their defensive positions. No-one closed him down and our adventurous full-back never needed to be asked twice to have a go. He was about thirty-five yards out when he took aim. His blistering right-foot drive exploded behind their goalkeeper, Steffen Iten, who didn't even move as the ball scorched high into the roof of the net. That was the boost we urgently required. Five minutes later we had doubled our lead when a back heel from Bertie wrong-footed the defence and Joe whipped a low shot wide of the goalie. It took a nick off a defender, but, from where I was standing, it looked a goal all the way.

We thought we had made it 3-0 bang on the final whistle when Joe, clearly onside, headed past their keeper from close range. We celebrated and the referee, a fussy Dane by the name of Frederick

Hansen, indicated the game was over. Was it a goal? We didn't know and the fans in the 50,000 crowd hadn't a clue, either. The match official simply pointed to the tunnel. Later we discovered he had blown for full-time a split-second before Joe planted his effort in the net. Now that's what I call precision timing. Swiss clock makers would have been more than satisfied. So, too, were the Swiss players. In the end, of course, it didn't matter. I was on the left wing again when we played the second leg at their place on October 5. Ronnie Simpson was a virtual spectator as we racked up a deserved 3-0 victory. Big Tommy cracked in another in the twenty-second minute and Stevie pounced to make it 4-0 on aggregate just before half-time. The Swiss probably wanted to skip the second-half and even more so when we were awarded a penalty-kick three minutes after the interval. Tommy dispatched it with his usual aplomb.

Next up came French outfit Nantes. Like Zurich, they, too, had a number of players in their line-up who had played for their nation in the 1966 World Cup Finals. I sat this one out with Jock changing the tactics and going with Bobby Lennox alongside Stevie and Joe. They gave us a fright by opening the scoring through Francis Magny inside twenty minutes, but we recovered our composure swiftly and Joe equalised and Lennox's pace paid off again as he raced through to notch a second five minutes after the turnaround. The French looked devastated when Stevie knocked in the third midway through the second-half. The game, though, belonged to Jinky. He was unstoppable as he hared up and down the right wing creating confusion and chaos in the Nantes rearguard. The French fans might not have enjoyed what he was doing to their team, but they had the good grace to applaud the Wee Man when he was in full flight. They nicknamed him 'La Puce Volante' which actually translates to 'The Flying Pea', but somehow that was changed to 'The Flying Flea'. I'm told if the French call someone 'Pea' it is actually a term of endearment. Thought I might clear that one up. Mind you, I don't know why they insisted Joe McBride was a Marlon Brando lookalike. That one's got me beat.

Jock went on record as saying the tie wasn't over and Celtic would continue on the offensive in the second leg. Again, there was no place for me and the manager brought Charlie Gallagher back in to bolster the midfield alongside Bobby and Bertie. Wee Jinky, aka 'La Puce

Volante', got involved in some deja vu to turn in another sparkling display and, in fact, opened the scoring in the thirteenth minute. However, a very talented French side pulled one back through Gerard Georgin and the same player gave us another fright shortly afterwards with a swerving shot that gave Ronnie all sorts of problems before he grabbed the ball on the line. Thankfully, normal service was restored and Stevie restored our three-goal advantage with our second just on the hour mark and Bobby Lennox slid about twenty yards to get on the end of a cross from Jinky to fire in the third. All things considered, we were quite happy with a 6-2 aggregate triumph. So, that was four games played, four games won with eleven goals scored and only two conceded. Not bad going for European Cup rookies.

We were drawn against Vojvodina Novi Sad in the quarter-final and, once again, the Central Europeans were a bit of an unknown quantity. What we did know, though, was the fact they had knocked out Atletico Madrid in a play-off in the previous round. They won the first leg in Yugoslavia 3-1 and we were intrigued to discover their goalkeeper, Ilija Pantelic, scored their second goal with a penalty-kick. They were beaten 2-0 in Spain and were trailing by the same scoreline in the decider after Atletico had netted twice in the opening six minutes. The Slavs might have folded after being hit by such an early salvo, but it was to their credit that Silvester Takac pulled one back in the twenty-eighth minute and Dimitri Radovic snatched the equaliser just after the hour mark. The replay went to extra-time and it was eventually settled by an effort from Takac in the 102nd minute. To come back and win in extra-time showed guts. And we were to find they had loads of skill to go with that vital commodity.

The pitch in Novi Sad for the first game was flint hard. Jock knew I could operate on such precarious conditions and I was back in at outside-left. Bobby Lennox was sacrificed, but ten of the other Lions were on display. We were doing okay with about twenty minutes to go and the game still goalless. Then Tommy attempted a passback that fell between Bobby Murdoch and John Clark. They hadn't anticipated our attack-minded left-back knocking the ball backwards and a pacy forward by the name of Svemir Djordjic latched onto it and squared a pass across to the unmarked Milan Stanic and he left Ronnie helpless with a swift low drive into the corner. Faither, hardly a serial swearer, came out with some words I'm pretty sure never figured figure in the Concise English Dictionary as he blasted our defence. He could be a bad-tempered old so-and-so when he conceded a goal - even in training! We kept it to 1-0, but we realised tough times were ahead in Glasgow.

A week later the Slavs were in town and the psychological warfare between the two managers went into overdrive. Jock refused to allow the Vojvodina players to train on Celtic Park the night before the game. Their coach, Vujadin Boskov, who would go onto manage Real Madrid later in his career, was furious. 'Sorry,' said Jock, 'it's been raining in Glasgow for the past few days and if you train on the pitch you'll ruin it. You can train at Barrowfield.' Helpfully, he added, 'I'll make sure the floodlights are switched on.' Considering we were now into March, it was quite a noble gesture by our manager! Boskov was making all sorts of threats, but Jock waved him away. 'You can train at Barrowfield or not train at all,' he said, defying argument. The Slavs had also predicted a win at Parkhead and that irked Jock somewhat. 'We'll see about that,' he said with menace.

So, the scene was set for a thriller at our place on a cold, mist-shrouded evening in the east end of Glasgow on March 8 as we fought for the right to play in the semi-final. Jock made one change - Charlie Gallagher replaced Bertie Auld - and I was told to get up and down the left wing all night and not give their full-back, a bloke called Rajko Aleksic, a chance to hit on the counter attack. I have to admit the Slavs settled into the confrontation right from the start. They passed the ball around with great accuracy and all their players looked comfortable on the ball. The first-half ended goalless and we rarely threatened their penalty-taking goalkeeper Pantelic which was as unusual as it was disappointing. 'One break and we're in,' observed Jock. 'Jinky, Yogi get yourselves into the game. We need width.'

And with that we went out for the second forty-five minutes with 63, 374 urging us to step up the tempo. Jock asked me to line up beside Jinky on the right wing at the restart. 'It'll give them something to think about,' he said. I didn't spend too much time on the right, though, and drifted back to the left as the game went on. We realised we needed to put more pressure on Pantelic and his back lot, but we were very mindful about the pace at which the Slavs could break forward. Like us, they were an extremely fit outfit. It was easy to see why they could beat Atletico Madrid in extra-time in their play-off.

My immediate opponent was fast on the turn and it was proving to be a difficult task to push the ball past him and leave him standing. However, I have always believed you will get one chance to get a cross in from wide and I kept plugging away. Just before the hour mark I saw an opportunity, without even kicking the ball, to open up their rearguard.

We were coming forward and I spotted Big Tommy really getting into his stride as he raced down the left wing looking for a pass. I decided to act as a decoy and take the right-back inside with me to give our left-back a clear run. It worked a treat. Tommy received the pass and swung the ball into the penalty area. Pantelic, who had looked so safe and sound, suddenly flapped. He mishandled the ball as Stevie came racing in and he couldn't miss with the goal gaping in front of him. The Slav defenders were completely taken aback. Obviously, they were used to their goalie, who was also their captain, dealing competently with such crossballs. However, he got his angles wrong on this occasion and Stevie was never slow to pounce. Momentarily, the Slavs were rattled and we knew we had to take any advantage we could against this team.

I had two tries well held by Pantelic as he recovered his composure. Wee Jinky squeezed in a shot, too, that was saved and Tommy tested the keeper with a long-range effort. We needed that second goal or else we were looking at a play-off in Rotterdam. With ten minutes or so to go, Vojvodina looked fairly satisfied with the deadlock, no doubt believing they could complete the job in a third game as they had done with Atletico Madrid. They stood off us and that was a mistake of monumental proportions. We continued our momentum as we probed and passed our way forward. In the final fading moments, with the Swedish match official Hans Carlsson checking his watch, Jinky won a corner-kick on the right.

It was like the charge of the green brigade - we wore an-all green strip that night - as we hastily took up our positions in the penalty area. Charlie rushed over to take it and looked as though he was going to knock a short one to Jim Craig. 'Get it into the box,' was the bellow from Jock in the dug-out. I've no idea if Charlie could hear the manager above the racket coming from the terracings, but that's exactly what he did. Charlie hit it sweetly, as ever, and the ball soared into the box. Pantelic moved off his line, but ran straight into Stevie who was blocking his path. The keeper was stranded in no-man's land when Billy McNeill rose majestically into the air to make perfect contact and his header flew into the top corner. I didn't realise it at the time, but the referee blew for time-up two seconds after Vojvodina kicked off again. We were elated, but shattered by the time that final whistle sounded. Jock said at the end of the season, 'Vojvodina were undoubtedly the best team we met in the European Cup.' I wouldn't argue with that summing-up.

So, Dukla Prague were dismissed in the semi-final and I took my place in the stand at the Nacional Stadium in Lisbon on May 25 1967, a date embedded in every Celtic-minded person's memory bank. The swelling in my ankle had gone down a little, but I had found difficulty in putting on my shoe. I cheered along with our unbeatable support as my team-mates came back from conceding an early penalty-kick goal to Sandro Mazzola to pummel Inter Milan into submission. Tommy equalised with a blockbuster in the sixty-third minute that even their tremendous goalkeeper Guiliano Sarti couldn't get near. When that whizzbang effort struck the net everyone knew Celtic were going to be crowned the European champions. Stevie turned in a low ball from Bobby Murdoch five minutes from the end and the most glittering prize in football was heading for Celtic Park.

Just take a quick look at the statistics for the match. Celtic had a remarkable forty-two attempts on goal with twenty-six on target. Two hit the bar while Sarti saved thirteen. The others were either blocked or deflected. Ronnie was required to make two saves. That's unbelievable. We forced ten corner-kicks and they didn't get one. It was as one-sided a football match as you will ever see. Inter Milan, acclaimed world club champions in two of the previous three years, just couldn't live with the Celtic players that day. My heart was bursting with pride in the dressing room afterwards. I looked around and all I could see were so many happy faces. The guys were genuinely delighted they had done it for Celtic. It wasn't about financial bonuses or personal fame; they had achieved it for the team we all loved. It was a special day in the history of an extraordinary football club.

In the midst of all the gaiety, the whooping and hollering, I couldn't help but thinking about how our fortunes had changed so dramatically and excitingly in such a short space of time. Just over two years earlier, in April 1965, to be precise, I had played in two back-to-back away league games. We were trounced 6-2 by Falkirk at Brockville and, a couple of weeks later, were hammered 5-1 by Dunfermline at East End Park. Billy McNeill, Tommy Gemmell, Bobby Murdoch, John Clark, Jimmy Johnstone, Bobby Lennox and Bertie Auld had been team-mates during at least one those embarrassing drubbings. And now they were the proud possessors of European Cup-winning medals. I looked at them and I felt a heady mixture of pleasure, joy and happiness for my team-mates. Like myself, they had been so much turmoil in a dark period in the club's past. Now they had conquered Europe.

If only I had been fit enough for selection in Lisbon. Fate, though, decreed otherwise. The players and team that triumphed that day deserve their special place in Celtic's rich heritage. I can always use my imagination, though.

Chapter 10

MISERY IN MILAN

For decades I have been haunted by THAT miss. I have been so tormented by a lost opportunity against Feyenoord in the 1970 European Cup Final defeat that I have stubbornly and steadfastly refused to watch film of the incident. The anguish of that moment is something I never want to relive. Nothing or no-one will ever persuade me to revisit it and it's painful even thinking about that particular instant in time which possibly went a long way to ending my career at Celtic.

God only knows how often I've been informed Jock Stein never forgave me for failing to score at the start of extra-time with the game balanced at 1-1 on that fateful evening on May 6 at the San Siro Stadium in Milan. I've lost count of the times it has been suggested my apparent penalty box malfunction hastened my departure from Celtic. True or false? Honestly, I haven't a clue. Big Jock was an unforgiving character, that's for sure, but would he have booted me out of the door because of a perceived momentarily lapse? Only one person can answer the question with any degree of certainty and he's not here anymore, so we will never know. That's the truth of the matter.

Okay, here's what I do remember of the incident that has been my personal albatross for so many years. The game had just kicked off for the extra half-hour when I anticipated a crossfield pass coming from the left. I intercepted it about thirty-five yards out and raced between two Dutch defenders towards goal. I charged into the penalty area and took a slightly heavy touch as their goalkeeper Eddy Pieters Graafland raced from his line. I connected with my right foot to flick the ball to his right as he spread himself to his left. My heart missed a beat, I was sure the ball was heading for the net. He stretched out his right leg, my effort took a deflection, but was still heading for its destination until a defender appeared from nowhere to block it. Even then it looked as though it might go over the line because he mis-hit his clearance and the keeper had to scramble backwards to throw himself full length to hold the ball right on the line. I've been informed the action was all over in six seconds, such a short passage of time that may have altered not just my football career, but my entire life.

And yet it could - and should - have been so different.

For weeks before the game Celtic fans were asking me for a prediction. We had just racked up home and away semi-final triumphs over Leeds United, the best team on the planet, according to the English media. It was daubed the 'Final before the Final' because no-one really bothered about what was happening in the other semi-final encounter between Feyenoord and Polish outfit Legia Warsaw. The outcome of those ties didn't matter because the winners in Milan would most assuredly come from our titanic tussles with Don Revie's outfit. And, of course, we walloped them 3-1 on aggregate.

'So, Yogi, what's going to be the score?' I was asked umpteen times by supporters, getting ready to celebrate Celtic's second European Cup victory in three years.

'Oh, I think it'll be 3-0 or 4-0,' I would answer regularly with the utmost confidence. I couldn't foresee any eventuality other than Celtic lifting that coveted silverware in the picturesque Italian city. I wasn't alone. Jock Stein clearly thought so, too. You haven't been required to read between the lines to get the notion that the Celtic manager and I didn't always quite see eye to eye, so please take my word for it that this is not a personal attack on Jock. However, he had to take his share of the blame for the shambles in the San Siro. It's no secret Jock enjoyed the spotlight and the glory that went with being an extremely successful manager. No-one can ever take that away from him. What he achieved at Celtic after returning in 1965, quite rightly, made him a club legend. That is not up for debate and he deserves undying credit. But there is a fine line between being praised and being pilloried in this game. Believe me, I know what I'm talking about because I've been there. One minute a hero, the next a zero. That's what they say, isn't it? Unfortunately, it's all too accurate.

Big Jock planned meticulously for the European Cup Final against Inter Milan in Lisbon three years earlier. He went into every detail in the most immaculate and minute manner. Nothing, and I mean nothing, was left to chance before that historic meeting. The players were told what and when to eat, how many minutes they were allowed to be exposed to the sun, when they could sit by the pool, the best time to take a walk and do some exercise. He left absolutely nothing to chance.

His mindset was completely different for the match against Feyenoord. It was evident to us all that he believed the trophy was as good as in the bag. That sort of attitude, bordering on arrogance, can get through to the players. He dismissed many of our Dutch opponents. We were informed Wim van Hanagem was a 'poor man's Jim Baxter' with no pace and wouldn't be able to keep up with play after half-an-hour or so. Swedish striker Ove Kindvall was dismissed as being 'too slow'. Their skipper and central defender Rinus Israel was 'cumbersome' and Bertie Auld was continually reassured his midfield opponent Wim Jansen wouldn't give him any trouble. Midfielder Franz Hasil was 'an ordinary player' and was only in the team because he was an Austrian like his manager Ernst Happel. Basically, he went all the way through the team, destroying the profile and shredding the reputations of the rival players. If he was attempting to inject super self-assurance into the Celtic players he was doing a fabulous job. Most of us had already worked out how we would spend our win bonus. Poor Feyenoord, they were wasting their time turning up for the spectacle.

Let's face it, though, there was reason for genuine optimism. We had not only beaten Leeds United, we had totally dismantled, completely destroyed the English champions who had been touted as being seemingly indestructible. Respective managers Jock Stein and Don Revie had been at their mind games as soon as the teams had been paired in the ballot. Revie, preparing for the first game at home, kicked it off by saying the playing surface at Elland Road would need to be returfed in the summer and it wasn't conducive to playing the ball on the ground. He knew, of course, that's the way we liked to play. If you took me out of the usual forward line formation you would be left with Jimmy Johnstone, Bobby Lennox and Willie Wallace and none of them was in the skyscraper category. Jock, of course, retorted in the vein of , 'good teams can perform on ANY surface. And Celtic are a better than a good team.' And so it went on right up until just before kick-off when a UEFA official came into our dressing room to say Leeds had complained about Celtic's white socks. Revie was claiming they would clash with his side's colours in their all-white kit. Why wait until virtually the last minute before making this observation? Our kitmen hadn't bothered to pack our green socks, so we had to borrow a set off our opponents. They were yellow and Jock smiled as we donned the new gear. 'Under the floodlights it'll look as though you're playing in green, white and gold,' he observed. 'That's a good omen.'

Within a minute - fifty-five seconds to be precise - we were a goal ahead when young George Connelly turned the ball goalwards, it struck a Leeds player and wrong-footed keeper Gary Sprake who remained virtually motionless. What a start. It remained that way until the interval and, incredibly, we had the ball in their net again within a minute of the restart, this time in forty-five seconds. Once again it came from the right boot of Connelly. The referee ruled it out, but there was no way Big George was offside. Jinky pulled the ball back from the by-line, so we can only presume he had strayed into a dodgy position. We were never going to get the benefit of the doubt at Elland Road. No matter. Leeds United rarely threatened Evan Williams in our goal and we went home happy with a first leg advantage.

The battle of wits between Stein and Revie continued. The Leeds gaffer said, 'We have been told that no team who are a goal down from their home tie in a European Cup semi-final have ever reached the Final of the tournament. But we won't let that worry us because we are history-makers, we are record-breakers. And if ever a record can go, this one can.' Caustically, Jock replied, 'Aye we've been known to make a wee bit of history at this club, too. Let's just see what happens in Glasgow.'

A crowd of 136,505 - still a record for the competition - turned out for the second leg at Hampden a fortnight later. What a breathtaking

Here's me doing my absolute best to look like a poster boy for Brylcreem.

Above: A rare reserve team photograph with the players wearing the now-defunct Shamrock strip. I'm seated on the left and my good friend John Divers is second from the right.

Below: Bang…it's a goal! I'm all alone as I smash a shot past the helpless Airdrie goalkeeper from close range at a packed Celtic Park. We won 3-0 on November 18 1961.

Above: *Head Bhoy! I get up above an Airdrie defender to bullet in a header to open the scoring in the 1961 Scottish Cup semi-final. I got another as we triumphed 4-0.*

Below: *The Famous Five! Here I am with Celtic team-mates Jimmy Johnstone, Bobby Murdoch, Stevie Chalmers and John Divers after a training session at Barrowfield.*

Above: *Russia here we come! We're ready to fly off to face Kiev Dynamo in season 1960/61. We drew 1-1.*

Left: *What a hat-trick! John Divers and I wear our Cossack hats as Mary and Eileen welcome us home at the airport.*

Below: *It's snow joke! Billy McNeill and I go through a routine at Celtic Park. Presumably, this picture wasn't taken in July.*

Above: *Aerial antics…or air we go! I'm out to prove I'm the head master to my grounded team-mates Alec Byrne (centre) and Charlie Gallagher.*

Below: *The Greatest! No, not the bloke second from the right, but the guy in the middle – Muhammad Ali, the world heavyweight champion who turned up at Parkhead on a publicity tour.*

5

Crash, bang, wallop…what a goal! Sprawling Airdrie keeper Lawrie Leslie doesn't stand a chance as I fire a shot into the roof of the net from close range.

Above: *ON THE SPOT No.1…I send Rangers keeper Billy Ritchie the wrong way with a penalty-kick in the 1965 League Cup Final at Hampden.*

Below: *ON THE SPOT NO.2…this time I strike the ball to the Ibrox goalkeeper's right for Celtic's second goal in a memorable trophy success.*

HIGH JINKS! I'm trying to rise and shine against the Rangers duo of goalkeeper Gerry Neef and skipper John Greig during another hectic Old Firm clash. This one ended goalless on January 2 1970.

Above: *The last hurrah…I'm just out of luck with a header in a 1-1 draw with the Republic of Ireland in September 1969 in Dublin - my eighth and final Scottish cap.*

Below: *Yogi Bear among the Teddy Bears! I'm outnumbered at the end our 1965 League Cup Final win. Dejected Gers are: Alex Willoughby, Jim Forrest, Kai Johansen, Willie Johnston and Ronnie McKinnon.*

Above: *The eyes have it…England goalkeeper Gordon Banks and I are a study in concentration as the ball drops into the danger zone. Unfortunately, the chance passed me by, but I still managed to score Scotland's goal in a 1-1 draw at Hampden in 1968.*

Left: *A Scotland fan tries to console me at the end of the game against the Auld Enemy. We had just blown the opportunity of getting to the European Championship Finals in Italy later that year.*

Above: *I help lift John Greig shoulder high after he scored the winning goal against Italy in a World Cup-tie at Hampden in 1965. Joining in are: Alan Gilzean, Ronnie McKinnon, Billy Bremner, David Provan, Bobby Murdoch, Jim Baxter, Neil Martin, Bill Brown and Willie Henderson.*

Below: *Twelve in a row! That's me at the back with team-mates Jimmy Johnstone, Willie Wallace, Bobby Lennox, Jim Brogan, Bobby Murdoch, Stevie Chalmers, John Fallon, Tommy Callaghan, Jim Craig, Billy McNeill and Tommy Gemmell.*

I have it on good authority I wasn't auditioning to become the fifth Beatle when this picture was taken. I'm third from the left of the back row. Rest are (back, left to right): Davie Hay, Jim Craig, Evan Williams, Billy McNeill, John Fallon, Tommy Gemmell, George Connelly and Tommy Callaghan. Front: Bobby Murdoch, Jimmy Johnstone, Harry Hood, Bobby Lennox, Stevie Chalmers, Willie Wallace, Bertie Auld, Lou Macari and Jim Brogan.

Above: *Heads I win…I dive in front of Leeds United centre-half Jack Charlton to score with a header to put us back in front on aggregate in the 1970 European Cup semi-final. We eventually won 3-1 overall after two truly memorable tussles.*

Below: *So near and yet so far. Gary Sprake goes down bravely at my feet to avert a certain goal at Hampden. Unfortunately, the Leeds keeper was injured in the incident and had to be helped off with bruised ribs.*

Above: *Celtic Bhoys and Ghirl! The Hughes clan take after their dad in supporting Celtic. Flying the flag are Martin, Joanna, John and Kevin.*

Left: *Brother Billy sporting a rather snazzy moustache during his days as a Sunderland player. He did well, too – winning an FA Cup medal in 1973.*

Above: *Brother Patrick leads from the front in this snap. That's John Divers in between us with Billy McNeill on the left. Mike Jackson is partially hidden behind Patrick.*

Above: *Happiness is…Theresa and I are all smiles as we pose for the camera. I met her in Majorca and we have been married for the last twelve years.*

Below: *Hughes a lucky boy! I'm pictured with the rest of the family for this happy snap. As you might expect, it's always great when we get together.*

Me and the Bear Cubs. Clockwise from the top: Andrew, Michael, Caiohme, Paul, Johannah and Martin. This is one of my all-time favourite photographs.

occasion that was, undoubtedly one of the highlights of my career. The grand, old stadium was super-charged for this encounter and our support was simply magnificent. The players had been aware of the build-up to the main event all day. We were a goal ahead, were ninety minutes away from a European Cup Final and we had home advantage with the backing of the best supporters in the world. The place was heaving by the time we walked out for the 8pm kick-off. Within fourteen minutes, the tie was all-square. Bertie Auld has already held his hand up to take responsibility when Billy Bremner zoomed a twenty-five yard screamer high past Evan into his top right hand corner of the goal. The ball cracked off the inside of the woodwork before flying into the net. Bertie might have done better in trying to close down Billy, but there were no recriminations among the players. We had conceded a goal to allow them back into the tie, but we also knew we had plenty of time to turn things back in our favour.

There are occasions in contests, though, when you realise you are going to scrap and fight for everything you achieve. Nothing was going to be served up on a plate and this was one of those encounters. Shortly afterwards, I won a ball up front, knocked it back to Big George and our elegant midfielder slid an inch-perfect pass in front of Bobby Lennox, cutting right through the heart of their defence. In a situation like that, you would put your house on the Buzz Bomb to score. Sure enough, he neatly clipped the ball over the outrushing Sprake and his effort was rolling towards the net when right-back Paul Madeley, with a superhuman lunge, managed to get a foot to it to knock it away. Before half-time, they failed to clear a right-wing corner-kick and it dropped to the feet of Billy McNeill at a tight angle on the left. Caesar was at his happiest attacking in the ball in the air, but he fairly sizzled in a low drive. It beat Sprake, but, on this occasion, left-back Terry Cooper materialised to whack the ball away to safety.

Although Dame Fortune was snarling in Celtic's direction, I didn't think for a moment we would fail to win. Sometimes you just get the feeling that it will come right in the end. I didn't believe for a moment they could withstand our assaults. We were coming at them from all angles and something had to give. I could hear the Leeds players shouting at each other, they realised they were on the ropes. Wee Jinky was striking terror into their rearguard every time he got the ball. Cooper was the England international left-back at the time and was rated as one of the best in the world. However, Jinky was tying him up in knots as he weaved his merry way down the right wing. I could hear central defender Norman Hunter shouting at Cooper, 'Kick that little bastard.' Cooper screamed back, 'You come over here and try to kick the little bastard yourself.' Jinky just smiled and maintained his special brand of torture.

Down the middle, I was giving their World Cup-winning centre-half Jack Charlton a hard time, too. Big Jack had played against me a few times, but really didn't know how to handle me or my style. If he stepped off me, I would attempt to push the ball past him and take him on for speed. It must be said he wasn't the quickest on the turn. And if he wanted to attempt to out-muscle me, I was more than happy to mix it in there, too. We gave them a first-half battering, but had nothing to show for our efforts which was tantamount to unbelievable. Something had to give, though. Thankfully, it did two minutes after the interval when I scored with a rare header. Jock had given Jinky the go-ahead to roam around because he believed he would scare the life out of them all over the pitch. Jinky was deep in his own half when he picked up the ball and rolled a pass towards Bertie on the right. Our irrepressible midfielder had been involved with their big, burly centre-forward Mick Jones just before the half-time whistle. His 'tackle' - if it could be called that - left Jones in a heap, writhing in agony in the centre circle and there was a doubt if he would be able to make an appearance in the second period. Thankfully, he did. Some of the Leeds players had words with Bertie in the tunnel as we waited to come out for the remaining forty-five minutes. I'm pretty certain they weren't asking for his address to send him Christmas cards. It was a waste of time threatening my team-mate. We were all aware he could look after himself.

Anyway, as Jinky's pass made its way towards Bertie, Billy Bremner appeared to take it upon himself for a bit of retribution on behalf of his team-mate. I don't think for a moment he attempted to get the ball as he launched himself at Bertie. He really should have known better. Bertie was cuter than any fox. He saw it coming , touched the ball to Davie Hay, going down the right, before skipping a couple of feet into the air and Wee Billy missed by miles. Bertie had the presence of mind to look back at the grounded Leeds captain and say something like, 'You'll have to do better than that.' Davie was a lot faster than a lot of people might have thought because of his straight-backed running style, but he could cover the ground. Hunter eventually caught up with him and was only too happy to prod the ball out for a corner-kick. My pal's speed of thought was every bit as quick as his legs and he took a swift short corner to Bertie who had followed up in support. Bertie took a touch, looked up and swept in as delightful left-foot cross as you will ever see.

Charlton was practically wearing the same shirt as me, but I took a couple of steps away from him and threw myself into the air at an angle. I flicked the ball off the side of my head and Sprake didn't have time to move a muscle. What an incredible feeling. The roof came off Hampden, the din was deafening. The power surge through my body was totally exhilarating as my team-mates rushed to congratulate me. We were back in front on aggregate and the Leeds players knew there would be no lifeline this time.

Unfortunately, I collided with Sprake five minutes later which led to the keeper being stretchered off. It was a complete accident and no-one ever suggested otherwise. I dummied Hunter as I turned to run into the penalty box. Sprake, very bravely, sprinted out to meet me and threw himself at my feet. It was a fifty/fifty ball and we both had to go for it, there could be no pulling back. There was a crunch as the ball went out for a goal-kick. I didn't think any more about it as I trotted back up the field to get into position. However, it was obvious the goalie wasn't going to resume and I went back down to have a closer look. Neither he nor his colleagues even thought to point the finger of blame at me. The Hampden crowd sportingly applauded the keeper as he was taken from the field. I was grateful to discover at the end that it was nothing more than bruising.

David Harvey, a future Scotland international goalkeeper, came on as substitute and the first thing he had to do was fish the ball out of the net. Bobby Murdoch surged forward to play a neat one-two with Jinky and then lash a low drive from the edge of the box under the body of the diving and helpless Harvey. Bobby leapt as high as I have ever seen him as he celebrated and there was no way back for our opponents after that.

However, there was something that everyone appears to have overlooked. I should have scored a third goal that night. Certainly, it was a far easier opportunity than the one I missed against Feyenoord. The game was in its fading moments when Evan thumped a long kick-out down our left. I hared after it as the same time as Hunter. My knowledge of playing on the wing served me well as I quickly controlled the ball and slipped it inside as the Leeds defender challenged and ended up on his backside. I took the ball into the box, Harvey came out and sprawled at my feet, but I touched it round him and lined up a shot with my right. I was aware Charlton was desperately trying to get back into position and I hit it quickly. Somehow, the centre-half managed to get a block on the effort and the ball spun away for a left-wing corner-kick. No-one ever rebuked me for that miss. No-one ever mentioned it. No, not even Jock Stein. If you pass up a chance when you win no-one cares. Miss one when you lose, well that's a different story, isn't it?

The final whistle went when Tommy Gemmell propelled the ball somewhere towards the Hampden floodlights. I swapped my jersey with that of Jack Charlton. I thought that was only fair - he had wanted to hold onto it all night. Seriously, he did say something like, 'Good luck in the Final.' He must have been hurting like hell and I really appreciated the sentiment. Later Norman Hunter said, 'Celtic are probably the best side I have ever played in Europe.' Years later, Allan Clarke, their striker who got nothing out of Caesar over the two legs, admitted, 'Looking back, they were the better team over the two matches. There's no doubt, though, we were jaded. That said, Jimmy Johnstone was magnificent.'

Caesar told me he bumped into Terry Cooper while on holiday a few years ago. Cooper admitted, 'I still have nightmares about Jimmy Johnstone. I reckon I had good anticipation and could tackle, but I could do nothing to get the ball off that guy.' With all the verbal sparring over and done with, Don Revie said, 'When we scored I thought we could do something, but Celtic are a very, very good side. I sincerely hope they win the European Cup again.'

Billy Bremner and Eddie Gray, two Leeds players who did their utmost to overthrow their favourite team, came into the Celtic dressing room to wish us all the best for Milan. We found out later that evening our opponents would be Feyenoord who had beaten Legia 2-0 in Rotterdam after forcing a goalless draw in the first game in Warsaw. That result meant nothing to us at the time. Who were

Legia who had made Feyenoord work so hard to get to Milan? What was their pedigree in European football? Actually, what we didn't realise was that the Poles possessed such quality players as Kazi Deyna and Robert Gadocha in their line-up. Not a lot was known about football in their country - remember we are talking about a bygone era - but it might have been worth giving closer inspection to the other semi-finalists. Legia had actually beaten St.Etienne 3-1 on aggregate in the second round which, on the face it, doesn't appear to mean too much. However, that performance is surely enhanced when you discover the French side had beaten Bayern Munich, Franz Beckenbauer, Gerd Muller and all, 3-2 in the opening stage. In fact, they came from two down from the first leg to completely overturn it at their place.

Feyenoord? Someone must have overlooked the fact they had dumped AC Milan, then the European Cup holders, in the second round. They lost 1-0 in the San Siro in the first leg, but Wim Jansen brought it back to level pegging when he netted in the sixth minute in Holland. Wim van Hanagem, who, apparently, would be knackered after half-an-hour, got the winner eight minutes from time. That was the same AC Milan team who had knocked out Celtic the previous season after winning 1-0 in Glasgow before going on to hammer Ajax 4-1 in the Final. It was clear, then, that the Dutch side would not be appearing in the Final to merely make up the numbers. Evidently, they were no dummies. As we were to discover to our cost.

Honestly, I still find it agonising to reminisce about that European Cup Final. It meant so much to the club, the supporters, the players and to me on a personal level. I was desperate to get my hands on one of those medals the Lisbon Lions were so proud to display at every opportunity. I wanted a share of that. It's not a well-known fact, but Big Jock reassured me I would play against Feyenoord long before the game. That was most unusual for our manager, but he was fully aware what missing Lisbon had meant to me. I appreciated that.

So, what went so drastically wrong? Were we that bad? Or were Feyenoord that good? It would be churlish of me to belittle the efforts of the Dutchmen. Unlike us, they had clearly done their homework. Their astute manager Ernst Happel worked out a strategy that would nullify Jinky. Sadly, it worked only too well and Big Jock never came up with a Plan B. That's not unfair criticism of our boss. Normally, he would have something up his sleeve, but not on this occasion. Again, it's so easy to be wise after the event, but I have to say I was not the only one who was mystified by his team formation for the San Siro game.

George Connelly had been immense against Leeds United. He sat in a midline of three alongside the more experienced Bobby Murdoch and Bertie Auld and it had worked a treat. Jock, for reasons known only to himself, changed the system. Big George found himself on the substitutes' bench and Bobby and Bertie were left to fend for themselves in the middle of the park. They had been world class against Inter Milan in Lisbon three years earlier, but this was an entirely different ball game. The Dutch swamped the midfield and our two creative guys were left with too much to do. They were overrun. And while they were toiling that meant the service to guys such as myself, Willie Wallace and Bobby Lennox wasn't up to its usual quality. We foraged around, but that wasn't our normal routine. Meanwhile, Van Hanagem, Jansen and Co were running the show. They weren't playing a man-marking game because we knew that was not Happel's outlook. Famously, he once said, 'If you want that sort of system all you have to do is put out eleven donkeys.'

Jinky wasn't being picked up, but he was being forced inside every time he got the ball and couldn't get into his stride down the touchline. They treble-banked him when he came off the wing and, almost inevitably, they would seize possession and start moving towards Evan Williams again. Thank goodness our goalkeeper picked that evening to have the game of his life. He was easily the busiest man on the pitch, but he looked as though he was coping with all that was being hurled at him. Our attacking full-backs, Davie Hay and Tommy Gemmell, were finding it difficult to cross the halfway line and get into enemy territory. Ove Kindvall was proving to be as ponderous as a cheetah and Caesar was under pressure from the word go.

Curiously, though, Celtic should have been two goals ahead by the half-hour mark. It has been ignored that Bobby Lennox drilled a drive past Graafland after coming in from the left. In real time, it looked well offside, but I have been assured by some pressmen, after sifting through TV footage, that it was onside. In fact, I've been told Bobby was played on by THREE defenders. That wee man was too fast for his own good sometimes. And, of course, we did get one that counted in the thirtieth minute when Murdoch, with a lovely little back heel, touched a free-kick to Tommy Gemmell coming in from about twenty-five yards and he blazed a first-time right-foot drive low into the net.

We weren't playing well, but we were in the lead. Not for long, alas. Our defence got in a flap when they couldn't defend a right-wing free-kick two minutes later. Caesar, normally imperious in the air, got under the ball and misdirected his clearance up instead of out of the box. Unfortunately, he moved off the lurking Rinus Israel to try to atone. A Dutch player got there first, knocked it straight back into the territory just vacated by our captain and Israel, completely unmarked, nodded the ball into the opposite corner with Evan, for once, stranded. If only we had managed to hold our lead until half-time. It wasn't to be and you could see Feyenoord's players visibly pumped up after their equaliser. They realised anything was possible in this encounter.

Another strange thing about this evening was the fact we could hardly hear our fans. It was a fifty/fifty split in the stadium and there were about 25,000 of our followers in the ground. No doubt they were giving it pelters, but we couldn't hear them because of the klaxon horns from the Dutch supporters. That was something we had never encountered before. Our fans were simply being drowned out and it actually felt like an away fixture. However, it was 1-1 at half-time and we had a chance to regroup and have a rethink. I can't recall too much being said during the interval. Certainly, despite toiling, we didn't do anything drastic with our permutation that I was aware of. Jim Brogan had been struggling from the first minute after sustaining a foot injury, but he was allowed to carry on. We had Connelly on the bench and he could have come on to partner McNeill in the middle of the defence, a position in which he had performed before. Big George did eventually come on in the seventy-seventh minute, but it was for Bertie, who had struggled, too, under the wave of attacks from our opponents.

The second-half pretty much followed the pattern of the first. Van Hanagem was running around with his socks trailing around his ankles which may have given the impression he was knackered, but I can tell you he was not. In fact, he contrived to do something I had never seen on a football pitch before - he had the cheek to nutmeg Jinky! The Dutchman pushed right into our half for most of that period and our goal lived a charmed life while Evan worked overtime in his efforts to repel their raids. Then it went to extra-time and the moment that has left me frustrated and irritated for far too long. We were only four minutes from a replay when Feyenoord, deservedly it must be said, got the winner.

Bobby Murdoch, true sportsman that he is, could have booted the ball for miles when referee Concetto Lo Bello awarded Feyenoord a free-kick about thirty-five yards into our half. Bobby was chasing the ball when the match official blew. He could have done one of two things; give it a nudge further downfield and let the Dutch retrieve it; or simply allow it to run on. Bobby stopped the ball and kicked it back to our opponents. They couldn't believe their good fortune. Their player put it down, looked up and saw Kindvall lurking behind Caesar. Because of Bobby's sportsmanship we didn't get a chance to erect a defensive wall and the ball was pitched forward. Caesar didn't have time to think as the cross sailed over his head. He stuck up a hand, stunned the ball and it dropped perfectly behind him for the inrushing Kindvall who lifted it over Evan as he tried to snatch it off his toes. The referee had allowed advantage, but I've little doubt he would have awarded a penalty-kick if the Feyenoord player had missed.

Equally, I have no hesitation in saying we would have beaten the Dutch in the replay. They caught us cold and we just weren't prepared for their tactics or the sheer quality of their players. That may sound ungallant because they were well worthy of their triumph on the night. There can be no argument there. However, if we had been given a second chance I must say I genuinely believe we would have taken it. Feyenoord would have seen the real Celtic and not that strange pale imitation that turned up in Milan that night.

As I prepared to leave the San Siro Stadium, I saw Wim van Hanagem posing for pictures with ecstatic Feyenoord fans outside the ground. He was drawing on a huge cigar. The bugger still wasn't out of puff.

Chapter 11

MAYHEM IN MONTEVIDEO

Trust me to get involved in one of the craziest orderings-off in the history of the game. I can only look back on it now, almost half-a-century later, and wonder what on earth I was thinking at that precise moment. I'm talking about the infamous brawl in the Uruguayan capital of Montevideo on November 4 1967. It was supposed to be a showpiece encounter against Racing Club of Buenos Aries, the exciting meeting between the acknowledged champions of Europe and South America. Sadly, the occasion manifested itself into one of the most shocking and sorry episodes in Celtic's proud history.

We had been goaded beyond tolerance by a motley collection of the dirtiest players I have ever encountered or witnessed. They kicked and spat on us in the first leg at Hampden where we won 1-0 with a superb headed goal by Billy McNeill from my right-wing corner-kick. We wondered how they would behave in their native country if that's how they abused us in front of 83, 437 of our fans in Glasgow. We soon got our answer. They were even more brutal in front of their maniacal support. Sir Alf Ramsey called Argentina's players 'animals' after England had played them in the World Cup quarter-final at Wembley the previous year. We discovered he wasn't over the top in his comments. We netted first in Buenos Aires with a Tommy Gemmell penalty-kick - an absolute stonewaller after Wee Jinky had been decked - but they came back to score twice to take the Final to a third game in a neutral country. By the way, their first goal by Norberto Raffo was only a mile offside!

In hindsight, we should have come home immediately. The chairman, Bob Kelly, was all for getting us back to Scotland and away from the madhouse that was Argentina. The Racing players provoked us on the pitch and their supporters urinated on us in the stand. Unfortunately, I became a target for these filthy cretins. I was sitting beside Bertie Auld and Joe McBride as we were showered from a terracing above us. The Racing supporters were taking it in turn to relieve themselves on us and there was nothing we could do to escape. We just had to sit there and get drenched by the these scum. Could anyone have blamed us if we had packed up there and then and made our way home? I don't think so.

However, one man was adamant we should play a third game in Montevideo. Jock Stein was determined that Celtic should be crowned the greatest team on the planet. Big Jock wanted us to show the world how football should be played. He also believed we might get some protection from the referee in neutral Uruguay. Some hope! The Paraguayan match official, Rodolfo Osorio, was even worse than the weak Uruguayan Esteban Marino in Argentina. Big Billy is one of the most circumspect and fair men I know, but even our inspirational skipper was convinced the referee was bent. It takes some motivation for Billy to make such an observation, but no-one would argue with that assessment.

If anyone has ever been in any doubt, they just need to have to look at his decision to send off Jimmy Johnstone. The ref got a good view of the incident, I think he was only about ten yards or so away from the scene of the so-called crime. Jinky played a one-two and was running past their player when the defender simply grabbed him by the neck to block his movement. Jinky had a temper, as the Racing players probably realised, and he tried to wrestle free. His arm caught the Racing defender and, of course, he went down as though he had been hit by an invisible train. That was all the match official required to send our wee winger packing. The Racing defender escaped any punishment whatsoever. Not even a slap on the wrist. In that one moment, any thoughts of fair play from the ref were dispelled. Bent? I agreed wholeheartedly with Billy.

What can I say about my own sending off? I've got to hold up my hands and plead guilty. Although I believe Big Jock thought I would be better off pleading insanity. What came over me? I can only say that I got caught up in all the chaos and confusion of the battle. There was very little football played that day and Racing were ruthless as they launched savage attacks on our players. Amazingly, the first Celtic player to be ordered off was Bobby Lennox. Bobby wouldn't say boo to a goose. He used to get some fairly heavy treatment from opponents in the Scottish game, but he refused to retaliate. He would take the punishment and get on with the game. His answer to the hackers and cloggers was to put the ball in their net as often as possible. I had never seem him react violently, yet he was first to go that dreadful afternoon. Everyone thought it must be a case of mistaken identity. Bobby was coming off when Big Jock told him to get back on. Our pacy frontman returned to the pitch, but the referee wasn't for changing his mind. Bobby about-turned to walk off when our manager signalled once again for him to get back into the fray. It was only when soldiers, with sabres at the ready, intervened that our player decided it was a good idea to ignore Big Jock and head for the safety of the dressing room.

Then off went Jinky and I was next to go for my moment of madness. Their keeper, Agustin Cejas, was wasting time as he picked up a passback. I thought I would try to force him to get rid of the ball a bit more quickly. I challenged him and you won't be surprised to be told he, too, collapsed in a heap as though he had been mortally wounded. I didn't do my cause any good when I confronted him again and tried to kick the ball as he lay writhing on the ground. It looked a lot worse than it actually was, but the keeper made the most of it as he rolled around. The referee wasn't slow in letting me know my work was done for the day. I was about to protest when I saw a couple of soldiers with their menacing swords about to come onto the pitch and I decided against it. Cejas, unsurprisingly, got to his feet and, unhindered, played the rest of the match.

I have been quoted often enough saying I didn't think anyone was watching. That's a bit strange when you consider it was the World Club Final - or the Intercontinental Cup, to give the trophy its correct title - and the action was being beamed live to just about every country on the globe, although, curiously, Celtic fans back home only got a highlights package later that evening. The match was edited by the BBC in London and they slaughtered Celtic. And, of course, the TV editors made a big thing of Tommy Gemmell's swinging right boot that had their player Raffo squealing during yet another lull in play. Big Jock was so furious when he saw the edited version he banned the Beeb from Celtic Park for about a year.

Of course, no-one can condone violence or retribution. But you had to experience what we were going through out on that field against a team consisting mainly of hoodlums in football strips who knew every dirty trick in the book. And some that weren't. Reason just flew out the window. I will always remember Big Jock stressing to us not to get involved in a kicking match. Unfortunately, that's easier said than done. Everyone's got a breaking point and the yobs masquerading as Racing Club players knew which buttons to push. I'm sure the patience of the most saintly among us would have snapped in that hellish environment. There are just so many times you can accept someone spitting on you or having a fly kick while the play is elsewhere. Yes, it was wrong, but there were mitigating circumstances to take into consideration. We allowed ourselves to be dragged down to their level and we paid the consequences. And the board clobbered each of the players with a £250 fine for our sins.

The actual game, if you could it that, was a shambles. They won 1-0 when a long-range drive from Juan Carlos Cardenas eluded our stand-in keeper John Fallon. In fact, when you think of it, the assault on Ronnie Simpson just before kick-off in the second match in Buenos Aires should have had us heading for the exits there and then. Mind you, with over 100,000 screaming, frenzied supporters in the Avellaneda Stadium there would have been every probability of a full-blown riot erupting all around us.

There has been a lot of speculation over what actually hit our keeper on the head that day. My view is it must have been the actions of a photographer who would have been able to hide the object in his camera bag. It would have been impossible to get something up and over the large mesh nets that were behind Ronnie's goal. It had to be done close-up and, of course, none of the authorities thought about searching the photographers' kit. So, that was game over for Faither after being clattered on the back of the head by some sort of metal object. And, of course, he still hadn't recovered by the time the third game was played. John Fallon made only four first team appearances that season and, amazingly, two were in two of the most important games in the club's history.

Unfortunately, that disgusting encounter in Montevideo is something I'll never forget. Do you know I had never seen any film of that match until a few years ago? I'm not a big fan of watching Celtic lose and I just wasn't interested in viewing any footage. However, I was working in my pub, The Condorrat Arms in Cumbernauld, one day when someone brought in a video tape. 'Okay, to put this on, Yogi?' I was asked by the customer. 'Just so long as it's clean,' I said. 'No problem,' he replied. 'It's just a football game from the sixties. You're involved in it.' 'Aye, put it on,' I said. And that was the one and only time I have watched that match. My sending-off escapade didn't look any better on film!

I also witnessed Bertie Auld's ordering-off for the first time. He simply lost his temper and appeared to throttle one of the Racing Club's serial offenders. The referee pointed once more to the dressing room where Wee Bertie was 'invited' to join me, Jinky and Bobby. Bertie point-blank refused to leave the field. A harassed match official actually restarted play with a free-kick to Celtic. That just about summed up everything. The games against Racing Club developed into one huge long drawn-out farce.

I was informed our reprehensible opponents were promised a bonus of £1,500-per-man to win the trophy. That was a fortune in Argentina back then. That must have been all the inducement they required to win by any means at their disposal. That's why they thought nothing of indulging in all sorts of black arts. They were an odious bunch supported by abominable fans. No, I don't look back on events in South America in 1967 with any fondness.

One observer remarked, 'Racing Club players would have trampled over children's bodies to get their hands on that £1,500 bonus.' I couldn't have put it better.

Chapter 12

THE PRIDE AND THE PAIN

I played eight times for the Scotland international team and it wouldn't have upset me if I had never pulled on the dark blue jersey of my country. Believe me, I'm as patriotic as the next Scot, but there are some things no-one should be expected to endure or embarrassments to suffer in any walk of life never mind in the pursuit of sport.

I'm talking about getting booed and jeered by your own supporters and, worse still, being spat upon by a so-called fan. That's what happened to me in Belfast after Scotland had lost 3-2 to Northern Ireland in only my third international appearance. It had been a miserable, bitterly cold October afternoon in 1965 and the players were in a collective foul mood following a dismal performance and a dreadful result.

I was singled out for particular abuse from a halfwit as the Scottish players made their way from the front door at Windsor Park to our waiting coach. Our playing kit, of course, would have been collected by Scottish Football Association staff, but the players carried their boots in separate bags. I recall Billy McNeill, Willie Henderson, Alan Gilzean and myself heading for the bus to take us back to the hotel.

This imbecile appeared in front of us, shouted something not too complimentary at me and then spat in my direction. The vile saliva splattered onto my jacket. That would have been a mistake at any time. It was even more of an error when I had two boots in a bag I was carrying in my right hand. Unfortunately for him, he was well within striking range. I swung the bag at his head. The guy with the death wish just happened to be wearing a Rangers scarf. Maybe that's why he didn't have a go at Wee Willie. Of course, wearing the colours didn't necessarily make him a supporter of the Ibrox club. He could have been a neutral fan with a weird sense of humour. Who knows? I've got to say, though, his rasping accent appeared to owe more to Govan than Glentoran.

Anyway, my improvised missile banged the guy right on the head; a direct hit. Unfortunately, I think it was the only thing I got on target all day. The nutter reeled back in astonishment. Did he really believe for a split-second anyone would accept that sort of abuse? Did he think it was acceptable to go around gobbing on people? Sadly, for him, he picked on the wrong guy. He stood there holding his head and muttering some ill-chosen oaths. For a moment, I thought about giving him another dull one.

One of Ulster's finest witnessed the incident and decided to have a word. The policeman came over and said in a broad Irish brogue, 'I saw that. I think that's assault.' At least, he didn't say with a deadly weapon. I wasn't in the mood for him, either. 'So, it's okay for that pillock to spit on me, call me a Fenian bastard and challenge me? That's not an offence in this part of Britain? Have you got different laws over here?'

I'm not sure if he was trying to make a name for himself, something to tell his mates back at the Belfast nick. 'I think that was assault,' he said again sternly. I looked around and there were no other cops in the vicinity. Momentarily, my assailant had gone into hiding. 'It looks like your only witness has left the scene of the crime,' I said.

There was a chorus from my team-mates that went along the lines of, 'We saw nothing, officer.' The cop looked at me. 'I could have you locked up,' he said through clenched teeth. 'Great,' I said. 'I defend myself against a moron showing a lot of aggression towards me and I get arrested? Don't think so, mate.' I stepped onto the coach with the rest of the squad and he stood there fuming.

We sat there for a few minutes and then the simpleton with the sore head appeared at my window. He kept up a steady stream of four-letter words, making all sorts of silly threats while going through the usual two-fingered routine. I looked at him more in pity than anger. Sitting alongside me were Wee Willie, Jim Baxter and John Greig. They were actually squirming in embarrassment. It was an unsavoury incident altogether and you may think I am being petty in bringing it up. I don't believe I am.

I was proud to be representing my country, doing the best to my ability and then some cretin wanted to cover me in spittle. Probably that was the start of the end as far as taking pleasure in playing for Scotland was concerned. Maybe that was the snowball that went down the hill to start the avalanche. The love affair was short lived.

When you play for Celtic you come to expect to take stick from some of those who have sworn undying allegiance to Rangers. Some of it's good-natured banter, but sometimes it's downright unpalatable bile. You accept that Glasgow is a divided city and you have to ride out the storm on occasion. However, there are just so many times you can take people having a go at your religious beliefs, your perceived political stance or whether or not your parents bothered with the small formality of actually getting married before you were born.

I suppose it's the same the other way around although I have to say I have always found most Celtic fans to have been blessed with a sense of humour while a fair percentage of their Rangers counterparts have struggled in the mirth department. Yes, I know I'll be called biased, but that's the way I have always seen it and that's the way I will always call it. Remember, back in those dark and unenlightened times, Rangers refused to sign a Roman Catholic. Imagine if Pele had offered to play for them for nothing? They would have been forced to knock him back. That stupid state of affairs hardly helped defuse a potential and ongoing powderkeg situation in what could often be a volatile city.

And I won't embarrass the individuals by naming them, but I have known Rangers players who preferred to perform away from home rather than run the gauntlet of mindless insults from their own support at Ibrox. I never felt that at Celtic Park. Not once. Okay, there were days when the ball just won't run for you, but, as far as I'm concerned, I never got anything other than one hundred per cent backing from our fans. There could be the usual moan and groan when something didn't come off, but that's part and parcel of the game. On the whole, the fans were prepared to tolerate and accept that fact.

Yes, I also realise it should be an honour to play for your country and I know how much it meant to my old international pal Denis Law. Nothing or no-one would ever have prevented The Lawman from turning out in the dark blue of his nation. And, of course, the fans idolised him. The subtle difference between Denis and I is that he played for both Manchester clubs, United and City, Huddersfield Town and Italian side Torino while he was representing his country. I played for Celtic. And that made me a target for the bigots. Before the Tartan Army came on the scene in the seventies, a massive percentage of the international support was made up of Rangers fans. It was almost like Scotland were their 'other' side. The players would be in the team coach heading for Hampden and we would pass thousands of supporters and so many of them were adorned in Rangers colours. Not a trace of tartan in sight. And, as you might expect, they wanted to see their club's players in the Scotland line-up.

If I played at outside-left it would normally mean there was no place for Ibrox favourites such as Davie Wilson or Willie Johnston. If Jimmy Johnstone was on the right wing it would mean Willie Henderson sitting in the stand. If Billy McNeill got the centre-half berth then Ronnie McKinnon was a no-show. And the so-called Scotland international followers were never slow to voice their disapproval at their idols being overlooked in favour of Celtic players. I was on the receiving end of some obnoxious remarks and nauseating gestures while playing for Scotland, particularly at Hampden. I felt like a stranger in my own city turning out for my country and being maltreated for my trouble. I could go to the touchline to retrieve the ball for a throw-in and be confronted by a sea of gargoyles as they spat out their vitriol in my direction. Believe me, it's all too easy to become swiftly disenchanted in that uncomfortable environment.

I'm not looking for sympathy. I don't run away from challenges. In fact, my entire life seems to have been a series of trials, on and off the pitch as you will discover as you read on. Obstacles are put in front of you and you have to confront them and then overcome them. I don't think these tests are unique or exclusive to me. However, if I am going to tell anyone that playing for Scotland meant so little to me then the least I can do is to attempt to give a detailed reason.

Have you ever wondered why a genuine world class performer

such as Wee Jinky only won twenty-three caps? How about Bobby Murdoch, another class act? He picked up twelve. That's a ridiculous amount for a player who could have walked into any international team in the world and I include Brazil. John Clark was one of the best defensive players I have ever seen. How many caps? Four. That total beggars belief. Even Kenny Dalglish was derided by a section of the support, but all that changed when he moved to Liverpool. Suddenly, he was being lauded from every corner of Hampden. Maybe he became a better footballer when he left Celtic.

So, most of the time it became more of an ordeal than a pleasure for a Celtic player to represent Scotland. Jock Stein capitalised on the situation. If Celtic had a big game coming up on the Saturday he knew he wouldn't have to work too hard in convincing a player to withdraw from the international squad for a midweek encounter. 'I'll get the secretary to call the SFA and tell them you're not fit,' he would say. Back then, medical certificates didn't have to be provided to prove an individual was injured. Normally, the international bosses were told you had a hamstring pull or a groin strain. These were the sort of injuries that could sideline you on a Wednesday and miraculously disappear by Saturday. It would probably have been pushing it a little to say a player had a broken leg yet could still turn out three days later. Surely even the powers-that-be at old Park Gardens might have had their suspicions aroused if that had been the case. And then again...

There was also a bit of 'Them and Us' on the international scene. If we were flying anywhere, the blazers, of course, went first class. The lucky ones among the players got to travel cattle class. If you were really unfortunate, you got a place out on the wing. To be fair, the SFA did provide gloves. Alright, a slight exaggeration, but you get the drift. Sometimes it looked as though there were more of the SFA contingent, wives, girlfriends, hangers-on etc, than players and, at the end of the day, we were the guys who would be pitched in at the business end. Chairmen of some of the mighty Highland League clubs - and, remember, this was before the likes of Inverness Caley Thistle, Ross County, Peterhead and Elgin City were allowed into the senior divisions - would swan around looking extremely important. No, I wasn't impressed. It wasn't quite what I had dreamed about as a kid.

I'll admit to being excited when I was called up for my debut against Spain in May 1965 at Hampden. Unfortunately, the incident in Belfast with the brain donor was only five months away. By happy coincidence, Billy Bremner, my adversary with the Stirlingshire Select all those years beforehand, made his international bow in the same game. It was a friendly encounter that had been arranged while the leagues in both countries were winding down and the international teams were preparing for World Cup qualifiers later that month. I'm afraid there was very little for the 60,146 crowd to get excited about as it ended goalless. I played at outside-left while Denis Law and Alan Gilzean operated as the main strikers through the middle. I recall we were captained by Billy McNeill. I was up against a bloke called Feliciano Rivilla who had won a UEFA Cup medal with Atletico Madrid three years earlier. He was different from what I had been used to in Scotland and manoeuvred the ball quite well when he was bringing it out of defence. He wasn't slow in putting in a sly kick every now and again while the attention of the referee and the linesmen was elsewhere. Over the years, I came to expect it just so long as they didn't squeal when they got some of it back.

Actually, most of the kicking and hacking was going on over at the other side of the pitch where it appeared a hard man named Severino Reija spent the bulk of the game attempting to hoof Willie Henderson out of the ground. Eventually, English referee Kevin Howley, who hadn't given my wee Rangers pal too much protection, had to point to the dressing room and banish the Spaniard. Ibrox fans in the crowd booed vehemently. It was a sound I would grow accustomed to at the national stadium.

Remarkably, Ian McColl, the manager who gave me my international baptism, was sacked by the time the next game came around - only a FORTNIGHT later! I was as stunned as anyone when Jock Stein agreed to take over the role in a caretaker capacity as Scotland prepared for the qualifiers for the World Cup Finals in England a year later. So, in the space of two weeks, I had played two international games under two different managers. Surely, that must be worth a place in the Guinness Book of Records. McColl was actually dismissed while he was at Largs getting Scotland ready for a vital qualifier against Poland in Chorzow. In stepped Big Jock and Billy remained as skipper while my old Celtic team-mate Paddy Crerand was brought in at half-back. We got a very creditable 1-1 draw with Denis cancelling out an earlier strike by Roman Lentner.

Four days later I was left out of the line-up to face Finland in Helsinki in another qualifier. Rangers' Davie Wilson took my place and, before you ask, no I wasn't given an explanation. Scotland won 2-1 with goals from Wilson and his Ibrox colleague John Greig and the main thing is that we won and took the points. The Home International Championships interrupted the business of the World Cup and I returned for the ill-fated confrontation in October to play Northern Ireland, George Best and all. It wasn't quite the return to the fold I had anticipated - before, during or after the match. Despite two goals from Alan Gilzean, we went down 3-2, Willie Irvine grabbing their winner in the last minute. I felt pretty frustrated and, of course, my mood didn't get any better when I was confronted by the idiot at the end.

Big Jock gave me my jotters when Poland arrived in Glasgow for their return World Cup-tie. Willie Johnston, my old foe from Rangers, made his debut at outside-left and it proved to be a woe-filled evening in Mount Florida. Billy McNeill opened the scoring early on with a shot into the roof of the net after the Poles failed to clear a corner-kick. Big Billy scoring a goal with his foot was as rare as finding sunken treasure at the bottom of your bath. Scotland led with that effort with only six minutes remaining when the roof fell in. A bloke called Jan Liberda equalised and, in the fading moments, Jerzy Sadek raced away to plonk the winner behind Bill Brown. It was a loss that would have catastrophic consequences.

I was back in the side by the time our main rivals Italy came calling on November 9. Big Billy was out and Jock brought in Rangers' Ronnie McKinnon so he could hardly have been accused of showing bias towards his club side. Tommy Gemmell had a chance of playing at left-back, too, but once again Jock opted for the Ibrox option and brought in David Provan. My only club companion on such a memorable evening was the masterful Bobby Murdoch, who fully deserved to perform on such a grand stage. It was a truly remarkable occasion with the Italians parading such exciting talent as Giacinto Facchetti, Sandro Mazzola and Gianni Rivera. However, a strike from John Greig right at the death gave us an astonishing 1-0 triumph. I had rarely seen Big Jock so animated and I think we were all taken by surprise when he, fully-clothed, jumped into the bath with the players at the end. Our World Cup dream was on again.

Less than a month later it was in tatters. Scotland were hit by a barrage of injuries and players were calling off all over the place. I wonder if Big Jock thought for a moment that possibly some of them were faking it! Anyway, Bill Brown, Billy McNeill, Willie Henderson, Jim Baxter and the talismanic Denis Law all withdrew from the crunch encounter in Naples. I think the best Scotland could have hoped for would have been a draw which would have forced a play-off and kept England 1966 in sight. Burnley's Adam Blacklaw, who was a fairly mediocre goalkeeper, took over from Brown, David Provan, a left-back, was switched to the right, Jim Forrest, a centre-forward, was moved to the right wing and Ron Yeats, the Liverpool centre-half, started the game with the No.9 on his shirt. Yours truly was at outside-left again in one of the strangest-looking Scotland teams in history. The expression 'snowball's chance in hell' sprung to mind. And so it proved. Enzio Pascuti pounced on an unusual piece of hesitancy from the normally-reliable Eddie McCreadie to fire the Italians ahead just before the interval. Facchetti, who, as an Inter Milan player, would meet up with Celtic in a certain occasion in Lisbon two years later, lobbed a thirty-yarder over the back-tracking Blacklaw for No.2 and the final nail in the World Cup coffin came from Bruno Morca five minutes from the end. See Naples and die, right enough.

I went into cold storage for over two years before I was recalled by Bobby Brown for a European qualifier with England at Hampden in February 1968. Scotland, of course, had beaten the world champions 3-2 at Wembley the previous year - how I would have loved to have been involved in that encounter - but in typical fashion had thrown away the advantage when they lost 1-0 to Northern Ireland in the next qualifier six months later at Windsor Park. My memory of that game was an unstoppable performance by George Best. He tormented the hell out of the Scottish defence and if it hadn't been for the heroics from my old pal Ronnie Simpson the result would have been even more embarrassing. Faither was superb and even saved a penalty-kick from Johnny Crossan. Bestie later said, 'I thought it was a game between me and Simpson. I kept firing in shots and he kept saving them. It was easily one of the best performances from a goalkeeper I have ever witnessed in my life.' Praise indeed. Unfortunately, even Ronnie was helpless when David Clements knocked in the sixty-eighth minute winner after a cross from Bestie had been diverted straight to his feet about six yards out.

So, there was all to play for when the Bear came out of international hibernation and a crowd of 134,000 crammed into Hampden that freezing winter's afternoon when we took on Bobby Charlton and Co. To tell you the truth, I shouldn't have been anywhere near the national stadium that day. Alan Gilzean was expected to lead the line, but he failed a fitness test twenty-four hours before the kick-off. I got the call, but I told Bobby Brown I, too, was struggling with a hamstring strain. However, as I wasn't as bad as Gilzean, I was told I was playing. That's the way it worked back then.

We made life difficult for ourselves when Martin Peters ghosted into a great position on the edge of the box and rifled an unsaveable effort high past Ronnie into the top corner of the net in the eighteenth minute. My big moment came just before the interval when I scored my only goal at international level. And I was absolutely overjoyed to beat a goalkeeper I rated as one of the best in the world, Gordon Banks. A cross was delivered from the right and, as centre-half Brian Labone hesitated for a moment, I got up to get my head to the ball to divert it low towards the net from about ten yards. Banksie took after it and flew across his line, but, thankfully, the accuracy of the header swept it wide of his right hand and I was the happiest guy at Hampden, probably all of Scotland, when I saw the ball nestle in the net. It ended 1-1 and Scotland missed out by a point on qualifying for the European Championships in Italy later that year.

However, for all the criticism I had to put up with, for all the nonsensical comments from so-called Scottish supporters and the poison that used to spill from those terracings, most of it was worth it in that one split-second to say I once scored against the utterly unflappable Gordon Banks, a true great among goalkeepers. Right up there with Faither!

My great regret as far as Scotland was concerned was never getting to perform in a World Cup Finals. What a thrill that would have been. But I'm in good company when it comes to missing out on playing in the most glittering, famous tournament on the planet. It's sad to believe George Best never got there, either, to show his skills to the world. Look at Ryan Giggs's record at Manchester United, too, but he never made it to that level, either. And what about the one-and-only Alfredo di Stefano, the Real Madrid icon? He played for three nations - Argentina, the country of his birth, Colombia and Spain - and still never got to strut his stuff in international football's ultimate competition. How come he got to represent three different nations? Maybe someone at FIFA might help clear up that one!

But I was in reasonably optimistic mood when I was chosen to play against Austria at Hampden on November 6 1968 as Scotland took the first tentative step towards a place in Mexico in 1970. We got a bit of a fright when our visitors hushed the crowd of 80,856 by taking the lead in the second minute through August Starek. He hit a speculative effort from about twenty-five yards and it moved all over the place in the air to completely flummox Faither. The Lawman flashed in a trademark header shortly afterwards for the leveller and Billy Bremner forced in the winner about fifteen minutes from time. I was all smiles when I came off at the end, victory secure and Hampden, on a rare occasion, united in its acclaim of the players. I never kicked a ball in a World Cup-tie again. At least, I went out a winner.

The curtain came down in a non-event bounce game against the Republic of Ireland at Dalymount Park, Dublin, on September 21 1969 watched by 27,000 fans. It ended 1-1 after Rangers' bustling striker Colin Stein gave us an eighth minute advantage that was nullified by Don Givens around the half-hour mark. And that was that. Eight games, two wins, two defeats, four draws, one goal and far too much hassle. My international career was over at the age of twenty-six. I would have loved to have played in the World Cup Finals and, alas, destiny dictated that I would never step onto the hallowed turf at Wembley.

For years afterwards international squads were announced and the name John Hughes was missing. I didn't shed a single tear.

Chapter 13

PUTTING THE
RECORD STRAIGHT

'Fifty per cent of the supporters swore by him and other fifty per cent swore at him.' That's the sort of criticism I have had to endure for decades as people have given their verdicts on my performances for Celtic. Apparently, I was either wonderful or woeful with nothing in between. Let me tell you right now that the observation is a load of nonsense. Utter rubbish. I don't accept the inconsistency theory and I've got the facts to back me up.

For a start, Jock Stein would never have chosen a player who was unpredictable. Jock agonised over selecting his line-ups and took everything into consideration before he pinned up his team sheet. He would dissect the opposition, where they were weakest and most vulnerable, he would take into account the weather and the underfoot conditions and he was a big fan of horses for courses. If he thought a player performed outstandingly well at, say, Tannadice, Tynecastle, Pittodrie or wherever, then there was every chance he would get the nod to play in those games on those particular grounds. He left nothing to chance.

So, does anyone really believe for a second Jock Stein would have chosen me as a regular in his team for six years when I couldn't guarantee a reasonable performance? Trust me, there was no chance of that happening. It didn't take Jock too long to make up his mind about a player's capabilities. For instance, look at Hugh Maxwell, an inside-right the club bought from Falkirk for £15,000 in November 1964, just four months before Jock returned to the club. The boss put Hugh into the team for two league games and, unfortunately for the player, the club lost them both - 4-2 to Hibs at home and 5-1 to Dunfermline away. That was the end of Maxwell's career as a Celt. Jock wasn't impressed and packed him off to St.Johnstone at the end of the campaign.

That seems incredibly harsh, but that was Jock's way, as you will no doubt have picked up by now. He shed no tears when he told players to pack their bags. Hugh Maxwell wasn't alone in getting the heave. Ian Young played at right-back in the 1965 barrier-breaking Scottish Cup-winning side, but a year later he was toiling for a first team place as Jock moved Tommy Gemmell to right-back before settling on Jim Craig in the No.2 berth. Young was out in the cold and remained there until he was sold to St.Mirren in 1968. Jim Kennedy was a stuffy left-back who moved to the old left-half position in latter years, but his style of play clearly didn't fit into Jock's plans for the team. He was sold to Morton in the November of the manager's first year. My pal John Divers suffered a similar fate. He did better than Kennedy, though - he lasted a year before being moved onto Partick Thistle.

And what about the 'now-you-see-me-now-you-don't' situation with Chris Shevlane? He arrived at the club in the summer of 1967 after being surprisingly released by Hearts at the age of twenty-five. Jock obviously thought there was still some mileage in the right-back and brought him to Parkhead. Shevlane played only three first team games before being freed a year later to join Hibs. It appeared Jock thought he was good enough one minute to don the hoops and the next he was surplus to requirements.

There's an entire list of the players who didn't suit the boss's ideals. He was totally uncompromising and I wouldn't have lasted six minutes never mind six years if he didn't believe I had something to offer on a consistent basis. Also take into account the fact that Jock selected me for eight Cup Finals and also had me in the team for the so-called World Club Championship play-off against Racing Club in Uruguay. I wouldn't have got a sniff if he didn't believe I could contribute.

Even before Jock arrived, I think I was more than paying my way in a fairly average Celtic team. I scored eighty-eight goals in my first four years with absolutely no coaching from my team-mates or the backroom staff. I have to say I am fairly satisfied with that record. I'm no big head, but that's an average of twenty-two goals per campaign for a rookie brought into the team from Shotts Bon Accord, so I must have been doing something right even in my early days. My total in eleven seasons was 189 to put me in seventh top place in Celtic's all-time top goalscorers' list. What's inconsistent about that? In fact, I might even have taken second or third highest position if Jock hadn't sold me to Crystal Palace in 1971. I was twenty-eight at the time and people consider a player hits his peak between twenty-eight and thirty-two. So, working on averages, if I had remained at the club for another four years and scored seventeen goals-per-season, I would have ended with a tally of 257 and that would have beaten third top Henrik Larsson's haul of 242. It would have been sixteen short of Bobby Lennox in second place. It's worth pointing out that I scored my 189 goals from 416 appearances while my old team-mate took 571 games to reach his total. I'll concede I would never have caught Jimmy McGrory's 472 strikes from 445 appearances. I would have given it a good try, though!

Yes, I realise all this is merely conjecture, but what I'm trying to get across is the fact I don't accept for a second that I was a hot or cold performer. There's no way you can reach those figures if you are erratic or your form is irregular. Absolutely no chance. Of course, there were days when I didn't perform at the highest level, but you could say that about every player who has ever kicked a ball. It's not possible to turn it on in every outing. It's only normal that any footballer's form will fluctuate. There were days when I felt unstoppable. I could get into my stride early on and I just knew somehow it was going to be a good day at the office. Those were the match days where everything I fired at goal hit the target. However, everyone has to accept there will be encounters where the ball just won't run for you. It was hardly unique to me. But I've been stuck with the label and I don't think it's fair. In fact, it makes me sick to the back teeth when I hear people talk about my apparent rollercoaster form.

Maybe the expectation levels among the fans were just a bit too high. I'm sure they would have loved to have seen me run amok in every game. Believe me, I would have settled for that, too. If I didn't hit the heights in every game it certainly wasn't for the lack of trying. When I pulled on that green and white shirt I had only one thought in mind and that was to do everything within my powers to help Celtic to win. If I scored a few goals along the way, then that was a bonus. I knocked in five goals in an 8-0 romp against Aberdeen in a league game back in January 1965. I only scored one apiece in the next three games, wins over St.Mirren, Kilmarnock and Airdrie. Did that mean I had hit a slump because I didn't produce the same scoring ratio as against the Dons? I suppose everything is relevant.

Remember, too, that I played a huge chunk of my career on the left wing. There's no doubt I would have scored a helluva lot more than 189 if I had been playing through the middle all of my career. I would like to think I set up more than a few goals for the likes of Bobby Lennox or Stevie Chalmers, who, by the way, is fourth in the scoring stakes at the club with 231 goals from 393 appearances. So, if I'm stuck with being a volatile, unreliable performer in my years at Celtic, I have to ask, 'Who was Mr Consistency?' I'm not going to point the finger at any of my former colleagues, but I can't think of anyone who guaranteed a top-notch display in every game. As I have said, that is just not feasible. We had some world-class performers in my day, but even those individuals put in exhibitions that I'm sure even they would admit were somewhat less than inspiring.

So, please do me a favour and let's get rid of the annoying inconsistency tag once and for all. I'm not being precious, anyone who knows me will tell you I am not that sort of person, but to be absolutely frank I'm fed up with the label. I feel I made a contribution in a huge percentage of my games for Celtic. The statistics surely back up my belief and I can only return to Jock Stein. If I hadn't been producing regularly and meeting his exacting standards I would have been axed early on. Simple as that. I had to be reliable to get into any of Jock's line-ups. Hopefully, this will once and for all bring a halt to the wayward assessments and unfounded observations that my form was up and down like a yo-yo.

Jock would not have accepted it back then and I'm not accepting it now. I don't expect to hear any more on the subject!

Chapter 14

FROM PARADISE TO PALACE

It took me precisely forty-five minutes to realise I had made a dreadful mistake in signing for Crystal Palace. I had just played the first-half of my debut against West Ham at Selhurst Park on October 30 1971 and I thought to myself, 'What the hell have I let myself in for?' We were toiling and trailing 2-0 and I was sitting in the dressing room at the interval expecting the team to get a deserved rollicking from manager Bert Head. I'm still waiting. Jock Stein would have gone ballistic after witnessing that lacklustre, awful performance. He would have ripped into the players and taken no prisoners. I discovered very quickly that was not the way things were done at Palace.

Instead, one of my new team-mates, an ex-Celt by the name of Tony Taylor, congratulated me on the way I had brought down a pass on my chest and charged forward all in one movement. I thought he was joking. We were getting turned over on our pitch in front of our own fans and that was his only first-half observation. It would be a monumental understatement to say it wasn't quite what I had anticipated at my new club. Willie Wallace, of course, had left Celtic with me in a double deal that was worth around £55,000 and he was sitting there, too. He was our substitute that day and took his bow in the second-half after replacing me. We looked at each other and I knew he was thinking the exact same thoughts as myself. Sadly, there were so many crazy happenings during my brief spell at Selhurst Park although it did have its sprinkling of memorable moments.

Bert Head had wanted to change the system in my first game. He believed Palace would be better suited to playing a man-marking game against our London rivals who still had class performers among their ranks such as Bobby Moore, Trevor Brooking, Harry Redknapp and Frank Lampard Snr although World Cup-winning pair Martin Peters and Geoff Hurst had moved on to Spurs and Stoke City respectively. Our boss worked on our master plan all week in training until he thought his players had perfected the new tactics. We were a goal down before we could blink. West Ham introduced a seventeen year old by the name of Ade Coker and he was left totally unguarded when the defence failed to clear a right-wing corner-kick. Before we could catch our breath, Billy Bonds was in splendid isolation about eight yards out and he couldn't fail to knock a header past our goalkeeper John Jackson for the second goal. What on earth had happened to the man marking? Who was supposed to be picking up Bonds? It's still a mystery to this day.

There wasn't a lot said during the interval, but I do recollect there was little or no direction whatsoever. The manager, though, still believed his man-marking strategy would work in the second forty-five minutes. I had my doubts and my fears were confirmed when the Hammers netted a third goal. Again, one of their players, a big, strong Bermudan by the name of Clyde Best, had the freedom of London to score easily at our back post. That completed the scoring in what was a debut to forget. Bert Head wanted to know why no-one was in the vicinity of Best when he claimed the third goal. A defender by the name of Mel Blyth had failed miserably to pick up the West Ham striker. He made this startling observation. 'Yes, boss, I could have got to him, but that would have meant me leaving the player I was marking.' I didn't know whether to burst into tears or burst into laughter. He was deadly serious, too. Big Jock would have bounced him off the wall for about half-an-hour and then booted him out the door. Bert Head nodded his head, almost agreeing with the defender.

I had struck a quick friendship with a midfield player at the club called Bobby Kellard. He was a jovial little Londoner who was in his second stint at Palace. In training the following week, we were discussing the obvious pitfalls of the man-marking system. Clearly, it hadn't worked against West Ham and, in fact, we agreed there was never any likelihood of it ever functioning properly. Mel Blyth's assertion that his man didn't score was just plain daft, but highlighted the flaws in the grand design. So, Bobby, who was the club captain, and I decided to go to Bert Head to voice our concerns. Let me say right here and now, such a notion would never have entered my head at Celtic. Big Jock's reaction would have been typical. 'What do you know about football? Get lost before I drop you forever.' And that's just the stuff that would have been printable.

But we were ushered into the manager's office and we discussed the tactics that had gone so cockeyed against West Ham. I still half-expected Bert Head to tell us to stick our opinions where the sun don't shine, but, rather remarkably, he agreed with us and concurred that things hadn't gone too well on the Saturday. 'Okay,' he said at length, 'scrap the system and play it your way. But if it doesn't work, don't blame me.' I was astonished. Once again, I wondered what on earth I had let myself in for by joining Palace. The difference between Celtic and the Londoners really was night and day.

When I left our club digs close to the ground on the Saturday morning for my debut game I told my missus I would be back by five. I was as good as my word - I got home at five in the morning! The Supporters' Club was right next door to the main entrance at Selhurst Park and, as we were leaving after our thrashing from West Ham, one of my new team-mates said, 'Hey, Yogi, do you fancy a drink?' He motioned to go next door to mix with the fans. Now, please remember, we've just been humped 3-0 on our own pitch by London rivals and this guy wanted to go and socialise with our support. I thought he must be barmy. If I had played in a Celtic team that had lost by three goals at Parkhead I would have gone into hiding for about a week. But that wasn't the way things were done at Palace. I looked at him. 'Are you serious?' I asked. 'Won't the fans be baying for blood? They've just seen West Ham wipe the floor with us. Won't they be spitting feathers?' He reassured me, 'No, Yogi, don't worry. Our fans aren't like that. In any case, they're used to us losing.' I shrugged my shoulders and went for the drink. The fans actually applauded when I walked in. I was swiftly getting the impression Crystal Palace might be more of a social club than a football club.

Over a couple of beers, some of the Palace fans were still raving about a game against Manchester United the previous year. 'You should have seen us that day, Yogi,' they said. 'What a goal Alan Birchenall scored to put us ahead. Alex Stepney hadn't an earthly as Big Alan's shot whizzed past him. Pity we've just sold him to Leicester City. You would have been great together.' I could see they were clearly excited at the memory of this particular encounter against Bestie and Co. 'And the United keeper didn't have a chance, either, when Bobby Tambling made it 2-0. What a striker, Yogi. You'll enjoy playing with him. He scores goals out of nothing. We paid only forty grand for him from Chelsea, you know. What a bargain. He's a Jehovah's Witness, so watch you don't use bad language in front of him.' They continued to reminisce and I wondered what was the full-time score. 'I take it you won, then?' I asked. There was a lot of head-shaking among the supporters. 'No, unfortunately, they gubbed us 5-3, Yogi,' they chorused. 'But we were two goals ahead for awhile.' Once again, I couldn't envisage the Celtic fans getting misty-eyed after conceding five goals on their own ground.

I realised I was now encountering football's version of The Twilight Zone, a whole new ball game, a world where supporters didn't contemplate throwing themselves under a bus after witnessing their team being demolished. The Palace fans could also afford to laugh at the club's former centre-half Roger Hynd, who signed from Rangers in 1969. When he was left out of the team, the player would sit in the stand and shout. 'Bring back Hynd' for the entire ninety minutes!

We had a Scottish coach at the club by the name of Dave Ewing and I have to admit I wasn't too impressed by his methods, either. By the way, I'm using the term 'coach' loosely. He understood as much about tactics as I did about the requirements of becoming an astronaut. There was one day we were working on attacking free-kicks. Dave, who had managed Hibs for one season in 1971/72 before getting the old heave-ho, thought it would be a revolutionary idea to put our two central defenders into our opponents' defensive wall. 'That'll confuse them,' he said, obviously proud of his strategy no-one had thought of before. 'Wait a minute, Dave,' I said. 'What happens if we don't score and the other team break upfield? Our two main defenders will be out of position, won't they?' Dave scratched his chin, even he could see the flaw in this ploy. 'Aye, you've got a point, Yogi,' he said. 'Let's scrap that idea.'

To be fair, the London side did attempt to entertain. They had

Charlie Cooke in the team when I arrived and the former Chelsea, Dundee and Aberdeen attacker was a real box of tricks. I had played alongside Charlie in the Scotland international team and I liked his style. He was such a graceful athlete, a genuine ball-playing winger. He was now about thirty years old and, unfortunately, we had seen the best of this one-time exciting individual. Apart from myself, Wispy, Charlie and Tony Taylor, there were a few other Scots at Palace. There was a former Kilmarnock striker called Gerry Queen. He figured in one of the greatest sporting headlines of all time when he was ordered off after a punch-up in a game against Manchester City. 'QUEEN IN BRAWL AT THE PALACE' was one of the wittiest pieces of newspaper journalism I have ever seen. Another in the Tartan Brigade was Sam Goodwin, who had signed from Airdrie a year before me. Sam was a good, hard-working midfielder. There was also Jim Scott, whose brother Alex played for Rangers. Jim was a pacy outside-right the club had signed from Hibs.

John McCormick, a centre-half who had started his career at Third Lanark before having a stint at Aberdeen, was already at the veteran stage when I arrived - I think he was about thirty-five - but he was a superb pro and played on for another year before moving to an English non-league side. There was a young Glasgow-born centre-half coming through. His name was Jim Cannon and he went on to have an excellent career at the club. He played from 1972 until 1988 and made almost 600 league appearances. He was a massive Celtic supporter, but never got the chance of realising his dream of playing for his favourite club. David Provan, the left-back often driven to despair by Wee Jinky in Old Firm games, had been signed from Rangers. Iain Phillip, another strong-tackling defender, arrived just before me from Dundee. His nickname was 'Aggie', but I never found out why. Sometimes ignorance is bliss.

So, I wasn't short of company at Palace. As I have said, I got on really well with Bobby Kellard from day one and there was another Londoner I liked called Bobby Bell, who had had spells at Spurs, Ipswich Town and Blackburn Rovers before arriving at Selhurst Park. I was chatting to him one day when he left me just a little flabbergasted. 'What a shame you didn't play too many games for Celtic,' he said. 'What?' I spluttered. 'Yeah, Yogi, Willie Wallace was telling us you were stuck in the reserves most of the time.' I don't know if Wispy was up to a bit of mischief, but I swiftly corrected that impression. Bobby was quite impressed that I had also scored so many goals.

And, of course, I will be forever remembered for a goal I notched against Sheffield United a couple of months after my move to Palace. Actually, I scored two that afternoon as we won 5-1, but no-one remembers the other one. I have got to admit the goal that day was one of the best I have ever scored. For me, it was a combination of pace and power and, at least, it gave the Palace fans a glimpse of the real John Hughes. I recall picking up the ball around the halfway line on the left wing following a short free-kick. I had no idea what would happen next. I decided to go on a run and see where it took me. It was a really heavy pitch on a typical December afternoon as I set off on my great adventure. I skipped past a couple of challenges before switching the ball to my right foot. I didn't break stride as I smashed the ball as hard as I could from an angle about twenty-five yards out. My effort simply zoomed into the top corner with their goalkeeper John Hope completely helpless. I remember being mobbed by my team-mates and a couple of them still hanging off me as I made my way back up the pitch for the kick-off. It was a fabulous feeling of elation, but, unfortunately, I wasn't in the same frame of mind by the end of the game.

It was just about time-up when I chased a ball into their penalty area. I was desperate to get my first hat-trick in English football and I thought the chance was on. Their keeper had other ideas as he raced from his goal. He launched himself with a two-footed challenge and caught me smack in the knee. Instantly, I knew it was serious. I heard the crunch and I collapsed in pain. You see players these days going through the 'dying swan' act and rolling around all over the place. I just lay there. A couple of concerned team-mates raced over and I remained flat on my back and yelled, 'Don't touch me!' They were well-meaning, of course, but I was in so much discomfort I didn't want to move. I'll give John Hope the benefit of the doubt and say it was a complete accident, but, at the same time, I have to say it was a most unusual attempt to win the ball. I'm fairly certain he would get a red card in today's game for his actions.

I missed the next two games against Huddersfield Town and Leeds United, but returned on Monday December 27. We lost 1-0 to Southampton and I still didn't feel right. There was no way I could have lasted the entire ninety minutes and I was subbed by Sam Goodwin. I was back on the treatment table for the first three weeks of 1972. The club paid to put me in a private hospital in London to seek a solution to my problem. My case wasn't helped by the nurses when the Palace club doctor came round. 'There's nothing wrong with him,' they chorused. 'He's just a big wean. He's always moaning.' It was a pity they didn't take back their 'expert' opinion on the day the bandages came off. There had been bleeding into the joints of my knee and three pints of blood had to be drained from the wound. I lost 10lbs while I was 'play acting' and I was on crutches when I left the hospital. Just to underline that Dame Fortune had it in for me, my eldest son Kevin closed the heavy door of my Audi on my right hand as he tried to help me into my seat.

I came back into the team for a match against Manchester City on January 22. We went down 2-1 and it was obvious things were far from okay with my knee. I just couldn't run away from defenders the way I had done throughout my career. Speed and power were two main ingredients in my game and I couldn't utilise either, much to my dismay. My season was in tatters as Palace battled against relegation. They had been second from the bottom when I joined, but, thankfully, just managed to beat the drop at the end of the campaign. The side completed the term with twenty-nine points, four more than both Nottingham Forest and Huddersfield Town who toppled out of the top flight. At least, I had played my part in keeping Palace up!

I was excited, too, at the prospect of my solo effort against Sheffield United being voted the Goal of the Year. The BBC had a panel of experts who deliberated on the decision at the end of the season and I knew I was in the running for the award. A certain Jock Stein was among the judges and I have to say I don't think for a second that my old Celtic boss would have voted for me. I really mean that. Sentiment wouldn't have come into it for Big Jock. I believe he would have actually gone the other way. I don't think he would have wanted me to get the honour after he had sold me, obviously believing my best days were behind me. As it happened, I had to be content with the runner's-up spot. The winner was Ronnie Radford's stunning first-time thirty-yard screamer in non-league Hereford United's sensational 2-1 FA Cup victory over Newcastle. Mind you, it was one of those efforts that if it had missed the goal it would have gone on for miles and probably landed in a farmer's field terrorising a herd of bulls on its way!

I had a couple of operations during the summer as physiotherapist David Coombe worked overtime in attempting to get me fit for the forthcoming 1972/73 season. I'm afraid his efforts were mainly in vain. I was in the stand on the opening day of the league programme when we lost 2-0 to Stoke City. In fact, that's where I remained until September 30 when Bert Head thought I was fit enough to play against Norwich City. I was getting fairly frustrated sitting in the stand every week and I was determined to get back to match fitness. I was looking forward to returning to action again, but it didn't take me long to accept I was labouring. We lost 2-0 and, sure enough, that was me back on the dreaded treatment table. The entire month of October passed without a show from yours truly. I worked hard in training and was rewarded when I was named in the team for a home game against Everton on November 4. I played at outside-right and got through the ninety minutes. Even better, we won 1-0 against a very competent Goodison Park outfit. It felt good to be back, but I was wary of being too optimistic. I didn't want my hopes dashed yet again.

I played in three successive games during November and we drew the lot against Derby (2-2), Leeds United (2-2) and Chelsea (0-0). I scored my fourth and final goal for Palace - I had also netted in a 3-2 loss against Chelsea the previous November - in a 2-1 defeat against Ipswich Town at Portman Road at the start of December. The highlight in the rundown to the end of my career in London was undoubtedly a game against Manchester United at our place on December 16. The players combined in sparkling fashion to give our loyal support an early Christmas gift as we hammered the Old Trafford side 5-0 in an overwhelming performance from the entire team. We really sparked that afternoon as United were taken apart. That was as good as it got for me at Palace. I felt great during that confrontation and had been told by Bert Head to continually switch wings with Don Rogers. Don was a flying machine the club had bought from Swindon Town for the princely sum of £147,000.

United were going through a poor phase under the management of Irishman Frank O'Farrell who had taken over on June 1971 and would be sacked only eighteen months afterwards. Like a lot of defenders, it would be accurate to say O'Farrell never got to grips with Bestie.

The superstar was AWOL on the day they turned up at Selhurst Park. Scottish internationals Willie Morgan, Martin Buchan and Frank MacDougall were in the team and Denis Law was on the subs' bench. They also had the likes of Alex Stepney, Tony Dunne, David Sadler and Brian Kidd in the side and, of course, they had all picked up European Cup-winning medals only four years beforehand when United beat Benfica 4-1 at Wembley. They also had top players in Ian Storey-Moore and Wyn Davies in their line-up, so they were hardly likely to be pushovers. However, that's exactly the way it turned out.

Palace had just paid £100,000 to Everton for a wee will-o'-the-wisp striker by the name of Alan Whittle just a few days before the game. He was desperate to mark his debut with a goal and he pulled me aside before kick-off. 'You set them up, Yogi, and I'll knock them in,' he said. I liked his confident outlook. I was pretty eager to stick one in the pokey myself. I came so close, too, after an exhilarating run in the first-half that saw me one-on-one with Stepney. I sidestepped the keeper and rolled the ball towards to the net. Unfortunately, their right-back Tommy O'Neil hadn't given up the ghost and got back to boot the ball to safety. Whittle came close after I had plonked the ball at his feet, but Stepney pulled off a marvellous save.

It was exciting stuff and our keeper John Jackson could have taken out a book and deckchair and caught up with some of his reading it was so one-sided. Our Republic of Ireland right-back Paddy Mulligan ventured into attack twice in the opening forty-five minutes and twice thumped the ball beyond the overworked Stepney. Don Rogers helped himself to a couple, too, and Whittle's big moment arrived when I knocked a pass in front of him in the box. He didn't hesitate as he walloped it high into the net for our fourth goal. I can't remember if he ever bothered to say thanks!

In true Crystal Palace fashion, though, we lost the next match 2-1 at Leicester City, but came back to hammer Southampton 3-0 on Boxing Day at Selhurst Park. My stay was coming to an end by the time I played against Newcastle at St.James's Park on January 20. We lost 2-0 and I knew it was time for a move. I went to see Bert Head to let him know of my intentions. To be fair to the manager, he didn't want me to go. 'Is it about money, Yogi?' he asked. 'If it is, I can have a word with the chairman. You're still very much part of my plans and the fans love you.' I was on £90 per week and that was topped up by appearance and bonus money. Actually, it wasn't about cash, so I thought I would hasten a move by telling him, 'Okay, I want £200.' I thought I was calling his bluff. The following day he asked me to go to his office. I was amazed when he said, 'I've had a word with the chairman. You can get £200. We want you to stay.' I didn't know how to respond. It had been a very generous offer, but my mind was made up.

I laid my cards on the table and the manager was very sympathetic. He realised I had made my decision and I would be moving on. It had been very interesting at Crystal Palace, but I wanted to kick-start my career elsewhere. Bert Head didn't have too long in the Selhurst Park hot seat to go, either, although he obviously didn't have a clue that he was about to be replaced. In March that year the flamboyant Malcolm Allison was appointed manager of Crystal Palace and Bert was 'kicked upstairs' until the end of the campaign. He left the club for good in May. He had been manager for seven fairly eventful years. I have to admit it would have been intriguing to have worked with Big Mal. He was in charge for seven games at the end that season and Palace lost five of them and were relegated. A year later, they were in Division Three. Jim Cannon put it this way, 'No other man could single-handedly take a club from the First Division to the Third Division and remain a hero.'

Big Mal was very publicity conscious and one day the unconventional football boss thought it would be a good idea to invite porn actress Fiona Richmond to share the team bath at Selhurst Park. Fiona stripped off and was photographed in the pool beside the rather eccentric manager, wearing nothing but an outsized smile. If I had still been around the club at the time, I reckon that might have taken some explaining to my missus. 'What did you get up to today, dear?' 'Oh. nothing much. Just shared a bath with a naked porn actress.' It wouldn't have been dull with Big Mal around.

However, a couple of months before his arrival, I was packing up and heading out of London for the last time. Little did I realise that I had only about fifteen minutes of football left in me.

Chapter 15

THE END GAME

I was just three months short of my thirtieth birthday when I signed for Sunderland in January 1973. I was looking forward with eager anticipation to another chapter in my career. I knew all about the Wearside club, of course, because of inside info provided by my brother Billy, almost six years my junior, who had been at Roker Park since 1966. He was a bit of a hero with the support and we both enthused over the prospect of teaming up at long last. The last time we would have been in the same side would have been in a wee kickabout on a park in Coatbridge.

In fact, Billy and I could have been colleagues at Celtic in the sixties. Jock Stein wanted him, but Billy was aware that comparisons would inevitably be made with me. He was a strong-willed kid and, despite our parents also wanting him to go to Parkhead, he dug in his heels and opted for Sunderland. In fact, he made his debut at the age of eighteen in a 2-2 draw with Liverpool on February 4 1967, the same day I was playing in Celtic's 3-0 win over Airdrie at Broomfield. Almost six years later we would line up in the same Sunderland team.

I was well aware the North East was a strong and passionate football area and, naturally, I had been used to that fervour and intensity during my eleven years with Celtic. Crystal Palace had been something else altogether, a bit of an eye-opener with different levels of expectation, but I enjoyed the experience. Now, though, it was time to get my career back on track and I had been offered the perfect opportunity by manager Bob Stokoe. He thought enough of me to sign a cheque for £44,000 to Palace and that represented a good bit of business by the London outfit. They had paid £55,000 for me and Willie Wallace back in October 1971, so they recouped a fair amount of their initial outlay on me alone. Everyone was happy. For the time being.

I liked Bob Stokoe. He was a real football man, the son of a Northumberland miner, a great enthusiast and his love for Sunderland was obvious as soon as I met him. The fans had forgiven him the fact he kicked off his career with the 'enemy', Newcastle United. I was told he had been an old-fashioned uncompromising centre-half. I took one look at him and I didn't feel the urge to debate the point. Remarkably, he had played in the same English FA Cup-winning team as my old mate Ronnie Simpson when Newcastle beat Manchester City 3-1 in 1955. He was only forty-two and had just arrived at Sunderland two months before I signed. He had managed Bury, Charlton, Rochdale, Carlisle and Blackpool before moving to Tyneside. The club were in the league's second tier at the time, but he had grand plans. 'We're a First Division team playing in the Second Division, Yogi,' he told me. 'It's only a matter of time before we're up there with the big boys again. Mark my words.' He didn't mess around with fancy jargon and I liked that, too. He was serious about his football and the thought of sharing a bath with a nude porn star while I was at his club never entered my head. Bob Stokoe had ambitions for Sunderland and those aims were only too evident. I wanted to play my part.

So, on the Saturday afternoon of January 27, a cold, biting winter's day on Tyne and Wear, I prepared to make my debut for my new club in a league encounter against Millwall. You only get one chance to make a first impression and I was committed to getting off to a flier. Sunderland had paid good money for me and they demanded an instant return. I found that totally acceptable. I had passed a rigorous medical and any thoughts that I might be carrying an injury from my Palace days were dispelled. I was at outside-left and Billy was playing through the middle. 'Good luck,' he shouted over to me seconds after the kick-off. Fate wasn't listening.

Only a handful of minutes into the game, a Millwall defender came steaming into the tackle and completely mistimed his challenge.

Bang! He got more of me than he did the ball. He hit me smack on the knee that had given me such trouble after my collision with Sheffield United goalkeeper John Hope in December 1971. I felt the pain drive through my body. Instinctively, I realised it was a bad one. I crashed to the turf and the physio was at my side in a matter of seconds. 'That looked sore from where I was sitting, Yogi,' he said. I didn't bother saying it was fairly sore from where I had been standing. He massaged it a little, used the good old magic sponge and asked, 'You okay to play on?' I got to my feet, jogged a little and replied, 'Aye, let's give it a try.' The game got underway and my knee felt as though someone had inserted broken glass between the joints. I was in agony, but I wanted to play on because this game meant so much to me. Every player yearns to make an impact in his first game for his new club in front of a fresh set of supporters and I was no different.

However, I was finding it fairly stressful just to run. I wasn't picking up passes and I couldn't get past their full-back. I wasn't even kicking the ball properly. The Sunderland fans must have wondered about the quality of the new signing. There were a few calls from the terracings and I didn't blame them. They couldn't have realised the amount of torment I was enduring. I was in a fair bit of distress and Billy knew something was drastically wrong. I took another bone-shuddering challenge and, once again, an excruciating jolt rattled through my knee. I had been on the field about fifteen minutes and I knew it was game over. What I didn't realise, of course, that it just wasn't the game that was over, but my entire career, too. I hobbled towards the touchline and a concerned Bob Stokoe came over. 'I've got John Nathan on the bench, Yogi. I'm putting him on. You better come off before you make it worse.' I could only reply, 'Thanks, boss.'

By the way, we won 2-0, but, in all honesty, that wasn't my main concern the following day. I had to have my knee diagnosed once again to discover the extent of the damage. In the darkest recesses of your mind, there is always the nagging thought that this could be the end. I tried to remain positive, but the fact of the matter was my playing time in England had been decimated and there was no denying it. I had left Celtic as a physically fit twenty-eight year old and I was looking forward to the next four years I had always insisted was the peak period for a footballer. Two of those prime time years had passed far too quickly and, with my thirtieth birthday coming up on

April 3, I was anxious to make the most of the next two and beyond. I hadn't put a ceiling on when I thought my playing days would finish, but I had hoped to still be able to cope with the rigours of the game until I was at least thirty-four and, possibly, another couple of years after that.

The club doctor took a look at the injury the following Monday and was clearly disturbed at the destruction of my knee joint. 'I'll need a second opinion, but I believe this is extremely serious,' he said. I could hear the words, but I couldn't take them in. 'What are you saying, doc?' I asked. 'How bad is it?' He grimaced and answered gravely, 'Very bad. I'm sorry.' I was whisked off to a private hospital and the prognosis was identical. There was far too much wear and tear in the joint. The advice was simple, 'Stop playing football or you could be on crutches for the rest of your life.' And that was that. Game, set and match and I had always believed and hoped I would be enjoying the best years of my career during that period. Instead, my knee was smashed beyond repair and even attempting to continue would be nothing short of foolhardy. Or, put another way, a complete waste of time. There would be no miracle comeback. It was the end of the road. Or was it?

No player accepts their career will end prematurely. Maybe there are more optimists among the footballing fraternity than in any other profession. However, despite getting the very best medical advice, I still thought there was a chance of proving the docs wrong. Before I left Sunderland for the last time, I had a word with Bob Stokoe and I think he was closer to tears than me. This big, hard man who took no prisoners as a player was hurting. But we were both forced to accept that my playing days at his club were over. After fifteen bloody minutes.

I packed up and prepared to return home to Scotland. I consoled myself with the thought I could always spend my Saturdays watching Celtic. After all, it looked as though I was going to have a fair bit of spare time on my hands. Then, completely out of the blue, came a telephone call from Davie White, the former manager of Rangers. He was now in charge at Dundee and had heard about my bleak news. I had played against Davie many times during his career with Clyde and then he became an Old Firm adversary when he took over from Scot Symon as boss at Ibrox in 1967. He had lasted only two years at the club before being removed. He left with the unwanted baggage of being the first Rangers manager never to win a trophy. That, of course, was mainly due to the Celtic team in which I played. But White still had a good reputation as a coach within the game and everyone knew it would only be a matter of time before he surfaced again. Following two years in football's wilderness, White returned as boss at Dundee in 1971. And now he was making a phone call to me.

After the usual pleasantries, he asked, 'Do you think there is a chance of you playing again?' I told him the truth. 'I've been advised against it.' But the Dundee manager was nothing if not persistent. 'Yes, Yogi, but how do YOU feel? Do YOU think you can still do the business?' Again, I was honest. 'It's a lovely thought, Davie, but I just don't know how realistic.' White wasn't fazed. 'Would you be willing to take a risk? Do a bit of training and see where it takes us?' I thought about it for a moment; it seemed like a reasonable offer from a manager in Scotland's top flight. 'Why not?' I replied. 'When do you want me at Dens Park?' He laughed, 'About two years ago.'

It was all hush-hush stuff as I arrived in Dundee, admittedly, more in hope than expectation. Thoughtfully, Davie didn't want to put any pressure on me. If the newspapers had got hold of it, there would have been conjecture about me returning to the game. Suddenly, I would have found the spotlight back on me. But, let's face it, I had nothing to lose. And there was a list of players who had been written off in the past who had somehow managed to make reasonable comebacks. I couldn't help thinking about the story of the boy who had been told he would never play football. He was an undernourished little waif, born in a ghetto and one of his legs was shorter than the other. He was deformed, too. His right leg turned inwards and the left pointed outwards. But he was adamant he could play football. He got his wish and we all saw what Garrincha could provide when he played in the fabulous Brazilian World Cup-winning teams of 1958 and 1962. So, I could always hope. As I've said before, strange things happened in football.

A chap called Eric Ferguson took the training at Dundee and, helpfully, he gave me a lot of his time. Eric didn't want me to rush anything, but he offered great encouragement. I trained away as I attempted to build up the strength in my knee. After six weeks, I was moving more freely and, I have to admit, feeling good about myself. I couldn't help but wonder if a comeback was feasible. A reserve game was due for a Friday night around that time and Davie White and his training staff thought it was time for me to take the plunge and test the knee. I went through a couple of light sessions and I was eager to get out there and show I could still do it.

On the Friday morning, though, the searing pain in my knee returned. I was in agony. The timing couldn't have been worse. Any thoughts I had of turning out in a reserve game were obliterated there and then. I phoned the club to break the news. Eric Ferguson tried to soothe my anxieties by saying, 'Don't worry, Yogi, it's just a hiccup.' Some hiccup! I was finished and this time I knew it. I was absolutely shattered by the setback. I had trained hard for six weeks in preparation for that moment and, without warning, the opportunity had been whisked away from me. I was sick. What really hit me was the suddenness of it all. One minute there was hope. The next there was none. It was very hard to accept.

While I had been at Dundee, I had kept an eye on what was happening at Sunderland. I had the consolation my brother Billy was getting rave reviews, especially in the FA Cup. My wee brother hit four goals in pushing the club all the way to the Cup Final at Wembley. He scored against Manchester City in a 2-2 draw at Maine Road and followed up that performance with two in the 3-1 replay victory at Roker Park. He headed in the winner as Arsenal were dismissed 2-1 in the semi-final at Hillsborough. His remarkable displays were helping me to keep my mind off on my own problems. And he would get to perform on Wembley, something that had eluded me all the way from my days as a schoolboy. I was delighted for him. I knew a member of the Hughes clan would get to play there some day.

Sunderland were due to face mighty Leeds United in the Final and Elland Road boss Don Revie was fulsome in his praise of Billy. Revie said, 'He is one of the most exciting players I have ever seen. He loves to go forward and runs straight at opponents forcing them to commit themselves. Also, he can shoot with either foot.' I could remember the days people used to say that about his big brother! I don't know what the Leeds gaffer thought afterwards, but Billy helped force on a header from Dave Watson from a left-wing corner-kick and Fife-born Ian Porterfield fairly smacked a first-time drive past the helpless David Harvey for the only goal of the game. Around the same time

Billy was being awarded his winner's medal, I was finally admitting that my career had reached the scrapyard and there was no chance of resurrecting it. Or was there?

I kept fit by turning out for the Old Crocks, teams put together by former players mainly for charity. They were supposed to be just friendly kickabouts, but, believe me, they could feisty at times. I think some old scores were settled in these encounters. I remember playing quite well in one of these encounters where the standard was at a reasonable level. We weren't talking about ex-players turning up still in their zimmer frames or anything like that. Some had been performing in the top league just a year or so before.

Anyway, one day I rolled back the years and scored eight goals in one of these games at Petershill Juniors' ground. Former Celtic team-mate John Colrain was also playing and I knew he was still friendly with Bertie Auld, who was by now the Partick Thistle manager. This was the same Bertie Auld who only passed the ball to me when he didn't have any other options! Colrain must have got in touch with Bertie because I received a phone call shortly afterwards. 'Yogi, I've got something I want you to think about,' he whispered down the line. I was intrigued. 'Okay, Bertie, fire away,' I said. 'I think you can play again,' he said. I wondered if he was at the wind-up because my ex-colleague was known to be a bit of a practical joker.

When I realised he was deadly serious, I laughed, 'No chance, Bertie. My playing days are well and truly over.' He wasn't convinced. 'Listen, sign for Partick Thistle and I'll only play you in the last half-hour or so. I wouldn't expect you to play the full ninety minutes. What do you think?' In situations like that, you can't help but ponder over the possibilities. Bertie added, 'Look, Yogi, I'll only put you on if we have to. If we're winning comfortably I won't play you at all. You can get paid for sitting beside me in the dug-out. What do you think?' I considered it for a moment before answering, 'Sorry, Bertie, but it's got to be no. I just wouldn't do justice to myself. I know that deep down. Maybe it's best to leave the past alone and let people remember me as I was.' 'You're positive, Big Man? That's your last word on the subject? You can't be tempted? Do you want a day or two to mull it over?' I smiled and answered, 'That's my final answer.'

And I never did pull on those football boots in earnest ever again. My knackered knee made sure of that.

Chapter 16

THE LYING GAME

I believe I lacked an essential ingredient when I tried my hand at football management. I was handicapped terribly by the fact I only possessed one face. Genuinely, I think it is a prerequisite of the job for a team boss to have more faces than Big Ben. I'm not stating that every single manager is a downright liar, but there's little doubt the ability to tell a porky is a handy commodity. Let's just say it's a strength to be economical with the truth.

It didn't take me too long to realise I wasn't cut out for life in the dug-out. When I was forced to quit the playing side of the game just a few months before my thirtieth birthday, I wondered what lay in store in the big, bad world. I toyed with a few ideas and took up an invite to coach Baillieston Juniors. I was offered the post by a friend of mine by the name of Jim Ross, who was on the committee. After what I had been used to at Celtic, I have to admit it was a bit of a culture shock. The guys were all earnest, honest individuals and there was little doubt that a few of them might have played at a higher level if they had applied themselves earlier in their life. But I got the distinct impression some of them might have enjoyed a cigarette break during the action and I doubt if too many would have complained if the club's bosses had installed free draught lager in the dressing room instead of the usual orange slices at half-time.

The best I achieved in my brief interlude at Baillieston was guiding the team to a place in the quarter-finals of the Junior Cup. I left and then, completely out of the blue, I received a message from Stranraer asking me if I was interested in taking the post as team manager. It was 1975 - I was thirty-two years old - and I asked for some time to think about it. Stair Park wasn't exactly on the doorstep and I had no affiliation with the club whatsoever. Why would they even consider me for the job? After a couple of phone calls, I found the answer. Jock Stein. The Boss I hadn't spoken to since the day I had left Celtic in October 1971 had recommended me for the role. I was astounded he even considered me as managerial material. I wasn't that puzzled, though, that Jock had been involved somewhere along the line.

A lot of clubs went to Big Jock to seek advice on such matters. He was seen as The Godfather of Scottish football and his guidance was followed more often than not. If he put you forward for a job, you were off to a flying start and there was every likelihood you would walk into the post. For instance, take a look at the Lisbon Lions who went into management. There's Billy McNeill straight away. I wonder who proposed Big Billy for the Clyde job in 1977 two years after he had retired and had cut all ties with football? There's no doubt Jock manoeuvred Caesar's return to the game. And it was mentor Jock who piloted Billy towards the Aberdeen job shortly afterwards when Pittodrie chairman Dick Donald was looking for a replacement for Scotland-bound Ally MacLeod. I'm reliably informed Dick Donald, who was a charming old character, sought out my old gaffer for some suggestions.

Bertie Auld had been doing a reasonable job at Partick Thistle while keeping them in the top division. He was certainly in Aberdeen's thoughts, but Jock deflected them in the direction of Billy who had been at Shawfield for all of two months. Of course, Billy got the Dons job and, while Bertie may have been disappointed, nothing more was said of the matter. Tommy Gemmell got the gig at Dundee when former Rangers boss Davie White was sacked in 1977 and Bobby Murdoch even had a two-year stint in charge at Middlesbrough before coming back to Scotland. John Clark tried his luck at Cowdenbeath, Stranraer and Clyde after having a stint as Billy's No.2 at Parkhead. Ronnie Simpson even had a short spell at Hamilton Accies before he settled down to coaching goalkeepers at clubs such as Partick Thistle and Dumbarton. Willie Wallace had a go as player/coach at Ross

County before teaming up with his old mucker Tommy on Tayside.

Jim Craig briefly managed Irish outfit Waterford in 1974. Ironically, he took over from another European Cup-winning right-back, Shay Brennan, who played for Manchester United in their 4-1 win over Benfica in 1968, the year after Celtic had made history in the Portuguese capital. Cairney was actually player/boss at the club, but I believe he only lasted five months before returning to his profession in dentistry. Bobby Lennox's marvellous career stretched until 1980 when he quit playing at the age of thirty-seven. I thought they might have to have Bobby put down before he packed in kicking a ball. He moved immediately into a reserve team post in November that year and occupied that role for a few seasons before giving that up. So, that left only two players from that all-conquering 1967 team who didn't bother with an alternative career in the game - Stevie Chalmers and Jimmy Johnstone. Stevie walked straight a job with the club's Pools Development. It was a fitting reward for the man who scored the winner against Inter Milan. I believe, though, he must have conducted a lot of business on the golf course!

Jimmy Johnstone? Football manager? My imagination would have to be stretched from here to Australia. His good chum Davie Hay, in fact, gave Jinky a role with the Celtic youngster in the eighties. Davie wanted to bring Jinky back into football in some sort of capacity, realising he was still such a fantastic name in the club's history. He thought the up-and-coming kids could learn a thing or two and be inspired by the wee maestro. Jinky agreed to the job and promised, as ever, to give it his best shot. On his first evening with the youngsters, Davie put him in control and gave him a routine to follow. An hour or so later, Davie returned to see how things were progressing with the hopefuls. Jinky was waltzing around with the ball glued to his toe, going through his full repertoire. The poor kids couldn't even get a kick of the ball! Davie had to laugh, but he asked his wee mate to remember his instructions regarding the potential stars of tomorrow.

This went on for a few months before Jinky chucked it. He wasn't enjoying the coaching side of things and was honest enough to admit it to Davie. The Wee Man sitting in a dug-out bellowing commands to his players is not an easy picture to conjure. It would be a lot more likely for him to say, 'To hell with this,' and get the boots on and race out there onto the pitch to demonstrate how it should be done. Jinky was a natural blessed with a helluva lot more skill than Sir Alex Ferguson, but the former Manchester United manager was a far superior coach. Obviously, there is no argument on that score, but it just goes to emphasise the chasm between talent and tenacity. Fergie possessed the ruthlessness required and was always destined to become a coach, but that side of the game just wasn't for Jinky.

I wanted to do the business at Stranraer and I was willing to work overtime in an effort to achieve something. Fergie, in fact, had kicked off his extraordinary managerial career at East Stirling only a year before I took over at Stair Park. So, the possibilities were there and I was eager to give it a real go. Unfortunately for me, Stranraer were run by a committee. You know what they say about a giraffe, don't you? It's a horse put together by a committee. That just about sums it up perfectly because everyone wanted to have their say and throw in their tuppence worth. I realised my time at the club was coming to an end when I had to inform a right-back he would be dropped for a game against Queens Park at Hampden. He hadn't been playing well and, to be fair, he accepted my decision. I thought that was the end of the matter. I was wrong.

As the teams lined up for the kick-off, there was the bloke in his usual defensive position. I wondered for a moment if he hadn't understood what I meant when I said, 'You're not playing.' Seemed fairly self-explanatory to me. However, a meddling committee member had overturned my decision and told the out-of-form player he was back in the line-up. I kept my temper in check, but it would be fair to say I was far from happy at this player's appearance at the national stadium that afternoon. I informed the committee I wanted to see them on Monday night. They seemed a little surprised because I think they had got away with such things when other managers were in charge. I wasn't standing for interference from these characters. I told them. 'You made me look a fool.' They looked aghast; someone was challenging them. 'If that's the way you want to run your club, that's fine by me. I'm leaving right now.' I walked out of their little board room to deafening silence. I doubt if anyone had talked to them like that before.

Another thing that upset me at the club was the lack of professionalism among a few of the players. Okay, I accept expectation levels were a bit different between Stair Park and Celtic Park, but I still hoped for slightly more dedication from some of the team. They could come in at full-time after losing to a last-gasp goal and, before I could say a word, someone would ask, 'Anyone know the score with Rangers?' It had me climbing walls some times. If you haven't already realised this fact, I was an extremely bad loser. It's the old adage, isn't it? Show me a good loser and I'll show you a loser. The Lisbon Lions were all sore losers and that was one of their great strengths, as far as I was concerned. They didn't even like drawing!

So, what was next on the agenda? Even I was surprised. A couple of years after quitting Stranraer, I was offered the opportunity by Willie Blaney, the association's president, to become the first international manager of the Scottish Junior FA. I was intrigued and decided it was worth a try. What had I to lose? My God were my eyes opened once again. It was such a parochial set-up that it was almost laughable. I quickly understood I was being asked to be 'politically correct' when I was selecting players from up and down the country for my squads. Naturally, I chose those I believed were the best men for the job, but that didn't always go down well with the Junior FA members. I would be told that the Ayrshire FA weren't too pleased with me when I didn't pick any of their players. 'I don't care in which region they perform,' I would say. 'If they're good enough, they'll get a place in my squad.' Then it would be the turn of the Aberdeenshire people to complain.

Remember, there were around two hundred Junior teams from which to select players. I refused to play favourites and I didn't want players foisted on me who were never going to get the opportunity to get a place in the team. Willie Blaney actually recommended a right-back from the North and persuaded me to play him in a game against the Republic of Ireland in Dublin. That was a mistake. I had to take the guy off after only twenty minutes he was so bad.

I did have some good players, though. There was Norrie Fulton, for a start. He was a dangerous striker and, in fact, scored Pollok's winner in their Junior Cup Final success over Arthurlie in 1981. His son Stevie played for Celtic, but no-one really believed my old mate Billy McNeill when he said he rated Stevie as the 'new Roberto Baggio'! That was quite a tag to live up to and, unfortunately, it was one that was well outwith Stevie's grasp. However, he had a reasonable career after leaving Parkhead in 1993 and played for the likes of Bolton, Falkirk and Hearts before calling it a day at Partick Thistle in 2005. Norrie wasn't a bad centre-forward, but, to be honest, I never saw him as the 'new Diego Maradona'.

Actually, I enjoyed my time with the Juniors, despite the running interference from the various associations. Eventually, I walked away after realising football management just wasn't for me. Quite apart from some of the obstacles I have already revealed, there were other things to be taken into consideration. And one was the ability to speak with a forked tongue. I know a lot of people don't like it when you tell them the truth. Sorry, though, that's just the way I am. I tell it like it is and if other people don't like what they hear it's entirely up to them how they deal with it. I wasn't prepared to bend the truth as a football manager. I wasn't going to tell a player what he wanted to hear if I didn't believe my own words.

Others required being mollycoddled and wrapped in cotton wool. Once again, I have to say sorry that's just not in my DNA. I had never any intention of acting as a nursemaid to any precious creature. No, management wasn't for me. When I quit as Scottish Junior FA boss I knew that was my last kick of the ball. The nearest I would get to a football pitch again would be in the stand at Celtic Park on matchday.

I never regretted that decision.

Chapter 17

PLAYING FAVOURITES

For incomprehensible reasons, some fairly mediocre footballers have legendary status bestowed upon them. These individuals are catapulted towards a stratosphere of acclamation that should be reserved for those who actually deserve the accolade. I'm talking about the personalities who have worked long and hard at the coal face of the game to merit the right to such an exclusive tag. I believe you have to earn the plaudits. It's all too easy in this day and age to term someone an icon. Under closer scrutiny, what they have actually achieved and the adulation that comes with it, do not compare favourably or satisfactorily.

Images can become romanticised. Look at Jorge Cadete, for example. The Portuguese striker had only one full season at Celtic, but I've seen him being termed as a club legend. Eh? Please don't get me wrong, he was an exceptional goalscorer and was an exciting player to watch. The fans loved him, of course, and he was the sort of entertaining frontman the club has always encouraged. He had a wonderful start to his brief career in the east end of Glasgow when he came on as a substitute against Aberdeen at the start of April in the 1995/96 campaign and, with virtually his first kick of the ball, netted a superb solo goal in a 5-0 triumph.

But I don't believe anyone should be elevated to superstar status after five minutes. I wish Cadete had hung around a little bit longer when Celtic really needed him. Rangers, under Walter Smith, were attempting to beat Celtic's record of nine championships on the spin. When Cadete came on the scene, the Ibrox side were only two full campaigns from achieving that feat. But there was hope because Tommy Burns was putting together a team well worth watching and it looked as though good times were on the horizon. Cadete, apparently, was to become a key player in the revival. To be fair, he scored thirty-three goals from forty-four games in all competitions the following season and that certainly deserved a rapturous and lengthy round of applause. Then there was nothing. He was off on his travels again.

Cadete was last seen coming off the pitch after a game against Dundee United. I laugh today when I see players kissing their club badge. A fair percentage of those guys wouldn't have a clue about the history of the club who are bankrolling their lifestyles. Cadete went one better - he kissed the Celtic Park turf. The supporters loved it, but you have to ask if the player knew all along he had no intention of returning for the next crusade. Brings a new meaning to the term 'kiss off', I suppose. I'm sorry, but the mantle of Celtic legend doesn't sit comfortably on Jorge Cadete, in my opinion. There are others who are more worthy of the recognition.

John Divers scored 101 goals in 232 appearances for Celtic - and never won a solitary medal. He should be one of the best-known players in the club's history, but he appears to have drifted off the radar. That's a real shame because JD was a top-class footballer and a performer who never received the kudos I believe he thoroughly deserved. You hear and read about footballers playing through the pain barrier and my old team-mate could give you chapter and verse on that topic because he played EVERY single game in torment. The only other person at Parkhead who was aware of his affliction was Celtic club doctor John Fitzimons. And he warned the player to keep quiet about his personal agony or he would undoubtedly face getting the sack from the club.

JD struggled throughout his career with a circulation problem. Apparently, his body didn't have the facility to produce a proper flow of blood. A vascular surgeon ran tests on my colleague and told him he possessed the legs of a seventy year old. JD was twenty at the time. Unfortunately, no-one knew of the anguish he faced going through even the less strenuous of routines. He was branded lazy by critics and JD had to bite his tongue. There were others who claimed he wasn't a good team man because he didn't put himself about. Again, JD couldn't enlighten them to his discomfort. And yet he still scored over a century of goals for the club and, at the time of writing this book, he is one of only twenty-eight players who have achieved that notable feat for Celtic in their 126-year history. Ironically, one of the players among that number is Patsy Gallacher, who is a genuine icon in the club's folklore. Patsy just happened to be JD's Great Uncle.

John Divers is not a name that immediately springs to mind when fans talk about prominent Celtic footballers. That's a pity. No-one else was ever asked to perform with the sort of burden with which he was saddled. He made his debut for the club in season 1957/58 - just a month after the unforgettable 7-1 victory over Rangers in the League Cup Final. And, quite rightly, he could say he was the man who kicked off the surge to nine consecutive Championship triumphs. It was JD who scored the opening goal in a 4-0 win over Dundee United at Tannadice at the start of the 1965/66 league season. It was his 100th goal for the club. It was also his last in the league. His final strike came in a 3-1 League Cup triumph over Dundee at Dens Park in September 1965. After his effort against United, JD played only two more league games for Celtic and, although he was still at the club until the end of that campaign, he didn't qualify for a medal.

The John Divers story could have been so different in the club's chronicles. He left after nine years at Celtic Park and, sadly, there was no fanfare of trumpets, no rousing send-off for a fabulous club servant who never once complained about his condition or ever sought the sympathy vote. In fact, there was a horrible black cloud over my old mate's final season at the club where his dad, also called John Divers, played between 1932 and 1945. He just failed to join the Celtic Centurians when his goal tally stalled at ninety-two.

JD was obviously no speed merchant and possibly some of the fans, admittedly in the dark about his state of his health, might have thought he wasn't giving 100 per cent in effort. Believe me, he was always striving to do his absolute best for the club. One look at his goals total should tell you that. But his perceived laidback style could have confused the paying punters who might have expected a more up-and-at-'em style of play from an old-fashioned inside-forward. There was no way JD was physically equipped to perform in such a manner. You might as well ask a Sumo wrestler to attempt the pole vault. Even Jock Stein, who had coached the player while he was a youngster in the Celtic reserve team, knew nothing of his ailment.

Unfortunately for JD, Big Jock decided to take in a reserve game against Morton at Greenock one night. My old mate, even by his own admission, wasn't exactly putting himself about on a quagmire of a pitch at Cappielow. The players came in at the interval covered in mud - with the exception of JD, whose strip looked in almost pristine condition. Big Jock stormed into the dressing room. He pointed his finger at JD. 'I hope you enjoy the next forty-five minutes,' he bellowed. 'They'll be your last for this club!' Big Jock was as good as his word. JD was cast adrift and wasn't even allowed to train with the first team at Barrowfield. As punishment, the manager made him exercise on his own at Celtic Park.

It's interesting to note that John Divers' last appearance for Celtic came in a 2-1 defeat against Rangers at Ibrox on September 18 1965. I scored with a penalty-kick that afternoon and JD was blamed for squandering an ideal opportunity to claim the equaliser in the fading moments. As I recall it, Billy McNeill got up above the Rangers defence to nod down a left-wing corner-kick. The ball went to an unguarded JD about six yards out. Nine times out ten he would have tucked that chance away with his usual precise finishing. On this occasion, though, the ball took a wicked bounce, JD swung his right foot at it and missed completely. In a matter of seconds the opportunity was gone and so were Celtic's prospects of avoiding defeat at the hands of our oldest rivals.

One of life's great understatements would be to inform you Jock Stein hated losing to Rangers. He may have been a Protestant brought up by a Rangers-supporting father, but Big Jock loathed the Ibrox club. He detested what they stood for and their refusal, at the time, to sign a player of the Catholic faith. If he wanted to buy one player from the choice of two with equal ability and one was a Catholic and the other was a Protestant, then he would sign the latter. Why? Big Jock knew Rangers couldn't sign the Catholic. That's an absolutely true story. I've been in dressing rooms after we had beaten, say, Kilmarnock, Motherwell or someone else by three or four goals and Big Jock would still have a go at the players. There would be something in our game that irked the manager and he was never slow to let you know. It was a different story against Rangers, though. We could be absolutely dire and sneak an odd goal win and we wouldn't hear a chirp out of him. Beating the Ibrox men was all that mattered and nothing more was said.

So, that may paint a picture of the mood of Big Jock after the loss in Govan that afternoon. He was furious and poor JD bore the brunt of his criticism. My mate deserved some sort of medal to be actually still standing with only a minute or so to go after another gruelling and punishing Old Firm encounter. As usual, he would have been knocked around by John Greig and Co. No prisoners were ever taken in the heat of the world's biggest and most frantic derby confrontation. JD said nothing although he was probably wracked in pain at the time. That was the end of his Celtic career, as far as the manager was concerned. It effectively came to a halt when the ball took a weird ricochet off the Ibrox turf and he had a fresh air swipe. A year later he was a Partick Thistle player. And I believe he realised he was heading for the Parkhead exit when he read the story in a Glasgow evening newspaper that he was being freed. There must be better ways of discovering you're on the way out.

John Divers should have been hailed as a true Celtic hero just for the sheer torture he was forced to endure every time he performed in that green and white hooped jersey, playing for the club that was closest to his heart. JD had made his debut three years before my first appearance against Third Lanark in August 1960. We teamed up for the first time that afternoon and I reckon we must have performed alongside each other almost twenty times throughout that campaign. I was either up front as a centre-forward or an outside-left and JD performed in either of the insider-foward positions, as they were known then. I thoroughly enjoyed being in the same team and I will never forget the kindness he showed me as a seventeen year old coming into the top side, although, in fact, there were only three years between us in age. John Divers should still be feted as a Celtic great, but, of course, that is not the case. If any tale underlines how fickle football can be it must be that of John Divers.

And what can I say about the one and only Ronnie Simpson? Now there is a name everyone knows and Faither is a genuine legendary figure in Celtic history. Quite right, too. What a romantic footballing episode in an often cruel and harsh sport. It's almost the John Divers tale in reverse. The story goes that the club's celebrated goalkeeper was on the verge of signing for Berwick Rangers before Celtic stepped in at the last minute to change the course of destiny. Jock Stein was the Hibs manager at the time and he was quite content to let Ronnie move to the club languishing in the old Second Division. The popular custodian was thirty-four years old and Big Jock obviously believed he was past his best. It came as a complete surprise to everyone, Faither included, when Celtic came on the scene. I knew we were looking for a back-up keeper to John Fallon with Frank Haffey about to sign for Swindon Town. Someone got wind that Ronnie was heading for Shielfield Park and diverted him to the east end of Glasgow, instead. The rest, as they say, is history. And wonderful history at that.

I played in the same team when Ronnie made his debut on November 18 1964. If he thought he was coming to Celtic to merely top up his pension he was given a rude awakening when he was told he was playing against Barcelona in the Nou Camp Stadium in a Fairs Cup-tie, the equivalent of the Europa Cup these days. The previous Saturday we had lost 2-0 to Dundee at Parkhead and John Fallon was dropped for the first leg of the European tie in Spain. In came Ronnie for what wasn't the most auspicious of starts. We lost 3-1, but I managed to score our goal to give us hope for the second game on home turf. We had to settle for a goalless draw, but it was obvious Ronnie Simpson was not quite ready for the knacker's yard. He and Fallon jousted for the first team place for the remainder of the season before Big Jock gave the vote to the veteran for the majority of the following campaign.

Ronnie was one of my favourite team-mates, a good lad on and off the pitch. He got everything he deserved from the game. To be honest, Celtic had toiled for a consistent goalie before Ronnie came on the scene and I don't mean any disrespect to John Fallon and Frank Haffey when I make that statement. Frank Connor, who later became assistant manager to Davie Hay in the eighties, played a handful of games, too, in season 1961/62 before moving on. And poor Dick Madden is in the history books for all the wrong reasons as a Celtic shotstopper. He made his debut against Kilmarnock at Rugby Park in March 1963. It was his ninety minutes of infamy. He conceded six goals as the Ayrshire side ran amok and he never got near the first team again. Thankfully, I didn't play that Wednesday evening, but another guy who did make his baptism for the club that night had better luck than Madden. Maybe you've heard of him - Jimmy Johnstone!

Ronnie, though, brought stability to the last line of defence. He was a safe pair of hands while being exceptionally dependable. He wasn't tall for a goalkeeper - about 5ft 10in - but Big Jock never expected him to come for every high ball that dropped into the Celtic penalty area. If we were defending against a set-play, Billy McNeill was given a free role. That was his domain and our other players kept a watch on opponents taking up threatening positions. Ronnie stayed on his line and gobbled up anything that came his way. He was never flashy and relied on his anticipation to repel our rivals. He was a bit unconventional, too. Ronnie thought nothing of kicking the ball off his goal-line instead of trying to get his hands to the effort. He would knock things away with his backside, his knees or his elbows 'Just so long as the damn things stays out of the net, that's the main thing,' he would say.

It's quite incredible to believe Ronnie was only fourteen years and 304 days old when he played his first game for Queen's Park. And some twenty-two years later, at thirty-six years and 196 days, he became the oldest player to make their debut for Scotland. As usual, Faither did it in style by helping our nation to their famous 3-2 victory over the-then World Cup holders England at Wembley in 1967. I suppose the biggest accolade I can give this fabulous character is the fact even Big Jock wouldn't have dreamt of dropping him. It was often said that Ronnie and the Boss didn't quite see eye-to-eye during their brief time together at Hibs. That would be supported by the fact Jock was only too willing to offload the keeper for next to nothing. Jock liked the players to sweat blood in training, but it must be admitted Faither adopted a more relaxed attitude as he prepared for the actual action on matchday. Jock might not have liked it, but there was little he could do. Ronnie's outstanding consistency when it really mattered kept him in the top side.

John Clark never received too many headlines for the way he went about his business alongside Billy McNeill in the heart of the Celtic defence, but he is another of my all-time favourites. Luggy, as he was known, was totally unspectacular. He scored three goals in his entire career which is hardly surprising because he rarely ventured into enemy territory. He was quite satisfied in his sweeper role at the back, tidying things up around Big Billy and filling in when the likes of Tommy Gemmell went raiding down the left. No-one ever saw Luggy even attempting to send long-range passes deep into the other team's half. He much preferred to clean up in his unfussy manner and push short balls to midfielders Bobby Murdoch, Bertie Auld or Charlie Gallagher and let them do their best work.

Luggy was unflappable. That would often be demonstrated when he was left holding the fort on his own if his defensive team-mates had been caught our of position. If two forwards were bearing down on Luggy, I would have put my last penny on him averting the danger. He was very, very clever in those situations. He had the uncanny knack of making the opposing player to do just as he expected. He would force them wide and be well aware of their next intention. When they made their move, Luggy pounced and, more often than not, came away with the ball. I say he was unflappable, but there was one incident when my wee mate almost blew his top. That came in the infamous brawl against Racing Club in Montevideo. I recall Luggy running to protect Wee Jinky after another Argentinian thug had clattered our winger. The Racing Club player must have been taking brave pills because he was ready to have a go at our defender. Luggy adopted a boxer's stance with his fists clenched and hands held up in front of his face. It wasn't quite the Ali Shuffle, but it got the message across. He looked poised to land a haymaker on the chin of the Racing defender who thought about the folly of his actions and simply ran away. Aye, those Argentinian ruffians could provoke even the calmest of all Celts.

Bobby Murdoch earned his nickname Chopper during that match in Uruguay. Bobby was a lovely guy blessed with an even temperament. He could look after himself, no doubt about that, and was Jinky's unofficial minder on the occasion the Wee Man was getting too much rough treatment. That said, Jinky wasn't slow in getting in his retaliation, either. But Bobby looked after the winger in an almost big brotherly fashion. However, he became Chopper against Racing Club because, like John Clark, he, too, lost his cool in the most demanding and unacceptable of circumstances against those hooligans. Do I need to draw you a picture about the origins of the moniker? Any Racing Club player daft enough to annoy our masterful midfielder that day soon felt his wrath. Chopper gave them some of their medicine in his own inimitable fashion. Big Jock hated that nickname. So, that made absolutely certain it would stick with Bobby for the rest of his Celtic career!

Of course, it is his sublime football ability that will always be remembered. He was one of the best two-footed players I have ever seen. People often talk about Lubomir Moravcik and his talent for kicking with equal strength in either foot. There's no doubt Lubo was a very professional exponent with right or left, but I believe Chopper just shaved it. And, of course, he scored the most spectacular of goals from distance. Goalkeepers facing Chopper and Tommy Gemmell back then would have had every right to demand danger money. I was known to thump in a long-range drive every now and again, if you don't mind me saying. Chopper mainly played on the right hand side of the midfield, but he would have been just at home on the left and would never have looked out of place.

Celtic fans might never have realised that Bobby took a sore one on his right foot at the start of the 1967 European Cup Final against Inter Milan. In fact, he was afraid to take his boot off at the interval because he feared he wouldn't be able to get it back on again to allow him to play in the second-half. He played virtually the whole game mainly with his left foot. Look again at the footage of the game and I bet you'll be amazed. Imagine performing like that on one foot. Simply incredible!

It's just as astonishing that Chopper was allowed to leave Celtic on a free transfer before he was even thirty years old. He was only twenty-nine when he signed for Middlesbrough in 1973 and many believed he still had a huge future at Parkhead. Bertie Auld, in fact, made the point that he thought Chopper could have played in the sweeper role such was his savvy in being able to read play. He wasn't blessed with pace, but neither was Luggy, who had left for Morton in 1971. Players such as Jim Brogan, George Connelly and Pat McCluskey had been tried in the position beside Caesar as Jock sought to put the defensive jigsaw together. He overlooked the ability of Chopper, who, Bertie insisted, could have been Celtic's answer to Franz Beckenbauer. I'm not too sure about that, but it would have been an intriguing possibility. It would certainly have been worth taking a calculated risk.

But Jock had yet again decreed that a player had to go and Chopper was another of the Lisbon Lions to be offloaded. The manager was changing the Celtic system of play and had opted for a more industrious performer in the middle of the park. He bought Stevie Murray from Aberdeen and he was a player who preferred running with the ball while Chopper made the spherical object do all the work. He could ping passes all over the place with outrageous accuracy, but Jock thought our opponents were beginning to wise up on how his team was set out to play. Strange, that. Celtic had just won their eighth successive title when Chopper was practically gifted to Middlesbrough's new boss Jack Charlton. My old Leeds United sparring partner is on record as saying Bobby Murdoch was his best-ever buy. Who would argue with that?

The Quiet Assassin was the nickname earned by another Celtic player I rated extremely highly. I'm talking about Davie Hay, of course, and he's one of the nicest blokes I've met in the game. I think he's been shown the door about three times by Celtic, but he still turns up to support the team on most matchdays. Davie didn't want to leave the club when he returned from having an outstanding World Cup Finals in West Germany in 1974. However, Chelsea had offered something in the region of £225,000 for my mate and that was too good an offer for Celtic to knock back. Davie, against his wishes, was on his way to London. Then he received his P45 in 1987 as manager of the club. He had won the league championship and the Scottish Cup in his four-year reign, but that didn't satisfy the board. Davie was really unlucky he was up against Graeme Souness's spending power at Rangers at the time.

Souness was given the funds to bring in the likes of England international skipper Terry Butcher and his fellow-countrymen Chris Woods and Graham Roberts. Davie was forced to scramble around at the other end of the market, although, to be fair, he was allowed to spend £440,000 on signing Mo Johnston from Watford during that spell. Wonder whatever happened to that player! Davie, being the excellent professional he is, came back as chief scout when Tommy Burns was in charge and helped to bring in the likes of Paolo Di Canio and Pierre van Hooijdonk. After Tommy left the club, Davie's role changed and he was closer to new boss Wim Jansen. Celtic were on their way to winning their first title in ten years, but Davie once again lost his job. You would be forgiven for believing those set of unfortunate circumstances might put Davie Hay off football for life, but he is still a regular attender at Celtic Park. That's dedication for you.

He was a wholehearted performer for Celtic. Big Jock liked to play him in the midfield when we were playing Rangers. John Greig had ruled the roost in that crucial area for far too long. He was an intimidating sight as he crunched into tackles and generally put his weight around. Jock decided to pitch in Davie, who had been playing at full-back, in a match at Ibrox. He wanted him to combat the power of the Rangers captain. He gave Davie a role in the middle of the park in the opening Old Firm league game of season 1969/70. Davie was only twenty-one years old at the time, but he was determined not to be bullied in the presence of Greig. There were a couple of bone-shuddering tussles early in the game and the Ibrox player realised he was in a game. Celtic won 1-0 with a goal from Harry Hood and 'The Quiet Assassin' was born.

Wee Jinky has got to be another of my most treasured Celtic team-mates. He was a real bundle of mischief - on and off the field. Like all the other guys I've mentioned, he was a very humble person, very self-effacing. Just to emphasise that point, he could barely believe the supporters had voted him The Greatest-Ever Celtic Player in 2002. Once he realised it wasn't a wind-up, he asked, with all sincerity, 'Me? The Greatest? I thought they would have given it to Henrik Larsson!' That really tells you all you need to know about Jinky.

The fans loved him and he, in turn, loved the fans. Jinky was a good trainer, but a lot of what he did on a pitch could never be coached into a player. A lot of the things he conjured up were completely off-the-cuff; a shake of the hips, a dip of the shoulder, a shuffle of the feet and he was off. That sort of mesmerising ability lit up many a dull winter's evening for the punters at Parkhead. Jock Stein is quoted as saying his greatest achievement was prolonging the career of the Wee Man. What a shame, though, that Jinky was still four months short of his thirty-first birthday when Big Jock gave him the news that his time at Celtic was over. I'm glad I wasn't around that day in May 1975. As I have already admitted, I was devastated when I was told I was being sold, so I can only wonder what was going on in Jinky's mind when he was given that bombshell news. Celtic had been his entire life. He had even been a ball boy at the club and never at any stage would he have thought of leaving although, of course, clubs all over Europe would have been falling over themselves to get his signature when he was at the peak of powers.

Jinky should still have been playing football into his mid-thirties. Someone once observed Wee Jinky could drink for Britain in the Olympics and guarantee us a gold medal. Aye, the Wee Man could put it away, but, like the rest of us, he trained like a demon and I think we won so many games in the latter half of the sixties because of our superior fitness. How many last-minute winners did we claim back then? Far too many to count, but that showed the perseverance and professionalism of the players. Tommy Gemmell gave him a chance to show what he could do at Dundee when he was manager of the Dens Park club in 1977. Jinky had a short spell in the States with San Jose Earthquakes after leaving Celtic and then had a couple of seasons with Sheffield United. I know Tommy practically bent over backwards to keep Jinky on the straight and narrow to resurrect his career. It was clear, though, that playing football for Jinky actually meant playing for Celtic. And no-one else. His heart lay with Celtic and he was merely going through the motions with other clubs. He lasted only a couple of months at Dundee before his contract was scrapped. Jinky, though, was another who deserved to go out on a high and never got the opportunity.

Another thing I liked about the Wee Man was his ability to laugh at himself. He told me the story of the day he was preparing to turn up to take his girlfriend - and future wife - Agnes out on one of their first dates. To make sure he made a favourable impression with the family, Jinky bought himself a new white coat which, I suppose, must have been a trendy fashion item at the time. Jinky duly knocked on the front door and one of Agnes' relatives duly opened it. She took one look at Jinky, resplendent in his new gear, and shouted, 'Mum, it's the milk boy!'

Jim Baxter could have been an ideal drinking partner for Jinky. I don't think it was a particularly well-kept secret that the Rangers player had a fondness of lager before going onto Bacardi and Coke most days after training. I'm told he got away with murder at Ibrox and upset some of the older and more traditional brigade who had always toed the party line. But Slim Jim was a one-off and another

I would find a place for in my personal Hall of Fame. Manager Scot Symon was only too well aware that Jim didn't quite put his back into training and, unlike John Divers, he had no medical condition to offer as a reason. However, Symon turned a blind eye to the antics of the Fifer, one of the most elegant footballers I have played against or watched.

'Gie's the ba',' he would scream to Rangers goalkeeper Billy Ritchie when he was were about to launch a clearance down the park. 'I can't, Jim,' Ritchie would say. 'You're being marked.' He would scream back, 'Never mind that, just gie's us the ba'.' He called his left foot The Glove and he could so all sorts of wondrous things with that sublime left peg. I hated playing Rangers back then when Slim Jim was in his pomp. He could run the show from his left-half berth and it was agony watching him go through his repertoire. But, at the same time, I had to admire his skill and awesome talent.

He would have been a helluva player to have had at Celtic. In the early sixties, he was very friendly with a lot of our players, most notably Billy McNeill, Paddy Crerand and Mike Jackson. I also knew he got on very well with Big Jock and, in fact, the Boss made him captain of the Scotland international team when he was put in caretaker charge for the 1966 World Cup qualifiers. There was a huge mutual respect between Jim and Jock and, of course, the player was up for grabs when he was freed by Nottingham Forest in 1969, only two years after his excellent display in Ronnie Simpson's international debut at Wembley. Will anyone ever forget his bout of keepy-uppy? That was so typical of Slim Jim.

Rangers signed him again when he was only twenty-nine years old, but it was obvious he was out of condition. The years of the good life while not training properly were taking their toll. One thing was certain - he would never be nicknamed Slim Jim again! He didn't even last a season with the Ibrox side. He was signed by Davie White, but when he was sacked and replaced by Willie Waddell the writing was on the wall for Jim. Waddell was known as a strict disciplinarian and that was bad news for the player. His contract was torn up and he was out of football before he even reached thirty. What a waste, but he would always get a place in any of my Dream Teams.

Willie Henderson was another Rangers player with the ability to make my life a misery in the heat of an Old Firm battle, but you can't take anything away from his talent. A lot of people likened him to Jinky and, of course, they were very similar in stature, but, for me, Willie was always a lot more direct than our Wee Man. It was rare to see Willie coming across the pitch. He saw his role to get past the full-back and sling over crosses and it was something he did far too well. Jimmy Millar and Ralph Brand were the main Ibrox strikers when I was coming into the Celtic team and I doubt if they scored double figures between them with efforts outside the box. They would loiter with intent throughout a game and wait for the inevitable cross from Willie that would present them with an opportunity from six yards or so.

He had searing pace, too, but I think his great drawback was his vision. Willie wore contact lenses almost from day one of his career and, obviously, they didn't hinder him during afternoon matches in natural daylight. It was a different story under floodlights, though. Willie still had the ability to terrorise a defender with his blistering speed, but even he admitted he wasn't too sure about the destination of his final cross into the box. 'If I heard a cheer, I just assumed we had scored,' he would joke. Like Jinky, he was just such an irrepressible character.

On the international front, I have to say I liked the style of Alan Gilzean. He was a class act and that much was obvious as soon as he came into the Dundee team back in the late fifties. He was a tall, rangy type of player who scored a fair percentage of his goals with his head, but he possessed fantastic close control when the ball was on the deck and I don't think he ever received the praise for his overall intelligent and creative ability. He scored well over one hundred goals for the Dens Park club and helped them to their title success in 1961/62. A couple of years later he was on his way to Spurs and what a prolific partnership he struck up with Jimmy Greaves.

I'm told the White Hart Lane players used to run for the hills when Gillie, Greavsie and Dave Mackay, another former international team-mate, organised nights out with the lads. This normally consisted of picking a nearby pub and then attempting to demolish the bar owner's stocks. I wish they had been around when I had one of my pubs. I could be writing this book while sitting on my private yacht moored somewhere off the South of France! What a player, though. Genuine class.

So, too, of course was Denis Law. Unfortunately, though, I didn't get the opportunity to play too often with the Lawman in the international set-up. I first met him when we were both with the Scotland Under-23s squad and I started four games beside him at the top level. He was such an electrifying footballer with amazing lightning-swift reflexes. Now there is a guy who deserved all the ovations that came his way. Manchester United and their supporters were so fortunate to have Denis, Bobby Charlton and George Best all around at the same time of their careers and performing at Old Trafford. Have you heard the one about the Scotsman, the Englishman and the Irishman? A lot of opposing teams didn't see the funny side when they took on United at their very best.

Okay, who's the best I've ever seen? There have been many discussions over the years about the merits of Diego Maradona and Pele, two of the most accomplished professionals to grace a football field. Who would get my vote? I would go for the little Argentinian wizard. I paid £10 each for tickets to take my sons Kevin and Martin to Hampden in June 1979 to see what all the fuss was about. By the way, £30 was a lot of money back then! I had heard about this so-called 'little genius' who was creating quite a stir in South America. A lot of players simply don't live up to the hype and I thought I would take the boys along to see Maradona in action. I was stunned. He was breathtaking. He was only eighteen years old at the time and playing against a good Scotland side with players such as the Liverpool double-act of Kenny Dalglish and Alan Hansen in the line-up.

He ran the show from start to finish. I was amazed by this portly wee guy who looked anything like a sportsman. But he was unstoppable that summer afternoon. His movement was incredible, his change of pace was extraordinary and his ball control was exquisite. He raced at players and left them in his slipstream. It was as brilliant a performance as I have seen from any individual. At one stage, I swear he shimmied one way and went the other while sending the entire crowd in the terracing behind the goal the wrong way. I had seen Pele play for Brazil in a friendly against Scotland on the same ground as Brazil prepared for the 1966 World Cup Finals in England. His performance didn't come anywhere near that of Maradona. Mind you, my wee mate John Clark was playing that day and he did his usual first-class marking job on the Brazilian.

But Diego Maradona was something else altogether. All I knew about Argentinian footballers before I saw him in action was that they liked to spit, punch and kick you. But Maradona came along to shatter that image and I'm so glad he did. I wonder if they would have changed the rules if he and Wee Jinky had ever got the opportunity to play in the same team.

We would have required two footballs, of course.

Chapter 18

DUELING WITH CAPTAIN CUTLASS

Bobby Shearer was known as a combative type of defender. I could think of other expressions for the Rangers captain. He had been playing for the Ibrox side for five years when I first came into the Celtic team in 1960. He was twenty-eight years old and would have played around two hundred club games by the time I met up with him. It would be fair to say he was an experienced right-back. And I can tell you he used every bit of that know-how when I played against him.

Oh, let's face it, he was a dirty wee so-and-so. I've talked about him elsewhere, but I have never revealed he was, in fact, the most difficult opponent I played against. Okay, I was only seventeen at the time and was hardly well versed in the less genteel side of the game. Bobby Shearer, over a decade older, was well aware of that deficiency in my make-up and he exploited it every time we came face to face in an Old Firm confrontation.

I could run quicker while wearing a deep sea diver's gear than the Rangers defender, so that aspect was never going to be a problem. I could get the ball at my feet and amble up to him. My game was about acceleration, pace and power and there would be no stopping me once I got away from Shearer and into my stride. Easier said than done. Bobby, who was built along the lines of a giant Corn Flakes box, would let me knock the ball past him and then he would simply take a step to the side and block me off. Blatant obstruction, of course, but I was amazed at the amount of times he pulled the stunt and got away with it.

I got wise to the obvious tactic and then he started to use his elbow. He found a spot just under my armpit and he would drive his elbow into that tender area. The referees either didn't see it or didn't think it was a foul in the first place, but, believe me, it was bloody sore. During the pace of the game, it might not have looked too obvious, but I knew it was a foul. So, too, did he, but he kept on doing it as long as he got away with it. That was for another five years and then he took his special 'skills' to Queen of the South in 1965. He only played thirty times for the Dumfries side and retired from playing the following year. That was good news for outside-lefts in the old Second Division. I wonder why he earned the nickname Captain Cutlass?

I hated playing against Shearer, but one bloke I did look forward to squaring up to was Dundee right-back Alex Hamilton. Actually, where the Rangers man relied on strength, Hamilton actually possessed skill. Someone, though, should have told him he wasn't as good as he thought he was. He was chosen to play twenty-four times for Scotland and was seen as a colourful character. He believed he was one of the top defenders in the business, but I never had any trouble when I faced him. Like Shearer, he was a lot more experienced than me and maybe he thought I could be talked off my game. He was wasting his time.

I would get the ball wide on the left and take it forward where he would be waiting. He would stand off me and say, 'Go on then, lad. You think you're fast? Hit it down the line and we'll chase after it. Let's see who wins.' The first time I heard him make that challenge I was just slightly taken aback. Was he really testing me in a race? It was one I was happy to accept. I pushed the ball down the line and hared after it. I could hear Hamilton trying to keep up with me. No chance. The next time I received a pass there was the Dundee defender in front of me again. Surely he had learned his lesson? Remarkably, he was throwing down the gauntlet again. 'Go on, lad, hit it down the line,' he urged and away I went. Time after time. He was an absolute dream to play against and I have to say spotlessly clean in his efforts to get the ball - whenever he got close enough to me. Thankfully, that wasn't too often.

Alex - whose nickname was Hammy - was in the Scotland side when I made my debut against Spain in 1965. I quite liked him, he was a bubbly sort of individual off the field. I thought he was pulling my leg when he informed me he believed he had a future as a pop singer when he quit football. He told me he was quite a good chanter. I took his word for it, but you can imagine my surprise when I later found he had released a record with his band called *'Hammy and the Hamsters'*. Well, what else would you call your band? Music lovers everywhere can now sigh with relief. *'Hammy and the Hamsters'* released only one record and was restricted to the Dundee area. You might recognise the name of one the backing singers in the band that never seriously threatened The Beatles. It was Craig Brown, who is probably better known as being the manager of the Scotland international team between 1993 and 2001.

Another bloke who always gave me a run for my money was former Ayr United right-back Dick Malone, who was a team-mate for all of fifteen minutes in my brief stop-over at Sunderland. Dick was tall for a full-back - almost the same size as me - and he played with the unfashionable Somerset Park side for six years between 1964 and 1970. He was a top-class athlete and I wonder what he might have achieved if he had got a move to a bigger club earlier in his career and I mean no disrespect to Ayr United when I say that. He played over 160 games with the part-time outfit before he got his chance in England.

Like Alex Hamilton, he played you the proper way. He didn't try to kick you or threaten to half you in two if you tried to beat him. We had a few good contests during his years at Ayr United. Ally MacLeod was there, of course, during his first managerial spell which started in 1965 and lasted until 1975 when he left to take over from Alex Ferguson at Aberdeen. Ally was an exuberant individual and I thought he was great for football. He was nicknamed 'Muhammad Ally' after his extravagant boasts about what his wee team were going to do to the likes of the Old Firm and other top sides. 'The Fastest Gums in the West' was another moniker. He talked up his team and, fair play to him, he encouraged them to play attacking football. That suited Malone because he liked to launch into raids up the flank and I had to chase after the defender to close him down. He was a strong, reliable player and Scotland must have had an awful lot of good right-backs during his playing days because his international appearances were restricted to one Under-23 cap. His story has a happy ending, though. He played alongside my brother Billy when Sunderland beat Leeds United 1-0 to lift the FA Cup in 1973. He certainly deserved that success.

I was glad Wim Suurbier played his club football in Holland with Ajax. I wouldn't have fancied meeting him two or three times a season. I played against him when Celtic beat the Dutch side 1-0 in a European Cup-tie at Hampden in 1971. I was completely impressed by his athleticism, reading of play and speed all over the place. He rarely misplaced a pass and was composed throughout. Mainly, I enjoyed playing at the national stadium with its wide playing surface. Most of the time, I could get some joy galloping up and down the touchline. Big Jock would roar from the dug-out, 'Run him, Yogi, run him.' I had to persevere and wait for that moment when my opponent made a mistake or took his eye off the ball. That was the moment to pounce and create havoc. As far as Suurbier is concerned, I'm still waiting for that first error.

His performance that evening in Glasgow was about as flawless as any I can remember from a defender in direct opposition. He just looked so comfortable on the ball, neat and tidy and his timing while coming forward was impeccable. Play could be away over on the opposite flank, but he instinctively knew when to belt forward and I realised I had to go with him to attempt to snuff out the threat. He was a complete professional and he won three successive European Cup medals with that fabulous Ajax team. He picked up sixty caps in a very strong Holland international team and I wasn't surprised to learn he was playing in the Indoor League in the States when he was almost forty years old. You require good control in that very fast game and Suurbier had that in abundance.

As I said earlier, thank goodness he made his living in Holland while I was still playing.

Chapter 19

LOOK ON THE MONEY SIDE

My take-home pay in my last year as a Celtic player in 1971 was thirty-three quid a week. My basic wage was fifty pounds, but that was soon reduced after income tax and national insurance. I wonder how Wayne Rooney would get by on that! Good luck to the Manchester United player who is picking up £300,000 per week for an annual salary of £15.61million. The deal will bring in the twenty-eight year old more than £70million over the next five-and-a-half years. He is worth £1,785 an hour and just under £30 a minute. He earns more than Barack Obama, the President of the United States. Those figures go beyond mind-boggling.

But back in my day, it was an entirely different story. If I wasn't chosen for the Celtic first team there would be no win bonuses or appearance money and that would mean a yearly salary of £2,400. The average annual wage for an adult in the UK in 1971 was £2,000, but, of course, for a lot of workers there was the opportunity of overtime or extra shifts to top up their earnings. Some professions allowed people to do 'homers' on the side. I had no such luxury as a footballer.

From the outside, I had all the trappings of success you might expect a player at Celtic to enjoy. I had just built a lovely house in Uddingston, a beautiful and spacious four-bedroomed property that even had a table tennis room in the basement. I believe it cost something in the region of £20,000 to put together. I had a car and my wife also had a vehicle. At the time we had two sons, Kevin and Martin, and, somehow, I could afford to send them to fee-paying schools. Also, as a representative of Celtic Football Club, I was always expected to look smart. The players realised they had an image to maintain. Tracksuits were garments to be used only while training. Report to Celtic Park for duty in anything akin to a shell suit and I'm sure an apoplectic Jock Stein would have sent you straight home to change. The Boss even frowned on longish hair and facial fuzz. I wonder what he would have made of Georgios Samaras!

So, to outsiders, it may have appeared that I was living the dream. In truth, it was a financial struggle. I had huge outlays and commitments, but I didn't complain. I was happy to play for Celtic although I knew there were fatter pay cheques to be had in England. The Anglos in the Scotland international set-up didn't exactly rub your nose it in, but they made you aware that their pay salary dwarfed your own. Even when Celtic were successful in the second half of the sixties, I believe Rangers players had a superior basic wage. Mind you, we received win bonuses and they didn't, so that meant we were always better paid!

When I was sent packing to Crystal Palace my pay poke, including appearance money, actually doubled. And, as I pointed out in an earlier chapter, when I told them I wanted to leave they offered me £200 per week - FOUR times what I received from Celtic. When you consider the London club had nothing like the fan base of Celtic and there wasn't a massive difference in TV money - Sky was merely something that was above your head in the seventies - you have to wonder how they could have afforded such wages. Or, put another way, Celtic couldn't. I'm sure the powers-that-be at Parkhead at the time understood that most of their players were, in fact, Celtic fans and it was a pleasure and a privilege just to turn out for the team. Certainly, that was the case with me and that's why money was never an inducement to leave the club. The only time I seriously pondered my future was before Jock Stein arrived in 1965 and I was in and out of the side. That was an unsettling time as I looked for regular first team football, but I stress it had absolutely nothing to do with finances. It was purely a football matter.

But I often got the impression Big Jock believed he was paying the players money out of his own pocket. We often asked Billy McNeill to have a word with the manager on our behalf. He was the club captain, our figurehead and our spokesman. But the truth of the matter is that Billy absolutely abhorred going to the manager's office for talks with Jock on players' grievances over cash. Nowadays, he admits he used to go and sit in a cubicle in the ladies' toilets, remain for about half-an-hour and then return and inform us, 'Sorry, lads, Jock says No.'

Of course, our concerns would normally centre on bonus payments. At Celtic, the players never knew what sort of extra inducement was on offer before a big game. The Lisbon Lions received £1,500 each for winning the European Cup in 1967, which actually measured up well with what the England players got for lifting the World Cup the previous year. So, there were no complaints from the eleven who turned over Inter Milan. However, we were disappointed when we learned what we were to receive after beating Leeds United home and away in the European Cup semi-final three years later. The board obviously decided that knocking out the English champions wasn't on the same scale as beating the Italians and we were to be given £1,000. After tax, that was pegged at £600. Now, I don't want to sound mercenary, but that amount didn't appear to tally up. Okay, we hadn't actually won the trophy, but we were in another prestigious European Cup Final, it was three years after Lisbon and inflation had to be taken into consideration. But £500 had disappeared off the total and the players were more than a little upset.

Big Jock was told about the rumblings of unrest, but when he met us it was clear he wasn't interested in taking up our complaints with the board. The cheques were in brown envelopes and the players left them on the treatment table. We said we weren't going to accept them and we told the gaffer we thought we were worth more. He looked around the dressing room at the players and was silent for a moment. Eventually, he said, 'Ach, do what you want. Take the money or leave the money, it's up to you. The cleaner will be here in ten minutes and I'll tell her just to sweep everything into a bucket.' We knew he wasn't bluffing. One by one, we picked up our envelopes and nothing more was said on the matter.

There was another occasion when we again felt let down over a bonus matter. Bobby Murdoch and Jim Brogan took it upon themselves to have a word with the manager. They duly went to his office, knocked on the door and were greeted with Big Jock's gruff voice, 'Come in.' My two team-mates hardly had a chance to speak when Big Jock asked, 'Where's Billy?'

'We're representing the players,' said Bobby.

Jock exploded. 'Get out of my fuckin' office and don't come back without your captain.' And was the end of those short and sharp bonus 'negotiations'. By the way, Jock rarely swore and when he did you knew it was time to look out the tin helmets and duck for cover.

I've also heard over the years that Celtic lost the 1970 European Cup Final before a ball was kicked against Feyenoord in Milan. There were all sorts of rumours about the players being disgruntled with the money that was on offer. We were also said to be distracted by the possibility of commercial deals with an agent. We've been accused of letting down the club because we weren't focused on the job on hand. That is simply nonsense and utterly untrue. As I have already stressed, the Celtic players never knew what sort of bonus to expect, so there was no way we could have complained about it before a game. And if there were any deals getting done with an agent to bring in extra cash, I certainly didn't know about them. And, considering I actually played in the San Siro Stadium that evening, presumably I might have got wind of these negotiations taking place. It's just a load of baloney. People may even be making it some sort of excuse to attempt to disguise the fact we were beaten by the better side on the night. Hard to swallow, I know, but that's the truth of the matter.

By the way, did anyone notice that our Dutch opponents actually won the Intercontinental Cup later that year? They beat Argentina's Estudiantes 1-0 in Rotterdam and came back from two goals down to gain a 2-2 draw in La Plata, which was no mean feat. So, Feyenoord had the silverware to prove they were the best club side in the world in 1971.

However, here's a thought for you to chew on. What would have happened if Celtic had beaten the Dutch side and then found themselves facing another trip to Argentina to play Estudiantes? Considering what had happened against Racing Club in Buenos Aires in 1967, would Celtic have fulfilled the fixture? Would they have made their excuses and pulled out? The governing football bodies FIFA and UEFA might have insisted upon the game being played and that could have brought an interesting reaction from the Parkhead board. If they refused to play the match, they could have been banned from European competitions for a year or so. Also, they may have faced a huge fine. It's all conjecture, of course, but it would have been a highly intriguing situation. I, for one, would never have been in a rush to set foot in South America again. I think all of my team-mates would have thought along identical lines. No amount of money would have swayed anyone's mind.

My brother Billy was down at Chelsea a year or so ago and, still sounding like an excited kid, he phoned me later to tell me about the amount of Rolls-Royces he had spotted in the players' car park. It made me think of my first car which I so proudly drove along London Road before parking outside Celtic Park. It was a Ford Cortina GT with wire wheels. And, naturally, it was second hand. I couldn't afford a brand new one just out the salesroom, but that vehicle was my pride and joy.

And that brings us back to Wayne Rooney and his personal pot of gold. I mean it when I say the best of luck to the England forward. He's an excellent player and Manchester United obviously believe he is worth a landslide of cash. There are mediocre players in England's top flight picking up enormous pay cheques and I have to say good for them, too. I believe the average wage for a footballer in the Premier League in 2011/12 was £30,000 per week. Let's face it, they are picking up a lot more money than they deserve, but some clubs are frantic as they square up to annual battle to remain in the top league, so they reckon they can pay top dollar to maintain that status.

I played in a different era with a diverse market and was paid accordingly. So, please, don't get the idea I thought Celtic were mean or tight-fisted. Let's just say, they were careful with the pennies. Here's a wee story that may help illustrate that point. I was with my team-mates Jimmy Johnstone, Bobby Lennox and Willie O'Neill in Bermuda when director Desmond White very kindly offered to take us out on boat he had hired. We accepted, but, after about thirty minutes or so, we were beginning to rue the decision. The waters were particularly choppy that day and the vessel was being thrown around all over the place. Jinky and Wee Bobby were violently sick. Willie soon joined them and, before long it was my turn, to start heaving. 'Please, Mr White, can you take us back?' I implored. He looked startled. 'Are you kidding?' he asked incredulously. 'I've hired the boat for the day and

I'm going to get my money's worth!'

Also, I certainly don't mean to portray myself or my colleagues as grasping, greedy individuals. The truth is that we got rewarded what the club so fit to pay us at the time. We were hardly paupers, but it was tough for an individual if they were out of the first team for any length of time. And you couldn't expect any sympathy if you were injured for a month or so. That was just your tough luck and there would be no win bonuses or appearance money coming your way. Mind you, you got a free seat in the stand on matchday!

I spent eleven years in the first team before I was transferred and a few folk have asked me over the years if I should have been granted a Testimonial Match. That would have been nice, I have to say. Remember, though, that such games in my generation were few and far between. Jock Stein didn't actually encourage them although, curiously, he received one himself against Liverpool on August 14 1978. An all-ticket crowd of 62,500 turned out and, a day or so later with a few grand in his bank account, Big Jock left to become manager of Leeds United. Billy McNeill received a Testimonial Match, too, against the Anfield side in August 1974 while Jimmy Johnstone and Bobby Lennox actually shared the gate in the game to honour the two Lisbon Lions against Manchester United in May 1976.

Before Big Billy's pay-day there were only four Benefit Games in Celtic's history. Jimmy Quinn, the club's fifth highest scorer with 217 goals, got the first in 1909, but it was another twenty-two years before another one was granted. That went to Patsy Gallacher, No 6 in the scoring charts with 192 goals. Jimmy McGrory, with the unbeatable tally of 468 goals, was rewarded two years later and Willie Maley also received one in 1953. You couldn't argue that he deserved the accolade - he had been manager of the club for FORTY-THREE years. In more recent times, there have been such money-generating games played for Danny McGrain (1980), Roy Aitken (1987), Tommy Burns (1987), Davie Provan (1987), Pat Bonner (1991), Paul McStay (1995), Mike Galloway (1996), Peter Grant (1997), Tom Boyd (2001) and Jackie McNamara (2005). I say good luck to all of them.

Henrik Larsson was given the opportunity to bow out in style after seven years at Celtic when he played against Seville in a specially-arranged game at Parkhead on May 25 2004. A packed house said an emotional and lucrative farewell to the Swede. I'm not a jealous guy - envy is a wasted emotion if you ask me - but how I would have loved the opportunity to have had such a send-off in my last game for Celtic. And forget the bumper pay day. Just to acknowledge those wonderful fans and, hopefully, be acknowledged by them in turn would have been more than enough.

That would have been the most satisfying and memorable way of bringing down the curtain on my career as a Celtic player. Unfortunately, I wasn't afforded the opportunity. You can't have everything.

Chapter 20

FEED THE BEAR

Wee Jinky positively thrived on playing to the audience when the Celtic fans began belting out, *'Jimmy Johnstone on the wing.'* That's when his team-mates realised we would have to wait until the supporters stopped singing before there was any remote possibility of a pass from the Wee Man. I can reveal I knew exactly how Jinky felt when the Parkhead choir were in full throttle. I loved it when I first heard the rumblings of *'Feed The Bear'*. In fact, it probably took a moment or two to dawn on me what the fans were singing the first time I heard the inspired jingle from the Jungle.

'Feed The Bear, The Bear, He's Every-Bloody-Where...Feed The Bear...Feed The Bear.' Actually, I've substituted the word 'bloody' for a rather naughty word, but you get the drift. It was heaven in Paradise when I heard the fans beginning that chant. I felt my chest swell with pride as strength pumped into my legs. It was a real adrenalin rush. All I needed was a cape and I would have taken off. Do you know, I haven't a clue who first nicknamed me Yogi after the famous TV cartoon character at the time, Yogi Bear? Originally, I thought it was because I was smarter than the average Ranger because Yogi was always getting the better of the Park Ranger in Jellystone Park on the telly. However, his catchphrase was actually, 'Smarter than the average bear.'

If I was going to be named after the cartoon bear I thought it was only right that I satisfied my curiosity and found out a little more about the character. I wanted to make certain that being called Yogi wasn't an insult! There was an American baseball star around at the time called Yogi Berra and he was a bit of a character. He was known for his amusing quotes such as 'half the lies they tell about me aren't true.' The producers of Yogi - the bear not the baseball ace - insisted they had not based the cartoon on the sportsman and, believe it or not, he took them to court for defamation. The TV people said it was just a coincidence and he lost his case. Yogi Bear? Yogi Berra? Aye, right!

Anyway, I took it as a compliment and I still answer to it today - over four decades after hanging up my boots. I have to say it is all a bit humbling. I can be tucked away in a little bar in Majorca on holiday and I'll hear a complete stranger say, 'That's Big Yogi, isn't it?' It's nice to be recognised all these years later. And it's equally amazing to listen to the fans as they recollect some of the goals I scored for Celtic. In truth, some of them appear to have total recall. They can go into the most remarkable detail and I've got to take their word for it. Mind you, I have absolutely no recollection of this goal from a posting I found not so long ago on a website. It read,

'I started following Celtic circa 1970/71 and I recall a goal Yogi scored from about 478 yards against St.Mirren at Love Street. The ball ripped the net, pulled the goal frame out of the ground, landing on Gilmour Street Railway Station, killing 115 people by knocking two approaching trains off their tracks.'

I'm fairly positive I would have remembered that one! There are still a few that crop up in conversation and I'm honest enough to say I expand with pride by being remembered in such a fashion. It's a lovely feeling to know I have given so much pleasure to so many people because those supporters gave so much back in return. I'm often asked about a goal I scored against Dundee United at Tannadice and it's one that I do recall with a lot of fondness. It was in January 1969 and the pitch was a mudheap. If there was any grass on the playing surface that winter afternoon, I failed to detect it. It was a typically hard-fought game against the Tayside outfit and they had former Rangers centre-forward Jimmy Millar in their side. He had been known during his Ibrox playing days as the 'The Old Warhorse'. He was a well-built character and used to sport a crew cut hairstyle favoured by American marines at the time. He was a tough cookie, that's for sure. Even one of his ex-Rangers team-mates admitted Millar was 'more suited to boxing than football'.

Millar had a spectacular scoring rate against Celtic in Old Firm games, netting thirteen goals in all including one against us at Celtic Park on New Year's Day 1964 that put a slight dampener on any celebrations the players had planned later that day. Me included. He moved back to his original position as a half-back - where he played for Dunfermline before Rangers bought him and stuck him up front to partner Ralph Brand - and he was in the team that beat Celtic 1-0 in the 1966 Scottish Cup Final replay. That was the evening Big Jock tore into me for not tracking back when Kai Johansen claimed the matchwinner. So, it was high time Yogi got his revenge on The Old Warhorse. I saw my opportunity in the mud and glaur of Tannadice and I seized the day.

Bobby Lennox had put us ahead and it was nip and tuck until I received the ball wide on the left about the halfway line. They had a right-back by the name of Andy Rolland and I quite enjoyed playing against him as I knew I could always beat him for pace. United would have recognised that fact and they were doubling up when I received a pass. It would be me against Rolland with Millar coming into the space behind the defender. He was a wily Old Warhorse, I'll give him that, and he used his experience to its best advantage. I realised he was cutting down the running area behind Rolland to prevent me getting into my stride. On this occasion, though, his timing was out and I spotted it immediately. I pushed the ball beyond Rolland and had the opportunity to pick up some pace. Millar dived in, but I neatly sidestepped him as he slithered past on the dodgy conditions. The Old Warhorse wasn't one for giving up easily, though. He clung to my jersey as I continued to run at goal. I couldn't shake him off. I dragged him along in the sludge before I took aim and battered an unstoppable drive into the net. I turned away to accept the congratulations and Millar was still hanging onto my jersey. 'You can let go now, Jimmy,' I said. 'I've scored.' He groaned and released his grip. We won 3-1 to complete a happy day.

Possibly one of the first goals I scored that brought me to the attention of the Celtic support was one I netted in a Scottish Cup-tie against Morton at Cappielow in January 1964. People talk of some players being great goalscorers, but not scorers of great goals. I was doing my best to combine both. The Greenock side were running away with the old Second Division title and I think they were the highest scoring team in Britain at the time. Allan McGraw actually went on to score fifty-eight goals that season. Obviously, they were a dangerous proposition and when we went into the game we knew we were on a hiding to nothing. Our best chance of a trophy was the Scottish Cup because we were already struggling in the league and we had failed to qualify from our League Cup section. So, we were on the high wire at Cappielow and there wasn't a safety net in sight.

Morton were well hyped up for the game and there was a huge focus on Greenock that afternoon. Once again, we were asked to perform on another morass of mud. The first goal in any game is absolutely vital, that goes without saying, but it's even more crucial when you are playing a wee team on their own ground in knock-out competitions. One slip and you're history. That was in the back of my mind when I got the ball deep in my own half. I looked up and didn't spot a team-mate in a particularly threatening position and just took off. I slipped three or four challenges before lashing out with my right foot. I wasn't too sure of the distance, but I decided to let fly. The ball took off like a rocket and flew past their keeper before rattling into the net. The newspapers the following day said it was from thirty-five yards. Jinky and Charlie Gallagher got two others as we won 3-1 and avoided a potential banana skin. Unfortunately, we lost 2-0 to Rangers in the quarter-final at their place after gifting them the lead with some sloppy defending. Another Scottish Cup dream demolished. Thankfully, I only had to wait another year before I got my hands on a winner's medal.

I was now aware that the fans were urging me to shoot from all sorts of distances when I had the ball at my feet. Maybe that's when the chants of 'Feed The Bear' first came to life. I've got to admit I never needed too much encouragement to have a pop at the opposition's goal. If I felt good and the ball was running true, I would give it a dunt and pray that it hit the target. I recall I got another against Dundee at Dens Park in a League Cup-tie in 1965. They had beaten us 2-0 at our place in an earlier game in the section. We wanted to turn that around on Tayside and it was another day where I was bursting with energy and stamina. John Divers had scored our first goal when I decided to go on a run and see where it led me. I was aware I had eluded maybe two or three tackles and once again I could feel the vigour and intensity in my legs. I let loose and once more the ball took off like a meteorite. Goal! And Joe McBride added another in a 3-1 win. That helped push the club into the next stages and I wasn't to realise the significance at the time. We went all the way to the Final where I slotted home two penalty-kicks beyond Rangers keeper Billy Ritchie and we lifted the trophy for the first time since the 7-1 triumph over our age-old rivals in 1957. I make no apologies for mentioning that particular scoreline on more than a few occasions!

By the way, some of the greatest goals ever scored have hardly had the acclaim they deserved. A team can keep possession for five minutes, spray the ball around, complete about one hundred passes and someone will knock the ball in from six yards. But those efforts are never quite as memorable as a screamer from long range that thunders into the roof of the net. Thankfully, I can claim a few like that.

If I had a good rapport with the Celtic faithful, the same couldn't be said for other fans up and down the country. Especially the lot from across the Clyde. They did their best to ruin the day I stuck two spot-kicks into the Rangers net for that League Cup success. Back then, the victorious team was allowed to do a lap of honour with the newly-won trophy. God knows our fans had to tolerate it on too many occasions during our wilderness years. I don't recall too much trouble. However, a reasonable percentage of Rangers fans just couldn't accept we had beaten their team on that occasion. We never intended going all the way around the running track in any case because that would have been suicide with one half of Hampden packed with our followers and the other half taken up by the Ibrox supporters. Billy McNeill and I held the trophy aloft as we took it behind the goal to parade it in front of the traditional 'Celtic end' at the national stadium. We were making our way back to the middle of the pitch when a fairly large collection of their fans staged a pitch invasion.

I haven't a clue how many were on the pitch at that point, but I was certain they weren't there to add their congratulations to our silverware-winning achievement. One halfwit actually threw himself at our right-back Ian Young. He knocked our bemused defender to the ground. I thought he might have wanted to clap Ian on the back - he scored their goal that day! Seriously, he might have done damage as Ian tried to collect his thoughts while lying on the deck. A quick-witted Tommy Gemmell grabbed the nutter by the neck and pulled him away. Then another moron raced up to Big Billy and me. If you're going to pick a fight with someone would you pick two guys who are over 6ft tall? I think the police dealt with that intruder. Trainer Neilly Mochan was attacked, too, and, in all honesty, it's incredible no-one was seriously injured.

Also, I believe the Celtic support deserve massive credit for not retaliating after the shocking outburst from their counterparts. They could quite so easily have got involved in a pitch battle and that wasn't anything Scottish football needed. By the way, what punishment did the SFA mete out to Rangers for the misbehaviour of their fans? I can't recall any sanctions being imposed. None at all. Oh, the soccer bosses did take some action - they banned laps of honour at Hampden for the next ten years. Now that's what I call SFA justice.

There was another instance when I came close to a confrontation with a Rangers fan. Or about forty, to be more precise. It was the day of an Old Firm game and John Clark had volunteered to be chauffeur to pick up me, Davie Hay and Jinky, who were, at the time, the Uddingston contingent. John took his usual route which passed by Calderpark Zoo and, as luck would have it, we were stopped at a set of red lights. That's when a coachload of Rangers fans pulled up beside us. Unfortunately, they spotted us and started to give us the expected abuse. We ignored them, as usual, but I'm afraid I didn't see the funny side when they began making grunting noises and pointing to the zoo. They obviously believed I should be in there with the rest of the bears. The traffic light seemed to be stuck at red forever when I snapped. 'Let me out,' I said, 'I'm going to sort out this lot.' Davie said, 'For Christ's sake, Yogi, there's an army of them and one of you.' Naturally, my travelling companions made it quite clear they wouldn't be joining in the prospective fracas. At that point the lights changed and John, who was always an extremely careful driver, took off like he was a Formula One racer.

So, thanks to all the fans who sang, 'Feed The Bear' with such wonderful, vibrant gusto over the years. I don't know your names, but I know who you are. Thanks, also, to the person who christened me Yogi Bear. Whoever you are!

Chapter 21

WORLD OF A DIFFERENCE

I have absolutely no doubt Celtic have it within their powers to become the biggest football club in the world. And, no, I don't possess a pair of green-tinted spectacles. I believe I am stating a clear and obvious fact when I make that observation.

I look at Celtic's awesome fan base and I know it has the capability of being even bigger than that of Manchester United. The same goes for Barcelona and Real Madrid. Obviously, those are massive clubs, but Celtic undoubtedly have the capacity to overtake all three. I'm not sure if there is a Celtic Supporters' Club in Timbuktu, but I would be surprised if there is. Martin O'Neill, during his time at Celtic, admitted the club might have to restructure the stadium at some point to add another twenty thousand or so seats onto the current 60,832 limit. I can see that happening some day.

Things will evolve in the future and Celtic will become far too big for Scotland, if that's not already the case. They will have to look elsewhere and England, of course, is right on our doorstep. I accept it could be a long haul and the club may have to forfeit playing in Europe for awhile to accomplish the feat, but I think it is more of a probability than a possibility. Clubs in the top flight across the border will allow Celtic into the Premier League as soon as turkeys begin voting for Christmas. Why would they welcome Celtic into their set-up? It stands to reason that once Celtic get into that league they will not be relegated. They will be there to stay, they will go from strength to strength and will be able to compete with anyone when it comes to paying top dollar.

Too often in the past my old club have sold players to mediocre English outfits. The likes of Swansea City, Southampton, Norwich City, Nottingham Forest and Crystal Palace have been able to cherry-pick some of Neil Lennon's first team squad with Ki Sung-Yueng, Victor Wanyama, Gary Hooper, Kelvin Wilson and Joe Ledley heading across the border. I hope they enjoyed their taste of Champions League football because they won't sample it with any of those teams. Can anyone persuade me Gary Hooper would prefer to play at Carrow Road - capacity 26,034 - or Joe Ledley would opt to turn out at Selhurst Park - capacity 26, 309 - instead of performing in front of a packed Celtic Park? Of course not.

Whether we like it or not, Celtic are a selling club at the moment and chief executive Peter Lawwell has done a fantastic job in keeping the club far removed from financial ruin. Quietly and without fuss, he and his fellow-directors have built a solid foundation upon which Celtic can prepare for an extremely bright future.

We only have to look across Glasgow to Rangers to see what can happen when people get reckless with cash. David Murray once infamously said, 'We'll spend £10 for every £5 Celtic spend.' It was a cheap jibe that has come back to bite him. Who on earth would sanction the £12million transfer for Tore Andre Flo? That's a record-breaking deal that will stand for some time. But it's cash the Ibrox club could do with today. I'm not gloating and that's why I believe Celtic have to be prudent with their finances. At the same time, though, I have no doubt the club will be able to flex their financial muscle if - or, more likely, when - they get into a new league.

Celtic's route to the English Premier League could well come through working their way through the divisions starting in the lowest tier. I think, though, it is more likely they could be invited into the Championship where the clubs do not enjoy the lucrative TV deals as the top boys. Teams such as Birmingham City, Ipswich Town, Blackburn Rovers, Leeds United and Middlesbrough would all get a spin-off with Celtic being in their division. There's no doubt their home gates would get a boost when Celtic come to town. At the end of the day, that's what it is all about - hard cash. Chairman love the sound of those turnstiles clicking and that could swing it for Celtic.

Look at the amount of Testimonial Games my old club have been asked to perform in across the border. I recall playing in Bobby Moore's big match at Upton Park on a wet and windy November evening in 1970. It was estimated that over 3,000 Celtic fans made the trip to London to watch a thrilling 3-3 draw. Remember, this was just a month before Christmas, but those supporters still dug deep to make travel arrangements, arrange accommodation and purchase tickets for what was a game with nothing at stake but pride. Yet Upton Park was sold out weeks ahead of the occasion.

Bobby Charlton asked Celtic to play in his Testimonial Match at Old Trafford and Ron Yeats did likewise against Liverpool at Anfield. There is an enormous list that pays homage to the attraction of Celtic and its pulling power. In more recent times, my old club have played for Alan Shearer at Newcastle United and Gary Kelly at Leeds United. It's easy to see why clubs in England fancy a visit from Celtic and their supporters. These games pass without the hint of trouble and I'm certain that would remain the case when the occasions were more competitive. It would be fair to say Celtic have won a host of new fans over the years.

Just have a quick glance at the amount of players who have asked Celtic to play in their Benefit Games: Roy Keane, Ryan Giggs, Lou Macari, Mark Hughes and Brian McClair (Manchester United), Neville Southall (Everton), Ian Rush (Liverpool), David O'Leary, Paul Davis and Sammy Nelson (Arsenal) and Jack Charlton (Leeds United). And let's not forget Alfredo di Stefano who wanted Celtic to play in his tribute game for Real Madrid a few days after we had won the European Cup in 1967. There are others, but I think you get what I'm trying to say. Celtic are an attractive and marketable proposition. Quite apart from the actual football, the commercial possibilities for the Celtic brand are also boundless. Everything is there and some day I am convinced the jigsaw will come together.

Look at Manchester United, for instance. Quite apart from other commercial aspects, the Old Trafford side pulled in something in the region of £108.6million in broadcasting revenue alone in 2013.14. And I believe that figure was actually down on the previous year! With guaranteed revenue like that streaming into the club, could you begin to image what Celtic could achieve at another level? Yes, it would be a whole new ball game, right enough.

Celtic made in three successive championship successes in season 2013/14 and deserved a lot of credit for doing so. But Neil Lennon must feel like a boxer with both his hands tied behind his back when he takes the team into the Champions League. That's where the big bucks count, but the advantage has always got to be with the clubs who can spend almost obscene amount of money on continually strengthening their squads. As I've already pointed out with Manchester United, the TV money is astronomical compared to what Celtic receive. In 2013/14 the total TV money in the Scottish League was £14million. There is no comparison with what is on offer just across the border. Their total was £1BILLION. At the same time, if a club kept its Premier League status in England they would get between £60-£70million. Celtic won the title and what did they receive? All of £4million.

And, of course, cash-rich individuals from other countries also pour money into fortunate English clubs. It's an expensive hobby for some, but the football teams benefit because they can afford to attract some of the biggest and most glamorous names in the game. Not that long ago, most folk wouldn't have known an oligarch from an ostrich. But we do now with Roman Abramovich's presence at Chelsea. It must be nice to have the fiftieth richest person on the planet throwing money at your club.

There are boundaries that are restricting the growth of Celtic at the moment, but barriers are being broken down all the time in life as well as sport. Once the shackles are removed, I am certain Celtic will surge ever upwards. If they are allowed to perform in England, I am sure they will reach the top flight eventually. I don't believe they would immediately begin winning titles, but I wouldn't see a top six finish beyond them. Once the acclimatisation period was over, I can only envisage good things in the future.

When they are allowed to perform on a level playing field against the likes of Bayern Munich, Real Madrid, Barcelona, Juventus, Chelsea and the Manchester clubs, United and City, it will become evident that Celtic have the potential to become the biggest club in world football.

I just hope I'm around to witness it!

Chapter 22

LAW AND LAST ORDERS

The guy wearing the multi-coloured balaclava looked quite menacing. The shotgun he was pointing at my head was fairly intimidating, too. Immediately, I sensed he hadn't lost his way to the après ski jamboree. This was Balornock, Glasgow, and I was standing at the bar of my pub, The Brig, confronted by the threatening sight of someone who gave the impression he had just wandered into my boozer after participating in the Gunfight at the OK Corral. I had a fair idea what his mission in life was this particular morning.

'Gie's yer fuckin' money,' he rasped.

I stood motionless, absolutely rooted to the spot. This wasn't exactly how I had hoped the day would pan out.

'Gie's yer fuckin' money,' he repeated, waving the weapon at my napper. His mean, dark eyes were fixed on mine, his finger curled round the trigger of the gun.

'Listen, mate, you could have picked a better time,' I said reasonably, trying to sound calm in slightly trying circumstances.

'Oh, and why is that, ya bastard?' asked the menacing masked man.

'Well, it's 11am and I've just opened,' I replied. 'The till's empty.' I felt like asking him to come back in twelve hours when he might have better luck.

He said nothing, but kept the shotgun trained at my forehead. At that precise moment, my barman Michael appeared from the stock room. The would-be robber pointed the gun in his direction. 'Don't fuckin' move,' he growled.

Michael froze for a moment. The next thing he did was quite remarkable. He smiled. Then he laughed. 'Oh, for fuck's sake, Jimmy, put the armoury away before ye dae yersel' a mischief. And take that fuckin' stupid thing aff yer heid.'

The gunman was speechless. Michael picked up an empty glass and began pouring a pint of lager. 'Put the fuckin' gun away, get rid of the daft balaclava, I'll gie ye a free pint and we'll say nae merr aboot this fuckin' nonsense.'

'Nae filth?' asked the slightly deflated failed mugger, looking less scary by the minute.

'Nae cops,' said Michael. 'Ah'm sure this is just a wee bit o' fun. Right, Jimmy? A wee lark to get the day aff to a good start?'

'Aye, that's right, Michael,' said the incompetent thief with the bad sense of timing. 'Just a wee laugh.' He took off the balaclava and rested the shotgun on the bar. 'Ah could ferr murder a pint,' he said.

I was beginning to understand this was not an abnormal incident in a particularly interesting locale of Glasgow. I hadn't spent too much time scouting the area before I bought The Brig boozer. It was up for grabs, my accountants and I had a look at the books, the figures stacked up and I thought it would be a sound investment. I had been warned about some 'tasty' individuals who roamed the streets of Balornock, but I figured I wasn't exactly taking over a pub in the Bronx. I didn't feel the urgent requirement to invest in a bulletproof vest while swapping my Audi for a Churchill tank. Anyway, I was over 6ft tall and it took a lot to scare me. Mind you, I hadn't figured on looking down the barrel of a shotgun which was levelled at my head.

I feared the worst as soon as I drove into the housing scheme on my first day. I hadn't even seen The Brig Bar and I was following instructions on how to get to my destination. I made my way to the Red Road Court where, sure enough, there was a row of shops. However, alarmingly, no sign of my newly-acquired pub. I looked again at the map. It should have been opposite the shops. I searched around and, completely baffled, I asked a little lad, 'Hey, son, can you tell me where The Brig Bar is, please?' The wee boy didn't hesitate. Helpfully, he informed me, 'It's doon that ramp, ya stupid big bastard.'

'Welcome to Balornock, Yogi,' I thought to myself.

Yes, an interesting place. Don't get me wrong, though. There were many fine people in the area and I enjoyed spending time in their company. But there were also more than a few renegades who took a wee bit of watching. These were blokes who, sadly, basked in their own notoriety and were quite fond of a little mindless violence to while away the hours. Actually, they were cretins who went out of their way to make life hell for everyone around them. Unfortunately, that included me. I think they must have been watching far too many gangster movies. I was often 'invited' to take out insurance for the pub. They were running their own protection rackets and it was a case of agreeing to give them a couple of hundred quid at the end of each week or the place would be wrecked, razed to the ground or become a suitable target for the pyromaniacs of the district. Real charmers. I told them to get lost. Or words to that effect.

There was one evening when I had been warned three or four neds were coming to pay what was euphemistically termed 'a wee visit'. Unfortunately, I had an unbreakable prior arrangement. Honestly! I couldn't be there to meet and greet these basket cases, but I knew the pub was in good hands. The bar staff could more than look after themselves which, rather sadly, was a pre-requisite of trying to earn a decent, honest living in less-than-salubrious surroundings. 'We'll be fine, Yogi,' I was told. 'We'll take care of business. Don't worry.' I half-expected a phone call that evening to inform me the pub was up in flames, but, thankfully, that wasn't the case. The following morning, I opened up and one of the bar staff arrived to start his shift. 'All quiet last night, then?' I asked. 'Oh, there was a wee incident, but we took care of it,' he replied.

I was curious. I wondered what came under the heading 'wee incident' in this part of the world. I asked him to elaborate. 'Aye, they came in, right enough,' he said. 'Four of them. Just as we were closing. They made the usual threats and I tried to reason with them. "Listen, lads, it's been a long day," I said. "I just want to get up the road and put the weans to bed. Okay? Maybe we can talk another time?" They didn't seem too interested in having a wee chat. So, I had to use the equaliser.'

'The equaliser?' I asked, somewhat puzzled. 'What the hell is the equaliser?'

'Oh, didn't you know, Yogi?' he said matter-of-factly. 'I keep a crossbow behind the bar.'

'A what?' I practically screamed. 'A crossbow?'

'Aye, I don't like guns,' he answered. 'I prefer the crossbow. Great weapon. Gets the job done close-up with the minimum of fuss. Whoosh! And there's an arrow in the bastard.'

'Have you ever used it?' I was genuinely fascinated by now.

'Well, I did last night.' Once again he could have been discussing the downturn in the climate or the price of milk. 'This halfwit, I think he must have been the leader, came up to the bar and demanded the contents of the till. I told him to fuck off, but he didn't back away. He fumbled for something and I thought he was going to pull a knife. I went for the crossbow. I pointed it at him and do you know what this daft bastard said, Yogi?'

'Go on,' I urged, anxiously awaiting the next thrilling installment of the gripping saga that had been played out in my pub the previous evening.

'He looked at the crossbow and said, "It's okay, lads, it's a fake!" I looked at the guy. "What the fuck are you talking about?" I said. "How can this be a fake? You can get a fake gun, but this is a fuckin' crossbow with a real arrow. It's not fuckin rubber, you moron." And then, Yogi, do you know what the arsehole said next?'

'Go on,' I repeated. This was better than any radio adaptation of a thriller.

'He said, "Go ahead and prove it!" That's what he said. Could you believe that? Prove it was a real arrow!'

'And?'

'Well, I fired the fuckin' arrow into his chest, didn't I? You should have seen his face, Yogi. It was priceless. His mates bounced off each other as they crashed through the door and left him standing there with an arrow sticking out of his chest. Honest, it was so funny. The halfwit looked at the arrow and then me and said, "Ya bastard. Ye've tried tae kill me." I could hardly stop laughing.'

'Aye, I could see how that might tickle your funny bone,' I said. 'What happened next?'

'Well, he stood there for a minute or so, just gawping at the arrow. There was a bit of blood and I thought he was going to faint. Eventually, he turned around and headed for the door. He kept saying, "Ye've tried tae kill me," all the way out. Actually, if I had pulled the twine to maximum strength, I might have wiped him oot. But I had left it fairly loose. Anyway, he managed to get through the door before he collapsed in the street.'

'Christ,' I exclaimed. 'You didn't kill him, did you?' I wondered for a moment what he had done with the body.

'Naw, nothing like that, Yogi,' said my barman with the William Tell instincts. 'Luckily for him, he fell on his back. If he had pitched forward, the arrow would have gone right through his chest and out the back. That would have been tricky. Naw, he was just lying there muttering to himself when I came out and stood over him. I said, "So, ya daft bastard, do you still think it's fake?" I pulled the arrow out of his chest and said, "You'll no' be needing this. I might get some more use out of it if you ever turn up again. Okay? I take it you won't be visiting our establishment ever again, will you?" The poor bastard just lay there looking up at me. He shook his head. I grabbed him by the shoulders, pulled him to his feet and booted him up the arse. "Fuck off and don't come back," I said. He stumbled off, clutching his chest and mumbling that I had tried to kill him. I don't think we'll see him or his mates again.'

'No, I don't suppose so,' I nodded. It would be fair to say my barman had engaged my attention with his little ditty. I came to realise this was merely part of Balornock's rich tapestry of life.

Actually, I had to laugh when I was talking to one of the residents only a few days after I had picked up the keys to The Brig. She introduced herself, told me she knew who I was and her husband was a Celtic fan. 'Aye, ye'll be seeing plenty o' ma man,' she said. I didn't know if it was a promise or a threat. 'Ye'll find yer way aboot, Yogi. Remember, Monday's the day for the fashion show ower at the bingo hall. A' good stuff, tae.'

Fashion show? In Balornock? It must have been one of Glasgow's best-kept secrets. I asked a cleaner at the pub. 'Oh, aye, get yersel ower there, Yogi. Great bargains. Whatever ye want, ye'll get it in the bingo hall.' Apparently, some of the lighter-fingered among the fraternity went out 'on the rob' at the weekend. They lifted all sorts of stuff; dresses, suits, shirts, blouses, coats, shoes. Anything that wasn't nailed down. They would hang the knocked-off gear on pegs in the toilets in the bingo hall on a Monday and there was always a queue to pay readies for the goods. Nobody asked for a receipt, apparently. 'Get there early, Yogi,' I was encouraged, 'before a' the good gear gets snapped up.' She looked me up and down. 'You're quite a big guy, aren't ye?' I gave her ten out of ten for her observational powers. 'Maybe they'll need to nick some stuff to order. Ah'll have a word with the lifters, if ye want.' I assured her I was quite content with the more conventional way of shopping for clothes and not once did I feel the urge or inclination to join the bargain-hunting throng at the bingo hall on a Monday.

Of course, there were other occasions when I had nothing to smile about. Another set of protection racket imbeciles turned up one day. They read from the usual script. 'Nice place ye've got here, Yogi. Spent a few quid daein' it up, Ah see. We're sure ye wid like to keep that way, eh? Ye don't want any trouble in here, de ye? We can sort it oot fur ye, nae problem. Ye unnerstaun?' I understood okay. Once again, I informed them I had no intention of paying them so-called insurance cash. 'I work hard for my money,' I informed them. 'May I suggest you do the same?' These guys probably thought shaking down unsuspecting folk to relieve them of their earnings was a legitimate occupation. They wouldn't have lost a wink of sleep after terrifying some poor innocent. They probably told everyone they were in the insurance business. What they wouldn't have added was that the tools of their noble trade were knives, guns, blunt instruments, pairs of pliers and blow torches. They were pathetic, something you would scrape off the sole of your shoe. Sadly, they didn't know any better. Either way, they were getting nothing off me. I had a doorman who was costing me £100-per-week to keep out the riff-raff and troublemakers. Then he got a bit greedy and told me he wanted £200. I informed him that was far too much and he would have to be satisfied with £100. I seemed to be getting squeezed from every angle and the threats were never far away.

When I repeated the fact that the protection racket hoodlums wouldn't get a penny out of me, they were actually stupid enough to look surprised. 'We're sorry to hear that, Big Man,' I was told. 'Ye know whit happened across the road, don't ye? Noo that wisnae very pleasant, wis it?' I was only too well aware that a shop not too far away had been totally ransacked by these yobs. The owner had suffered the consequences of not handing over his hard-earned cash to these knuckle-draggers. His place was closed for months as the builders tried to put it back together again. All very sad.

I knew the name of the guy behind all the rackets, the so-called Mr.Big. He was the individual who controlled the local nutcases. He was making quite a good living out of doing nothing. I wasn't about to contribute to his ill-gotten wealth or his quality of life. 'Get lost,' I said to the brainless dolt and I fully realised he would promptly be on the blower to his boss. I had a fair idea what would happen next. By coincidence, I had been invited over to Belfast for a function with the John Hughes Celtic Supporters' Club. While I was there, one of the locals came over to have a wee chat. 'How's business, Yogi? Everything good in Glasgow?' he asked. I knew the bloke reasonably well and had met him at a few functions. I had the notion he was well-connected. I don't mean a member of an organisation or anything like that, but just a character who could take care of himself.

'Not so good,' I answered truthfully. 'There are a few would-be gangsters giving me a bit of trouble back home. There's nothing the cops can do, either. These idiots tore a place apart not so long ago. Just up the street from my pub.'

He nodded his head as he listened to me. 'I don't suppose you know the name of the leader, Yogi?' he asked.

'As a matter of fact, I do.' I then passed on the name. The guy smiled broadly. 'We know this name, Yogi. Aye, it crops up every now and again. We can sort this out if you want.'

I wasn't too sure what 'sort out' meant precisely. 'I don't want any trouble,' I said. 'I would just like the guy to bugger off and leave me in peace to get on with running my pub.'

'Perfectly understandable, Yogi,' said my new-found confidant. 'Leave it with me and we'll see what we can do. I'm sure we can help.'

I had a good weekend in Belfast, but, at the back of my mind, I wondered what was going on in Balornock. Would the pub still be standing by the time I got home? Would it be reduced to rubble? I told the head barman to get in touch if anything serious occurred while I was away. I didn't want any shocks waiting for me when I returned. I was relieved to see The Brig was, in fact, still intact. I asked one of the staff, 'Everything okay? No hint of trouble?'

'Funny thing, Yogi,' he answered. 'You know those guys who are always in here making a nuisance of themselves? Those fuckwits that try to get cash off people?' I nodded. I knew them only too well, of course. And their boss. The barman continued. 'Strangely enough, there's been no sign of them. Not a single one. Why do you suppose that is?' I couldn't prevent myself from smiling. 'I don't think we will be getting too much trouble from them in the future.' And, thankfully, so it proved. My friend in Ireland had obviously got a message to the self-styled Mr.Big. I can only guess at what might have been said. I will never know for sure and maybe it's best not to know. Whatever was conveyed across the North Channel did the trick.

My doorman was still insisting he should get a 100 per cent pay hike from £100 to £200. I had been happy to leave it as the original arrangement, but he wouldn't listen to reason. I pulled him aside one day. 'Are you still demanding £200?' I asked. 'Aye,' he answered bluntly. 'You won't change your mind?' I enquired. 'Nae chance,' he insisted. 'Then in that case, you can go. I won't be requiring your services in the future. Goodbye and thanks for all your sterling work in the past..' He just stood there looking astonished. 'You need me,' he practically wailed. 'No, I don't,' I said. 'You've just shot yourself in the foot, my friend.' So, my chance meeting with one of the John Hughes Celtic Supporters' Club in Belfast had put a stop to all the protection racket hassle from the neighbourhood pests, introduced some harmony to the pub and saved me £100 on a bouncer who didn't do much for his money in the first place. Yes, rank has its privileges, after all!

I'm still not too sure how I first started in the pub business. When I was forced to quit football just before I turned thirty, I really didn't know what I was about to face in the outside world. To be honest, I hadn't prepared for the eventuality. I couldn't have anticipated that my career would be over and done with so quickly. In 1970 I played in a European Cup Final and three years later I was all washed up. It was all so quick, ruthless and unexpected. My old team-mate John Divers went to Strathclyde University when he packed up playing after three seasons at Partick Thistle following his move from Celtic. Like me, he was twenty-nine at the time and hadn't prepared for life in the real world. But fair play to JD. He embarked upon a new career and actually became a teacher at Braidhurst High in Motherwell, St.Bride's in East Kilbride and Our Lady and St Pat's High in Dumbarton. I really wish I had taken the same route. Goodness know where I would be today, but, of course, instead, I got into the pub business.

Actually, that was hardly surprising when I look back at the amount of colleagues who took the same route. Bertie Auld and Joe McBride had a pub not far from Celtic Park and, over the years, guys such as Tommy Gemmell, Davie Hay, Bobby Murdoch, Jimmy Johnstone, Evan Williams, Danny McGrain and Bobby Lennox all went into the licence trade. In fact, I took over the lease of Billy McNeill's old pub in Queen's Park for a short spell not too long ago. Even Big Jock, very discreetly, invested in an off licence on the south side of the city. Big Jock didn't drink, of course, but he didn't mind selling booze to the punters. Now that's what I call covering all bases.

As you will have noted by now, it was far from mundane running a pub. The first one I owned was in my native Coatbridge and was imaginatively named 'Yogi's Bar'. How's that for originality? Took me ages to come up with that name! The boozer was on Canal Street and, as you might expect, one of the more regular jibes among the clientele was, 'Dae ye get yur lager oot the canal?' I moved around until I bought The Brig and that was a real eye-opener. There were high rise flats surrounding the pub and I recall one of my first days in Balornock when I was almost hit on the head with a flying television! Some rental firm had delivered a telly to a bloke on the fifteenth floor, but, unfortunately, it wasn't the one he had ordered. The solution was simple. As the two delivery guys were heading back to their van, the dissatisfied customer in the flat above simply opened the window and chucked the offending TV set out while shouting, 'This isnae the wan Ah want.' It crashed to earth smashing to smithereens not too far from where I was standing.

I spent one of the worst years of my life as mine host of a pub called the Tudor Inn in a place called Halfway in Cambuslang. I was actually in partnership with Celtic director Jimmy Farrell at the time. We looked the place over and, once again, it appeared to be a reasonable investment. Neither Jimmy nor I knew anything about some of the populus at the nearby Circuit, a place that made Balornock look like Valhalla. The local neddery soon made their presence felt. They were an aggressive bunch and my heart was in my mouth most of the time. Trouble could flare for no apparent reason and I always had to be on my toes. I wondered if I should possibly invest in a crossbow! Jimmy was a lawyer and was a sleeping partner in the venture. He proved to be smarter than the average Bear by staying away from the premises.

Three guys used to drive me to distraction every single night. They would order a pint each and stand at the bar the entire evening without a refill. With about an hour or so to closing time, they could be the only people in the pub and they would be nursing a mouthful in each pint pot. I had to remain at the pub right to the end and wait until after last orders before they eventually drained their glasses and left. This rigmarole went on night after night, week after week, month after month. It was infuriating, believe me. It was driving me up the wall when I finally exploded one evening. It had been the usual story. A pint each, their place at the bar and no second helpings. I don't know if they were doing it deliberately to annoy me, but, if they were, then it certainly worked. Just before the last bell, I walked over to the door and locked it. I turned to the three of them and said, 'Okay, the only way you guys are getting out of here tonight is through me. I've had enough of this nonsense.'

They didn't say a word. Then one of them, rather nonchalantly I may add, went to his back pocket and pulled out the biggest knife I've ever seen. It looked more like a sword. If you've seen the movie *Crocodile Dundee* you'll know what I mean. There's a moment in the film when a New York mugger pulls a knife on Paul Hogan, playing the title role as an Aussie on tour in the States. The bad guy says something like, 'Give me your money, punk. I've got a knife.' And good old Crocodile Dundee then fishes out this enormous blade, smiles and says, 'No, THIS is a knife.' The thief then takes off like an Olympian sprinter. Anyway, this bloke from the Circuit might have shopped at the same hardware store as Crocodile Dundee. He looked at me and I got the drift he wasn't about to peel me a grape. So, what's a guy to do in these sort of unwelcome circumstances? I couldn't run away. It was my pub, after all. I realised I had to stand my ground. If only I hadn't locked the damn door behind me! There was no shouting. There were no threats. Just an eerie silence. Me and three hard men and one of them was holding a blade the size of a lamp post.

'Put it away, Andy,' said one of the trio. I can't tell you how delighted and overjoyed I was to hear that simple little sentence. Now I had to hope that Andy would heed the words of his mate and take his advice. He swithered for a moment or two and then, with my heart about to leap out of my rib cage, eventually nodded and tucked the weapon back into the pocket. We looked at each other and neither of us blinked. Nothing further was said. They scoffed the remnants of their pints, I unlocked the door and they left without a word. I then poured myself a rather large vodka.

It was always quite lively in the Tudor Inn. There was another night when it was just getting a bit too rowdy and I decided to throw out about four or five blokes who were completely out of order and also completely out their brains. I ushered them to the door and said something like, 'Come back tomorrow when you're sober.' One of drunks looked at me and said, 'Sorry, Yogi. Our fault.' He offered me his hand. And as I shook it he pulled me forward and stuck the head on me! I was so surprised, I just stood there as he showed, plastered or not, he could shift as he raced into the night. Lesson learned.

The pub was also the meeting place for two nuisances who I soon to find out were the local money lenders. They were Cambuslang's very own Wonga.com. And probably with a higher interest rate, too. I wanted to bar them, but, in truth, they hadn't done anything wrong apart from conducting their business in my howf. I kept a wary eye on them, but couldn't catch them in the act. I realised they were messing people about and they upset the women customers, too. Not too sure what they were getting up to, but, after awhile, I understood they weren't good for business. There was always a bit of animosity when some of the punters were slow to repay the loans. The last thing I needed was the place turning into one of those John Wayne-type bar room brawls from the old Wild West. Eventually, I got a phone number for one of them and got in touch. I didn't want a scene in my pub, so I arranged to see him in the car park. He turned up and was all smiles. Maybe he saw me as a potential customer/mug and he was about to rip me off in the same manner he did the others. 'And what can I do for you, Yogi?' he beamed. 'You can do nothing at all for me,' I said, putting on my best no-nonsense voice. 'But I'm going to do something for you. I'm going to save your liver. You're barred. Don't come back to the pub. Understand?' He looked shocked, but got the message.

So, that was one money lender down and one money lender to go. I knew I would catch up with him in the end. I got a home number for him, too, and made the call. Again, I wanted to conduct our little chat away from the pub. Now, remember, to run a money-lending business in a place like Halfway in Cambuslang you required a certain street cunning. I was well aware this bloke could take care of himself. Maybe he even possessed a 'Crocodile Dundee' knife in his back pocket. I would soon find out. He brought along one of his cronies for our meeting. The guy was about 9ft 8in and he was obviously intended to scare the hell out of me. The ploy didn't work. We met in the car park and I broke the news he was no longer welcome in my establishment. What happened next astonished me. This wee hard man, who was apparently afraid of no-one or anything, almost burst into tears. He began stamping his feet like a kid in the playground after someone had stolen his last sweetie. 'Ye cannae bar me, Yogi. This is so unfair,' he wailed. 'I've been going into that pub for years. You can't do that. Oh, this is so unfair.' I almost felt sorry for him, but I didn't change my mind. Good riddance to bad rubbish, as they say.

Then there was the day I thought I had been robbed of £1,000. I turned up early one morning to do the books and I brought along my little Westie called Murphy. I loved that little dog and we were good chums. Anyway, I went to the safe this particular day to get some accounting done. I left the safe door open for a moment as I went to make a phone call. When I came back, I settled down to count the cash. It was after the weekend and I knew we had had a good couple of days and nights. The Tudor Inn had a huge bar area and there was also a massive function suite upstairs. There had been a wedding that weekend and, as you might expect, the tills had worked overtime with punters working up powerful thirsts as they did their John Travolta impersonations on the dance floor. Geriatrics really shouldn't do the twist, should they? I wasn't complaining, though, as I counted the dosh. My smile evaporated when I realised we were £1,000 short in the takings. I checked again. And again. There was £1,000 missing. You could say I wasn't feeling that grand!

All sorts of thoughts come to mind in this sort of situation. Had one of the staff helped themselves? I trusted my employees and I thought the possibility was most unlikely. Had I been robbed? And, if so, how could a thief get into the safe, take the money and lock it again? And why wouldn't they take the entire stash? Where was Columbo when you needed him? I scratched my head in bewilderment. A fiver or a tenner can go missing, but not £1,000. My cleaner arrived and I told her about the missing cash. Obviously, I wasn't accusing anyone, but she still looked slightly affronted. 'Oh, Mr Hughes,' she said, 'you've got the best staff in the business. They all love working for you. I don't think they would take anything.' I agreed, but, at the same time, I was £1,000 down on the deal. Where was that bloody money?

I puzzled over it for about an hour and couldn't figure it out. The cleaner was going about her duties upstairs when I heard her shouting excitedly, 'Mr Hughes! Come up here, please!' I wondered what on earth had got her so animated. I bounded up the stairs and she was standing with a bundle of cash in her hands. 'I think I've found your £1,000, Mr.Hughes,' she exclaimed. 'This was behind a cushion in that row of seats.' Relieved, I took the money, counted it and it came to £1,000. It was the missing takings. How did it get from the safe, upstairs and planted behind a cushion in the lounge? There was no need to put a call into Peter Falk. The answer came in the shape of a small, four-legged creature who thought he would indulge in a little bit of mischief. Murphy wagged his tail playfully as the thief was unmasked. I was grateful for my cleaner's honesty and I gave her £100. I almost had to fight with her before she took it!

That was a rare moment I actually enjoyed being in the Tudor Inn. After a year, I decided to put it on the market. I told Jimmy Farrell about the problems I was encountering and we both agreed to get shot of it. It wasn't up for sale too long when I received one of the weirdest phone calls in my life. The telephone shrilled and I picked up the receiver.

'John Hughes here,' I said.

'John Hughes here,' came the answer.

I thought it was someone having a laugh. I repeated, 'John Hughes here.'

'John Hughes here,' came the same reply.

I wasn't in the mood for any shenanigans. I gave it one last try. 'John Hughes here,' I said somewhat grumpily.

'John Hughes here.' I was beginning to wonder if I was in an echo chamber.

'I'm about to hang up,' I said.

'Oh, don't hang up,' came the reply. 'You've got a pub to sell, haven't you?'

'Yes,' I answered. 'Who am I talking to?' I wanted to know if the would-be purchaser was genuine or another time-waster.

'John Hughes,' he answered.

'Oh, for God's sake, don't start all that again,' I said impatiently.

'No, honestly, that's my name. I'm John Hughes.'

Once we had sorted out the identity clash, I arranged to meet my namesake. It turned out he was an electrician from Dennistoun who had been working in Saudia Arabia. There were no airs or graces with the guy, but, as ever, you have to find out if they can walk the walk after talking the talk. We met and he said immediately. 'How much for the pub?' he asked. 'Eighty grand,' I replied. 'Okay,' he said, 'it's a done deal.' Just like that. 'We'll need to sort out the paper work,' I said. 'Of course, that'll be no problem,' he answered. He could have been ordering a pint of beer. 'You'll need a survey,' I said. 'No problem there, either,' he replied. 'The money'll be with you tomorrow.' You can't help thinking that in such circumstances that you are possibly dealing with someone with a kooky sense of humour. My fears were dispelled when I walked him to his car, parked just round the corner from the pub. I was confronted with a gleaming cream and blue Rolls-Royce. I was impressed. My new best mate said, 'Aye, nice, isn't it? I buy one new every year. As soon as it hits 800 miles on the clock I trade it in.' I liked his style and, at the same time, puzzled over how much an electrician could earn in Saudia Arabia. Obviously, I had wasted a huge chunk of my life kicking a ball about for a living.

I was completely honest with the guy. I told him he would need someone on the door, particularly at weekends. 'Oh, don't worry about that, Big Man,' he said. 'Everything will be hunky dory. It's not your problem any more. I'll take care of business.' The deal was signed off about twenty-four hours later and I went for a short break with the family. When I returned I thought it was only good manners to pay one last visit to the Tudor Inn to see how the new licensee was faring. The place was wrecked! A party in the upstairs' function room had got just a little out of hand. There had been stabbings and assaults. It had been an orgy of violence. The police had been called. 'I'll learn as I go along,' said the new owner with a shrug of the shoulders. Aye, it wasn't my problem any more. Thank God!

I hope he managed to sort things out. I met the bloke he had just put in charge of the pub and he pulled me aside. 'How do I work a fiddle?' he asked. I presumed he wasn't talking about taking violin lessons. 'Pardon?' I asked. 'How do I manage to get a few quid under the table? Know what I mean?' I looked at him and said, 'That's your first mistake, my friend. I think you should be straight with your boss. I get the impression he's a decent guy and will look after you.' The bar manager certainly took the other John Hughes for something. He ran off with his wife! The last I heard, John Hughes Mark Two had bought a big hotel in Birmingham. I hoped he found better luck in the Midlands.

There was another time in one of my pubs when I was evicting a pest. He looked at me and said, 'Ah'm gonnae go and get a shotgun and Ah'm comin' back to blow yer fuckin' head aff. Ah'll see you ramorra.' I responded in kind. 'That's fine. I'll get a gun, too, and we can have a wee shoot-out in the car park and we'll see how's still standing afterwards. Let's find out who shoots who. On you go. See you later.' It's only now when I recant these stories that I realise how crazy they are. But, back then when you are mixing with some rather strange people, the abnormal becomes normal. Thankfully, the would-be gunman never returned. I was never that quick on the draw!

There were some interesting individuals who frequented the London Road Tavern when I owned that howf for awhile. Most of the clientele were Celtic supporters who were happy to reminisce about the good old days. There were a few other shady characters, however, I didn't welcome. For a start, they were costing me a fortune to drink my beer. They came up with a simple enough scam. They would order a pint, pay nothing and get change for £20. My barmaids at the time were so terrified of these blokes they simply did as they were told. I had to put a stop to that.

My car became a target for the vandals, too. My tyres were slashed on a regular basis and some bright spark came up with the idea of gluing my car doors shut. I don't know what substance they used, but, unfortunately, it was effective. I would be relieved when I walked to my vehicle and observed there was no damage. Then I would try to get into the car and that was another story. There weren't too many funny stories to relate about my time at the London Road Tavern. One incident did make me smile, though. I had been a bit late in paying my rates for the pub when I received one of those threatening letters from the tax people that inform you they are about to arrest your wages. I read the notice and realised they were getting me confused with the other John Hughes, my namesake who had played for the club in the season 1995/96. He even inherited my nickname of Yogi. He was manager of Falkirk at the time of this summons and they were informing him they were about to take his wages from the club if he didn't pay up. That would have been interesting. Needless to say, I settled the bill. The debt collectors should have known better - there is only one Yogi!

I had a good clientele in a Glasgow city centre pub called McConnell's in Hope Street just opposite the Theatre Royal. It was a good-going concern without even the hint of trouble. I was learning that was a major plus in the trade. One day this young bloke came in, ordered a pint and said, 'I hear some footballers drink in here. I'm a Celtic man myself. Do you know of any players who come here?'

'I do,' I answered as I poured him his beer. It was obvious the guy hadn't a clue who I was. He said nothing as he sipped his drink. I went through to the lounge and, shortly afterwards, one of my waitresses came though. She looked a bit mystified. 'That guy you just served, Mr.Hughes,' she said. 'He's asking me about a Celtic player I've never heard of. Can you help me?'

'If I can,' I said.

'It's someone called Adoo. You ever heard of him?'

I had to laugh. 'I do' had translated to 'Adoo' to this guy. I put him out of his misery when I told him who I was. He had the decency to acknowledge me. Apparently, his dad was a big Yogi fan!

Then there was another bloke who came into McConnell's. He knew me and we chatted about a few Celtic matters. One day, though, he looked a little puzzled. 'Yogi, can I ask you a personal question?' he queried. 'Go ahead,' I said, 'just so long as it's not too personal.' He thought for a moment before asking, 'What height were you when you were playing?'

Aye, it was certainly never dull in the pub business. Cheers to one and all for the memories.

Chapter 23

MY BATTLE WITH BIG C

On a July morning in 2008 I was diagnosed with cancer. Originally, I had gone to see my doctor to complain about severe pains in an ear. I thought little about it at the time, but decided to let the medical people have a look because the discomfort was so persistent. I was preparing for a short break and I didn't want anything to spoil the holiday. I was surprised to be told by the doc, 'The affliction could actually be coming from your teeth.' That was a new one on me, but I still wasn't too perturbed.

I have a friend by the name of Harry O'Donnell, a first-class dentist in Coatbridge. I went along to see him the following day. Harry X-rayed my mouth and the plot thickened when he said, 'Whatever is causing the pain, John, it's not your teeth. I can't see a single problem there.' I was baffled because the throbbing in my ear simply refused to go away. It was annoying the hell out of me. Harry pointed me in the direction of a Dr Black, who worked at the Whitevale Medical Care. He had a look, too, and was mystified. I was advised to go and see a specialist in an effort to solve the problem. I explained I was booked up and ready to go on holiday with my wife. 'There's no rush,' he said. 'Enjoy your break and see the Ear Nose and Throat folk when you get back.'

Completely ignorant of my medical condition, I went with Theresa to my favourite haunt in Majorca for a welcome vacation. I was still suffering, but put everything to the back of my mind and was determined to have a good break. When I returned home, I had an appointment to see a Mr Kenneth McKenzie at the ENT Unit at the Royal Infirmary. One of my sons, Martin, is a consultant at the hospital and he introduced me to Mr McKenzie. He did some tests and asked me to come back in a week. I was due to return on the Tuesday when I received a phone call from Martin on the Monday night. What he said will forever stick in my mind.

'Dad, what do you expect from the results?' he asked.

'Don't know,' I replied.

Then came the chilling words. 'You do know you can get bad results as well as good ones?'

Before I could answer, Martin added, 'I'll come with you tomorrow.'

What exactly was my son trying to tell me? It was obvious Mr McKenzie had passed on some information about my condition. What was Martin preparing me for? It didn't sound too clever and I admit I didn't sleep too easily that night.

The following morning, Martin and I met up at the Royal. Mr McKenzie looked a bit grim faced. He asked, 'Are you a smoker, John?' I told him I had never put a cigarette anywhere near my lips in my entire life. He nodded. 'I've got a concern over the polyps at the back of your tongue.' Basically, there was a small growth in that area. Immediately, I asked, 'Are they cancerous?' He didn't hesitate. 'I'm afraid they are,' he informed me. I have always had the feeling I can cope with anything and everything that life throws at me. I have had my fair share of heartaches and disappointments. This was something else. I had just been told I had cancer. I was motionless for a few moments as I tried to take it all in as a fog settled on my brain. I'm told people can often feel anger or resentment when they receive such news. 'Why me?' they might ask. I didn't feel those emotions. In fact, I didn't feel anything. I just sat there trying to take it all in. Martin and Mr McKenzie were having a discussion, but I haven't a clue what was being said. All I knew is that I had been diagnosed with the dreaded disease of cancer. Eventually, my mind cleared. 'What's the next step?' I asked after awhile.

Martin's wife Sheila is a GP and, fortunately, her parents were friendly with a specialist at the Beatson Hospital in Glasgow. If I felt sorry for myself, that grim mood disappeared as soon as I walked through the front doors of the Beatson. Some of the poor souls I saw made me want to weep for them. Confronted with these brave folk, I was made to feel humble. Certainly, in an instant, it put life into perspective. I was determined to beat the illness. At no stage did I believe I would die.

Well, those were my thoughts back then, but I now have to admit I might not have been so positive if I had known the full extent of the tumor. It's only when I have been putting this book together that I have discovered the remarkable truth. Initially, Martin had been told the tumor was a lot smaller than it actually was. My son was then informed it was reasonably advanced. In fact, I have now just found that there was a 75 per cent chance of me dying. I didn't have a clue. Martin, thankfully, elected not to update me on the developments. If he had done, I'm not so sure I would have remained so upbeat about my chance of survival. Let's face it, only the most optimistic or the craziest people would be confident when they are told they only had a 25 per cent chance of being cured. Ignorance is bliss, right enough. By remaining silent, Martin went a long way to saving my life.

Mr McKenzie told me afterwards, 'Your stoicism pulled you through.' He would have been better off saying it was my stubbornness because anyone who knows me will tell you I have that commodity in bundles. Look up the word 'stubborn' in the dictionary and you'll see a picture of me.

In such trying circumstances, you feel some sort of inner strength you may not have been aware of before. A resolve comes into play. 'I'm not going to let this thing kill me,' I thought. 'I'll fight it. And I'll beat it.' That was my positive train of thought at the time. I just don't know if I would have been so encouraged to take on cancer if I realised there was a 75 per cent chance of failure.

My treatment started in September 2008 and was completed five years later in 2013. Those were five long and harrowing years. Luckily for me, I didn't have too many adverse affects to the chemotherapy apart from my hair falling out. I was left completely bald and my daughter Joanna actually bought me a wig. I didn't wear it and I got used to the Kojak look in hospital. Remarkably, it's grown back completely and I have a full head of hair again.

I had radiotherapy for five days a week over the course of almost two months. That was absolute torture. I had to wear a mask that was moulded to fit my face while the docs concentrated on the affected area. Eventually, I lost all my teeth through the treatment. That was the least of my problems. I also shed over four stones in weight and must have looked a real sight lying in a hospital bed with tubes stuck up my nose. Yet, in my ignorance, at no stage did I believe I was on the way out; not even at my lowest point. I had a belief I was going to survive. I can't put it down to anything else other than my in-built stubbornness.

Theresa and the family were magnificent. I knew they were walking on eggshells whenever they came to visit. They said all the encouraging things you would expect of them. I've been in their position far too many times as a bedside visitor. You do your best to make positive noises to cheer up the patient, but when you get outside you say something like, 'God, he's not looking good.' It was in my thoughts that some of my visitors may have thought I was dying. I now realise what must have been going through Martin's head. But who could blame anyone for believing the worse when you consider my condition? Lying flat out on the bed, having lost four stones, all my hair, my teeth and with tubes feeding me liquids through my nose. Not the most inspiring of images, is it?

The tubes up my nostrils kept falling out, so Martin arranged for me to have a tube inserted in my stomach. Obviously, I couldn't eat anything, I couldn't even drink water and everything had to be fed through the spout in my side. It took fifteen hours a day to feed me and I slept with the thing stuck in my gut. Not too pleasurable, I can assure you. However, when I looked around the ward, I realised only too well I was one of the more fortunate ones. Once I finally got rid of the tubes I was moved onto liquids. My throat was as thin as paper and too narrow for anything other than fluids. It was just too bad if I fancied a big steak. Prior to going into hospital, I rarely touched soup. Now I have a bowl of soup every day. I'm hooked on it!

I had to go through an operation to have my throat stretched and widened. That was painful in the extreme, but I knew the people working on me were top-class professionals in their field and I was so grateful to them every day for their care. Mr McKenzie was wonderful and I will never be able to thank those good people enough for the attention they offered me in such dire moments in my life. I was left with a swollen face after that op and Theresa very kindly suggested I change my name to Desperate Dan. Thanks, Theresa. People can find humour in the darkest of places. Theresa also had a brush with the disease a few years ago when she was diagnosed with bowel cancer. Thankfully, like me, she's not a quitter and she beat it, too.

I'm fully recovered these days. That's the good news. The bad news is that I can't sing! With all the work done on my throat, I can't hold a note. I used to be one of the first up to the microphone on karaoke nights, but now I've got to sit it out. Actually, that may be welcomed by my friends. My life turned upside down in those five years. However, the kindness of my family and those in the medical profession will never be forgotten.

I'm still amazed that I did not know the full extent of the tumor. Had I been informed at the time, I'm not sure even I would have had the strength or the stubbornness or the stoicism to survive. Honestly, I had no idea how close I was to death when I set out to write my life story. Undoubtedly, Martin made the right call. Thanks, son.

Life is a magnificent thing. Make sure you enjoy it to the full.

Chapter 24

FACING UP TO SORROW

It was late afternoon on Christmas Day 2012 when the phone rang. I thought it was one of the family or a friend getting in touch to pass on the compliments of the season. Within an instant, I realised something dreadful had happened. My sister-in-law Rhona sounded absolutely frantic. 'John,' she practically shrieked. 'It's Patrick. Something's wrong. Patrick's collapsed.'

I tried to calm her down. 'Okay, Rhona,' I said, trying to hold onto my composure. Patrick was my brother, two years my junior. 'What do you mean collapsed?' Rhona was verging on hysterical. She couldn't stop crying and I could barely make out what she was trying to say through the heavy sobbing. The best thing to do was to jump into my car and get across Glasgow to their house. 'I'm leaving right now. I'll be there as quick as I can.' My mind was in a whirr as I told my wife Theresa I had something urgent to attend to. Before I could offer too many explanations, I was in my car and negotiating my way through the snow of a heavy winter. All I could think about was Rhona's words. 'Patrick's collapsed.' Had he taken a bad turn? I knew it had to be serious judging by my sister-in-law's anxious tone.

I got from Sandyhills to Coatbridge in about twenty minutes and was alarmed to see an ambulance, with its lights flashing, already on the scene. I ran into the living room and was immediately confronted by medics trying desperately to administer CPR - cardiopulmonary resuscitation - to my brother. I took one look and realised it was too late. Patrick was gone; my little brother had passed away. It had been so instantaneous. Later, Rhona told me they had been sitting at the table tucking into the festive fare. Patrick finished his meal, pushed the plate aside and said, 'I thoroughly enjoyed that.' And with that he slumped off his chair. The medics told me he would have been dead before he hit the ground. Patrick was sixty-six years old when he died of a fatal heart attack.

His son Paul asked me if I was going to the hospital. I shook my head with the desperate understanding that it was too late. There was nothing we could do for Patrick. It's in moments like that you realise how resilient the human being can be. You know you must be practical. Obviously, I was numb, heartbroken, totally shocked by this horrible turn of events, but I still had to take in the situation. I had to think of Rhona and Paul. I switched onto automatic pilot. I began making telephone calls to relatives and friends who had to be told the awful news. That wasn't easy, but it was a task that needed to be carried out. A grim silence settled on Patrick's home. It should have been an evening of entertainment and making merry. Instead, we were all plunged into mourning. It was the most dreadful of experiences.

I thought back to growing up alongside Patrick. He was the middle brother. In fact, Billy, the youngest, was preparing to celebrate his sixty-fourth birthday only five days later. I remembered Patrick wanted to be a footballer, too. Of course, I had signed for Celtic, Billy had gone south to Sunderland and Patrick was desperate to complete the Hughes hat-trick. He signed for St.Mirren from Baillieston Juniors in 1964. However, he only played seven games for the Paisley outfit before being transferred to Darlington. Effectively, that was the end of his career. That was a pity because he did have talent and ability, but it was never realised.

I could also look back on the days later in life when we would meet up, usually about twice a week. We would watch the horse racing at his place and the football at mine. We would have a couple of beers and just do the sort of things brothers do. Then he was taken away so suddenly. I still miss my wee brother and my very good friend. We had some great times together. He may be gone, but he has left me with a treasure trove of happy memories. Sadly, I never got the chance to say farewell.

Yes, life can be tough, can't it? People may look in from the outside and think, 'Oh, he's a famous footballer, what does he know about the real world?' Believe me, being able to kick a ball about for a living doesn't make you immune to the horrors of everyday life. My marriage to Mary ended in divorce in 1985. We had been married for twenty-two years and had four wonderful children in Kevin, Martin, John and Joanna. But we drifted apart and I can't blame anyone else but myself. It was my fault entirely. I could hardly believe my ears when Mary, obviously at the end of her tether, told me the marriage was over. I was dumbstruck. However, upon reflection, who could blame her? I was so immature that I didn't see the warning signals. I didn't realise cracks were appearing in our relationship.

Mary had been my childhood sweetheart at St Patrick's Senior Secondary School in Coatbridge. I was twenty years old and already a first team player at Celtic when we got married. Everyone told me I was too young, but I ignored them. I had made up my mind that Mary was the one for me and that was the end of it. My stubborn streak came to the fore again. And, of course, we were blessed with our first born, Kevin, a year later. Everything looked idyllic, but it was obvious that Mary didn't think so near the end of marriage. When she told me it was over I was shattered. I'm not too proud to admit that fact. I wondered what I had done wrong. I immediately gave up alcohol, although that wasn't the cause of the break-up. I think my utter selfishness was the main contributory factor. I just wanted a clear head as I attempted to piece things together. I didn't drink another drop for about six years. I've never been a believer in finding answers to problems at the bottom of a vat of booze. So, I deeply regretted the end of my marriage, but, deep down, I could see Mary's point. I couldn't argue with that. It took me a long time to come to terms that it was all over.

Thankfully, Mary and I are on friendly terms these days. In fact, my second wife Theresa, Mary and I were all over in Ireland in March 2014 for my granddaughter's eighteenth birthday. That may appear odd to most folk, but it was perfectly normal for us. There is no animosity and that's the way it should be. I had never really seen myself as a single bloke, but I wasn't desperately seeking to get wed again, either. That changed, though, when I met Theresa while we were both on holiday in Majorca. I was fifty-six at the time and had no thoughts of getting hitched. I first encountered Theresa - or the current Mrs Hughes, as Sir Terry Wogan would put it - at a karaoke bar, of all places. I probably belted out some of my favourites and I was very much aware of this attractive female. I could only think she must have been tone deaf. Anyway, we got chatting. I liked her straight away. I was struck by her pleasant outgoing attitude. We arranged to meet for dinner a night or so later and, again, I was impressed by her likeable manner. She just seemed so easy to get on with. That was fourteen years ago and we've been married now for twelve. I can be quite an impulsive guy. Happily, I can reveal I'm definitely not in the market for a third Mrs Hughes!

We live a quiet life and that suits us both. Theresa and I like to get away about twice a year and, thankfully, neither of us has fallen out of love with Majorca. We have a good social circle and many genuine friends. We dine out every now and again and we watch a fair bit of TV - sometimes together! And, of course, we have the enjoyment of our children and our grandkids. It's so special to see them all growing up and developing personalities. Mind you, I don't suppose Theresa will want any of them to develop any of my traits. She continually tells me I'm bipolar. I don't think she means it as a compliment and I don't believe I have mood swings from one to another. Co-author Alex Gordon asked me to describe myself in one word. I said, 'Crabbit'. It's a good old Scottish word for grumpy or miserable.

I'll take crabbit over bipolar any day!

Chapter 25

TV OR NOT TV?

I quickly realised I was not about to become the new Archie Macpherson or the new Arthur Montford after I was asked to give the live match summary on the Celtic v Rangers Scottish Cup Final back in the seventies. I was geared up and ready to go when a humourless BBC producer approached me. 'Will you please remember not to say anything bad?' he asked, straight-faced.

'What?' I replied. 'Yes, we don't want to be negative,' he said. 'What if I criticise a player for making a mistake?' I queried logically. 'What if someone's having a stinker? Am I not allowed to say so?' 'Oh, that wouldn't be good,' I was informed. So much for controversy. I reckoned if I couldn't give an honest opinion or a genuine appraisal then football punditry would be better left to Gary Lineker and Co. That was the end of any thoughts I had of following the likes of Saint and Greavsie into the world of TV football. It was a gag I didn't find funny.

I watched a Real Madrid v Barcelona La Liga game on the telly recently and I can understand why they call it El Clasico. Even while sitting in my own front room watching the goggle box, the atmosphere and the tension were quite awesome. I was informed the action was going to be watched by over 400 million people worldwide. Wow! I wondered for a moment what it would have been like to give my views on such an encounter. And then I remembered what the BBC man had ordered. 'Don't say anything bad.' I might have been sitting in the TV gantry making all sorts of observations that didn't quite sit comfortably with what I was watching and what was developing on the field of play. Over 400 million folk would have been thinking, 'Did he actually play football? That daft bugger knows nothing about the game.' I wouldn't have minded a stab at the telly, but, as you may have discovered by now, I'm quite an opinionated bloke and to be told to keep my thoughts to myself on such occasions would just be a waste of everyone's time. So much for free speech.

I don't suppose David Attenborough ever had to work under such instructions. I'm a huge fan of nature programmes and I think Attenborough is a first-rate broadcaster. His show is one of the oldest on TV and I believe it has endured for over fifty years. That's testimony to the man's excellent style in presenting such an engrossing package. He really grips your attention when he introduces his 'subjects'. It could be a herd of elephants in the Congo, penguins in the Antarctica or mountain gorillas in Rwanda, he really delivers something fairly special in every episode. I've enjoyed '*Life on Earth*' and '*The Trials of Life*' over the years. He can even make '*Living with Plants*' seem interesting and that must take some going.

I also liked '*Crocodile Hunter*' before the unfortunate presenter, Steve Irwin, was killed by a stingray. Actually, I watch all sorts of documentaries and I can sit with the TV controls and flick around merrily before I settle on something I think might be worth a view. I can even find myself watching '*Location, Location, Location*', '*Fantasy Homes by the Sea*' or '*Escape to the Country*.' Before you ask, yes, we have two TVs at home and the missus can watch her favourites such as '*Columbo*', '*Poirot*' and '*Miss Marple*'. I'm not a big fan of Agatha Christie and I could never get the magic of Humphrey Bogart, either. I've heard all about his presence in front of a camera and I've watched movies such as '*The Maltese Falcon*' and '*The Big Sleep*', but I just don't see where the charisma is supposed to be coming from. That's just my opinion, of course. And because this is my life story, I am allowed to express it in book form. The Beeb would never have allowed me to criticise Christie or Bogart!

I thought Jack Nicholson was absolutely brilliant in '*One Flew Over The Cuckoo's Nest*'. Way over the top, but wonderfully enjoyable. I also appreciated Charlton Heston in the epics such as '*Ben Hur*', '*El

Cid' and *'The Ten Commandments'*. He probably looked more likes Moses than Moses did. I can watch all sorts of movies; westerns, thrillers, war, mysteries. *'The Quiet Man'* with John Wayne, Maureen O'Hara, Victor McLaglen and Barry Fitzgerald was magnificent. It's about a retired American boxer who returns to the village where he was born in Ireland and, of course, falls in love. The actual pub that was used in the film was up for sale a couple of years ago and it would have been interesting to take over that one. Commuting might have been a problem, though.

Move over Barry Norman. I've also been entertained by the likes of *'Gladiator'*, *'The Wolf of Wall Street'*, *'Rambo'* and *'The Shawshank Redemption'*. I've laughed at the *'Airplane'* spoofs and with a name like *'The Green Mile'* I had to like that one, as well. On TV, I'm a big fan of the American cop shows such as *'Law and Order'* and the *'CSIs'*. I've really savoured *'The Following'* which is a bit different. I was hooked from episode one. I watch *'Judge John Deed'*, too, and I think Martin Shaw is superb in the title role, a fine acting performance. It's a bit different from *'The Professionals'* when he sported a crazy perm and shot up half of London with his sidekick Lewis Collins. Good old Gordon Jackson was Cawley, their boss in CI5, who tried to keep them under control. By the way, I have just about forgiven Jackson for giving the game away in *'The Great Escape'* when he blurted out something in English in front of a German officer. That led to a few of the escapees being rounded up and subsequently executed. David Attenborough's brother Richard was among them. Glad David was never asked to face a firing squad!

I can't abide soaps. *'Coronation Street'*, *'Emmerdale'* and *'EastEnders'* are not welcome in my wee part of Chez Hughes. I'm more likely to see which Roman Legions Spartacus is planning to attack than find out the price of a local newspaper in The Kabin newsagent in Weatherfield, Corrie's fictional location. Or so my missus Theresa informs me! So, as you can see, I am fairly quick on the draw with the TV remote.

Do you know I have been to a concert in my entire life? Not once. I like music, but I've never been tempted to take in a live show. Actually, I don't have an out-and-out favourite singer or band. My music collection at home is fairly varied. I enjoy listening to Nat King Cole, Shirley Bassey, Cliff Richard, Michael Ball, Matt Munro and, of course, Celtic's very own celebrity fan Rod Stewart. The Beatles and The Eagles are easy on the ear, too, but I have no time for Mick Jagger and the Rolling Stones. Frank Sinatra doesn't do much for me, either. And, no, it's got nothing to do with his nickname of 'Old Blue Eyes'. Sinatra seems to be a performer everyone is supposed to like, but count me out. I don't fancy his style one little bit.

I can get engrossed in a really good book, but, believe it or not, I'm not a big fan of sports publications. Until now, of course! You're more likely to find me with my nose stuck in a Wilbur Smith tome. I've read just about everything he has ever written. They are mainly set in 16th and 17th Century and depict the adventures of the settlers in the southern territories of Africa. I've read everything from 'A Sparrow Falls' to 'When The Lion Feeds'. His two best-known movies are probably 'Shout at the Devil' and 'Dark of the Sun'. Lee Child is another favourite. His real name is Jim Grant and he was born in Coventry. He only took up writing novels after he was made redundant from his TV production post with Granada. His first book was 'Killing Floor' which came out in 1997 when he was forty-three years old. A bit late to kick off a new career, but thank goodness someone thought he was surplus to requirements in the world of TV. Of course, everyone knows all about the 'Jack Reacher' books and movies these days.

Alistair MacLean was another thriller writer who liked to add a little twist to his books. Like Lee Child, he may have come to book-writing a little late in his career. He had been a teacher in a Rutherglen Primary School when he had a short story published in the Glasgow Herald. Someone at Collins publishers in Glasgow spotted the tale, got in touch with MacLean and the rest, as they say, is history. He had his first book 'HMS Ulysses' published in 1955 when he was thirty-five and he followed that up with 'The Guns of Navarone'. Hollywood beckoned and he went on to pen books and films such as 'Where Eagles Dare' - a particular favourite of mine - 'Ice Station Zebra', 'Bear Island', 'When Eight Bells Toll' and 'Fear is the Key'. All great novels, all fabulous action-packed movies.

Billy Connolly makes me laugh - and I'm not just saying that because the Big Yin took the trouble to pen the foreword to this book. Or the fact he is a Celtic fan. He is a complete original. When he first came on the scene in the early seventies he took us all by storm. He's older than me by about five months, but he is still touring and splitting sides everywhere with his unique brand of humour.

I used to play a lot of golf, mainly with one of my sons, Martin. Actually, my middle boy, sandwiched in between Kevin and John, was quite a good sportsman. He was extremely good at athletics and represented Scottish schools in the 800 metres and at youth level in the 800 and 1,500 metres. He played badminton at a reasonable level and turned out for Lanarkshire. I'm sure he could have made a name for himself in some sporting capacity, but he gave all that up when he took up medicine as his chosen profession. We were quite competitive on the links, but I developed a foot problem that made walking for hours on end extremely uncomfortable. Eventually, I was forced to quit the game and I gave my clubs to Martin's son. I hope he gets as much enjoyment out of them as I did.

Most footballers like a punt or two and I was no different. Mainly, I bet on the horses, but I'm glad to say the gambling bug never took a hold. I've seen too many people lose their wages on the turn of a card and that wasn't for me. I would stick a couple of quid on a nag, but I wasn't suicidal if it didn't come romping in first. In fact, most of the horses I backed would have been better off pulling stagecoaches.

The bookies rolled out the red carpet when they saw me approaching their shop. They just loved taking my money.

Chapter 26

A CELTIC MAN

I didn't give Mo Johnston an ounce of sympathy when he was branded 'Judas' by the Celtic support. I still believe he got all he deserved after making a fool of the club by signing for Rangers in 1989. There has never been enough money printed for me to even consider such a possibility. I could have been offered the keys to Fort Knox and I would have handed them back. Nothing and no-one would have persuaded me to ever play for that club.

The entire Johnston situation left an extremely bad taste in the mouth. One minute it appeared he was returning to Celtic after his two years with French outfit Nantes. He was sporting a huge grin and wearing the green and white hooped jersey, the most famous in the world in my opinion, when he was photographed along with Billy McNeill at Celtic Park. We were informed he was coming back to the club that was always closest to his heart. That affection disappeared when Graeme Souness came on the scene with his cheque book. God only knows what was going through the player's mind when he agreed to ditch Celtic and join their oldest rivals. Did he even give a second thought to what he was about to do? His agent, Bill McMurdo, was well-known for his allegiance to Rangers and would have done everything possible to nudge his client in the direction of Govan. Maybe Wee Mo didn't need much persuasion once the topic of cash was raised.

Remember, this was the same player the Rangers fans loathed and despised. He even made a half-hearted attempt at the Sign of the Cross when he was sent off in the 1986 League Cup Final against Souness's team. The Rangers legions were spitting bile at him that afternoon. Of course, on the day the sensational news broke, the more bigoted among the Ibrox support turned up at the stadium to set fire to their season tickets, scarves, tammies and anything else that was blue, red and white. Who in their right mind would want to perform for a support who used to go apoplectic when you played against them? They gave him dog's abuse, but, for a few extra quid, Johnston thought it was reasonable to sign for Rangers and give everything he had for them. He sold out big-style and I thought his actions were a complete disgrace. Okay, I realise football is a short career - if anyone knows that it should be me. I also accept that a footballer has the right to go anywhere he can to earn the best living for his family. That's all perfectly acceptable. However, Mo Johnston will never be forgiven by the Celtic fans for the manner in which he performed the most extraordinary u-turn in sport.

He really rubbed Celtic's nose in the dirt by defecting to Rangers. Graeme Souness knew exactly what he was doing when he signed Mo. Forget all the religious malarkey, I'm not buying into any of that. Souness saw the opportunity to put one over on Celtic and he seized it. Joe Miller had wrecked Rangers' hopes of a domestic Treble when he netted the only goal of the game in that season's Scottish Cup Final. I'm told the Rangers manager was raging afterwards in the Hampden dressing room and was vowing to get back at Celtic. He did that by signing Mo Johnston, the player everyone thought had agreed to rejoin Celtic only a fortnight or so earlier.

Here is what Mo Johnston is quoted as saying on the day he 'signed' again for Celtic from Nantes. 'I didn't want to leave Celtic and I don't intend to now. There was some rubbish about me wanting to join Manchester United, but it never entered my head to play for any other club. In fact, there is no other British club I could play for apart from Celtic.' I wonder if his nose was growing at that point.

Of course, there have been other players in the past who have crossed Glasgow's Great Divide. Alfie Conn did it when he joined Celtic in 1977 after starting his career across the Clyde at Ibrox. Importantly, though, Alfie had played for Spurs in between. All connection with

Govan had been severed for the best part of three years before Jock Stein took him to Parkhead. I believe Conn when he admitted it was the lure of playing under the guidance of Big Jock that persuaded him to join the club.

He put it this way. 'He was one of those managers I always wanted to play under. Rangers hadn't come back in for me and I thought I could still learn a lot. So, when Stein asked me, I didn't hesitate. Several people warned me against it, but it was only after I signed when I flew back to Glasgow, with all the Press and TV, that I realised it was bigger than I first thought. That's when it hit home. It wasn't easy hearing the fans of the team who used to cheer for me throwing insults.'

Steven Pressley is another ex-Ranger who, of course, signed for Celtic, but he also played for Coventry City, Dundee United and Hearts. There were actually twelve years in between Pressley packing his bags at Ibrox and arriving at Parkhead. And it was a similar story with goalkeeper Mark Brown. He made just five first team appearances for Rangers before moving to Motherwell in 2001. He spent only one season at Fir Park and then five years at Inverness Caley Thistle before Gordon Strachan signed him for Celtic. Kenny Miller was with Rangers in 2000 when they bought him from Hibs, but the striker was only a year at Ibrox before he was loaned to Wolves and, of course, the Molineux club then made the deal permanent. He was with the Midlands outfit for five years before he joined Celtic on a Bosman. Ironically, after going nine games without a goal, he got his first against Rangers. And he celebrated as though he has just scored the World Cup winner. He never became a first team regular and was sold to Derby County in 2007, but a year later Walter Smith took him back for his second spell at Ibrox.

So, Mo Johnston was far from unique in playing for both sides of the Old Firm. What is still disturbing, though, is the way he went about it. No real Celtic man with the club at his heart would have even contemplated that switch. It would have been utterly unthinkable. I could have been in the grubber and offered a King's Ransom and I would have knocked it back. I really mean that. I would never have played for Rangers. End of story.

And don't brand me a bigot, either. I welcomed the likes of Alfie Conn, Steven Pressley and Co to Celtic. They were bought by managers who reckoned they could do a job for Celtic. For me, it didn't matter a jot they had once earned their living playing in the light blue of Rangers. But the Mo Johnston situation was something else altogether; a completely unacceptable act of betrayal. FIFA actually came down on Celtic's side when there was all the wrangling going on about the transfer. Before his secret was revealed, Mo actually said something along the lines of that he would refuse to play for Celtic, the supposed team of his dreams. The club, at that stage, could have dug in their heels with the world football governing body insisting he was a Celtic player.

If Mo hadn't played for Celtic he wouldn't have been able to play for anyone else. In effect, he would have been finished with football and would have had to seek alternative employment. That would have been interesting. Unfortunately, the board agreed to scrap the deal and - hey, presto! - Wee Mo was suddenly on Rangers' payroll. I wonder if he ever regretted his action. Or did it just not occur to him what he was actually getting involved in? Either way, Celtic supporters got a good look at someone who had always said he was one of their own. Until a couple of quid was waved under his nose.

Nowadays, I am a Celtic fan and, like everyone else, I like to voice my opinion. So much so, that a Celtic security officer once had to ask me to quieten down! I was in one of the hospitality boxes when I decided to give it a little bit of 'advice' to a Celtic player. Actually, it was Aiden McGeady and I thought he was overdoing the ball-playing bit without any end product. He was on the wing and players were getting into good positions in the penalty area, but he was dwelling on the ball and failing to get in crosses. I barked out something from the window and a couple of minutes later one of the security lads came into our box. Someone had complained about the racket coming from next door. 'Who's doing all the shouting?' he asked. I turned round and answered, 'Me. Why?' He just stood there. 'Sorry, Yogi,' he said. 'Any chance you could lower the decibel rate?' We both laughed, but I tell the story merely to underline what Celtic Football Club means to me. I'm not one of the 'prawn sandwich brigade', as Roy Keane once famously named the well-heeled among the Manchester United support. I'm a Celtic fan and I celebrate when we win and I hurt when we lose.

I loved watching Martin O'Neill's teams. They were exciting and entertaining and, of course, had such prodigious talents up front in Henrik Larsson, Chris Sutton and John Hartson. They were always good for a goal or two and Henrik quickly became a firm favourite. How I would have enjoyed teaming up with that guy. I was in Seville for the 2003 UEFA Cup Final and I thought the Swede was simply outstanding. That was a masterclass in striking and he was so unlucky to be on the losing team. That was the first time I had heard the name Jose Mourinho. The extrovert Porto manager talked a good game, but surely even he would admit his team got lucky that evening. The ball just didn't run for Celtic in Seville, every break seemed to go the way of their Portuguese opponents. Just take a look at their winning goal in extra-time to see what I mean. The effort might have been kicked off the line by Ulrik Laursen, but it took a nick off Johan Mjallby and left him completely wrong-footed.

The referee, Lubos Michel, of Slovakia, was incredibly weak, too, but he didn't hesitate when it came to sending off Bobo Balde six minutes into the first period of extra-time. Their left-back Nuno Valente was eventually red-carded in the last minute, but he had been a serial offender right from the start. For him to remain on the pitch for almost two hours will remain one of football's greatest mysteries. I agreed with Martin O'Neill when he summed up the antics of the Porto players when they celebrated each of their three goals. There was a huge running track at the Olimpico Stadium and the Porto players left the field of play to run miles to celebrate with their fans. O'Neill smiled and said, 'I thought they were going into town for a drink to share in the salute.'

I didn't always agree with the words or wisdom of Brian Clough, but I thought he got it bang on the button when he said, 'I would have booked every single Porto player who left the pitch without permission. If they had done it again, I would have issued another yellow and sent them off.' At that rate, Porto would have been left with only goalkeeper Vitor Baia against Celtic! I was proud of my team that night, but also extremely disappointed. We came so close to winning a second European trophy, but it just wasn't to be. I hope to be back in the stand the next time we get to one of these Finals - and this time I hope to be celebrating along with the rest of the Celtic fans. It's high time the club put down their marker at this level again because Celtic are a club who deserve to perform regularly at soccer's summit.

I have to admit that when I played for Celtic I didn't understand exactly what winning and losing meant to the man in the street. I joined the club straight from school and was too immersed in playing for Celtic to look in from the outside. However, it was an entirely different story when I left the club and that's when my thinking changed rather dramatically. I wasn't one of a playing squad of twenty or so players doing their business out on the pitch; I was one of several thousand supporters cheering on the team from the stand. It's not quite the same as playing in the green and white hoops, but it's the next best thing.

I've often been asked how I would like to be remembered. That's an easy one. I would quite happily settle for being known as 'A Celtic Man'.